SLOW ESCAPE

SLOW ESCAPE

27 Years to Freedom

BY
LORIE WILLIAMS
AS TOLD TO
LAUREL MACON

A MEMOIR

Oaker Press

Battle Creek, MI

Oaker Press
P.O. Box 2032
Battle Creek, MI 49016-2032
Phone: +1 (269) 282-1290
Email: oakerpress@gmail.com

Disclaimer:
This is a work of creative nonfiction. The events are portrayed to the best of Lorie Williams' memory. While all the stories in this book are true, some names and identifying details have been changed to protect the privacy of the people involved.

Publishing and editorial team: Author Bridge Media,
                              www.AuthorBridgeMedia.com
Project Manager and Editorial Director: Helen Chang
Publishing Manager: Laurie Aranda
Design: Six Penny Graphics

Library of Congress Control Number: 2016910320
ISBN: 978-0-9977076-0-1 – softcover
        978-0-9977076-1-8 – ebook

Ordering Information:
Quantity sales: Special discounts are available on quantity purchases by corporations, associations, and others. For details, contact the publisher at the address above.

To
Tammi Lawrence
Who courageously began this journey two decades ago

&
For
Claire Ott

Acknowledgments

I am deeply grateful to Tammi Lawrence, educator and author, who graciously shared her body of work with me. Her interviews with Lorie were a comfort to the young twenty-seven year old who had just broken free from her abusive father's grasp. It was Tammi Lawrence's insights and Lorie's readiness to share her story that launched this book. Tammi began this work two decades ago. I am honored to finish this story.

My thanks to editor Helen Chang at Author Bridge Media. Local writer Anne Holcomb was instrumental in getting *Slow Escape* ready to publish. Claire Ott supported me throughout the process and her editorial tips were only surpassed by her friendship. Sherry Holland, cover designer, gave a face to this story. I appreciate the encouragement from Pat and Louis Gibson, my cousins Roxanne Loudenslager and Darcy Barghols, and my book club members.

To my husband Harold and my children Hayley, Adam, and Gabe, who supported me throughout my entire journey with Lorie Williams: thank you for not losing sight that I was with you in spirit even during the most demanding times of helping Lorie during her battle to get her children back.

~ Laurel Williams Macon

There is no easy walk to freedom anywhere, and many of us will have to pass through the valley of the shadow of death again and again before we reach the mountaintop of our desires.

~ Nelson Mandela

CONTENTS

PROLOGUE

I thought I had put it to rest. For twenty years that day haunted me like a bad dream—a cliffhanger that never had a resolution, at least not until now. It's an unforgettable story that deserves to be told.

It was 1974. I was still a young teacher, but I'd already experienced many moments of joy in our school, a nearly century-old building in an urban setting. Today was not to be one of those days. The teaching tools I'd learned in college a mere five years ago felt pretty useless when a fellow teacher pulled me aside that afternoon: she'd heard that one of my second-grade girls might have been sexually abused by a fifth-grade boy over the weekend.

After finding a private spot to talk to the girl, I cleared my throat and said, "Lorie, I heard that a boy was bothering you this weekend. He may have touched you inappropriately or hurt you in some way." I kept my voice calm and even. My young student wouldn't meet my eyes. She stared up at the ceiling of our school.

My eyes were fixed on my student. She was one of the shortest children in my class; her thick brown hair framed her blue-green eyes and strong features. Yet there was such an aura of sadness about this child, a determined little tomboy whose toughness was clouded by a vulnerability that set her apart at times. I wasn't sure that she trusted me enough to answer my question.

"Is there anything you want to tell me?"

Her face became hot and flushed. The urgency of her answer stunned me as the words tumbled out. "My brother does it to me!"

I put my arms around her and bent down so our faces were level with one another. "You don't have to put up with that. There are laws to protect you. We will help you. We will make him stop."

Minutes later we were in the school office where she told the story to our principal and then to a female police officer. She went home that very day with a foster mother. I didn't know at the time that this day would haunt me for two decades to come.

Within a matter of days, a doctor agreed that Lorie showed signs of sexual abuse. The judge sent her abusive teenage brother to live with relatives. I tried to put the issue to rest and get back to the job of teaching. The girl never returned to our school after that, but many times I still found my thoughts turning to her, wondering about the twists and turns her life may have taken.

Two decades after that day, while casually listening to a newscast, I froze when I heard a report about an incest case, the biggest one in the history of the state. Without hearing a name or seeing a face on my television screen, I knew it was her. The report said a twenty-seven-year-old woman and her father were arrested. They had been living together as husband and wife for sixteen years. The daughter had given birth to eight children. Both had been placed in jail on July 10, 1994.

A little investigating on my part sadly revealed that my gut reaction was right. It had been my student, Lorie, whom they were referring to on the news report which was rapidly getting national attention. Why was she being arrested? What had happened to her in the last two decades?

I managed to find Lorie, and she shared her story with me. It's a story like no other. No fiction can compare. Fifteen pregnancies and eight live births, all from her biological father, a man she tried desperately to escape.

Years later, she told me she felt strong enough; she was finally ready for her story to be told. This story is her gift to the world. It is proof of what the human spirit can overcome and a testament to what faith in God can do. After years of forced silence, Lorie can finally tell her story. In her own words, with her uncanny memory for detail and inner strength like I've never seen before, her story comes out of the secrecy of darkness and into the light. This is Lorie's story.

CHAPTER ONE

My first day of freedom begins the day I go to jail. As the door to my cell closes and locks me within, I take my first step away from a life of bondage.

Today is my twenty-seventh birthday, and also the day of my arrest. It is 1994. I am placed in the County Jail for Women, and my father, Walter, is sent to the men's jail across the road. Through the prison walls I feel as if I can still sense the heat of his hostile stare. Walter is my biological father. He is also the father of my six children, as well as my two children who died in infancy, several miscarriages, and the ones he forced me to abort. I experienced fifteen pregnancies. It is hard to understand the control this man has had over me without knowing the whole story. Even then, my story strains the limits of belief, but it's all true. I had no way of knowing that the statute of limitations had expired and Walter would not be held accountable for the things he had done to me. I didn't even know that incest between adults was not illegal in my home state. I had no idea that my bond was $10,000 and Walter's was exactly twice as much as mine. I only knew my prayer that I would escape the hands of my father had been answered. Yet any thoughts of the legalities of my situation were washed away by the ache I felt from being separated from my children.

There are nine other women crammed into this small jail cell with me. We each have a cot. At night, there are a dozen of us. Some of the women are allowed out on a work furlough and return only to sleep. On my very first evening of incarceration, a guard parades all twelve inmates out of our cell and down to a room that has a television. We are told to sit down and watch the news. I can see by the other women's reactions that this social event is very unusual. It isn't long before I realize that my situation is the big story in tonight's news. As my picture appears on the screen and my life's secrets are announced to the world, all I can do is watch helplessly. My fragile safety net shreds as the women all turn toward me with sneers on their faces. I'm dumbfounded by the realization that I have just become Public Enemy #1 in this women's prison. I am stung by my fellow inmates' words as day one of my incarceration begins: "Child abuser! What kind of mother tries to starve her own baby?"

Thanks to our escapade in the TV room and a newspaper the women are passing around, the other inmates know the charge I am brought up on: *child abuse*. A doctor said my baby showed signs of malnutrition. Maybe that is true, or perhaps it was just a way to get Walter behind bars. I don't know for sure.

I wonder, *if I told my fellow inmates the truth, would they believe me?* Over the next few days, the things the other women say to me not only hurt, they even scare me. Then, a week into my stay, and just days before my release, I hear an inmate say the first kind words about me: "Stop treating her like this. You don't know her story."

Her kindness touches me. No one knows my story. The sad irony is that no one was interested in my story before today. I spent my whole life trying to get someone to notice my situation: social workers, police officers, school counselors, anybody! Now we're on the six o'clock news and in the newspapers. I'm no longer invisible, but for me the big question is, will this publicity finally be the thing that will keep me safe? I kept my story hidden away and locked in my heart my whole life. Now I am ready to open the door.

CHAPTER TWO

I was not born into a happy family. My parents' relationship was rocky, even before their marriage began. They were both teenagers, both with abusive fathers. The conception of their firstborn child, Carl, is what brought an angry Walter Williams and a desperate Elaine to the altar.

Elaine was the youngest of eight children and the only girl. She used to tell me about the happy times she remembered when her mother was alive, but my grandmother died when my mother was only five years old. Elaine's father remarried a woman who was a drunk. She had seven children of her own. During her childhood, Elaine was expected to take care of her stepmother's seven kids, along with her own seven brothers. The only thanks she got from either parent were beatings. Maybe they beat some of the goodness right out of her.

My dad, Walter, was always small for his age, slim and dark haired. Growing up, he was bullied a lot. Those bullies sure taught him well, because he eventually became a master bully himself.

By the time Walter became a teenager, his father had tired of his troubled son. The regular beatings my grandfather had given him didn't appear to straighten Walter out, so he hoped that military service would do the trick. Even though Walter was too young to join the U.S. Army, his father insisted he lie about his age and sign up.

My parents met at a drive-in where Elaine was a carhop. The year was 1957. Sixteen-year-old Walter was waiting to be deployed to Korea. Elaine was broken hearted over a recent breakup with a boy. Mom didn't know at the time that she was pregnant by the boy who'd jilted her.

Walter returned to that drive-in a second time to ask Elaine to join him at a party given in his honor before he was to be shipped overseas. I guess you could call Walter's going-away party their first date. My father drank heavily that night. When he left to take Elaine home, he stopped the car on a deserted road. Elaine didn't fight much when Walter forced himself on her. Afterwards, they drove back to town. Walter felt he had a bit of a trophy from this first date. He hung Elaine's panties on his rearview mirror.

Elaine realized that she was pregnant not long after Walter left for Korea. When she found out how far along she was, she realized the baby wasn't Walter's child. But when my mother thought about returning to her abusive parents, the endless childcare and the mountains of work that waited for her, she decided to tell my grandfather the baby was Walter's.

When Walter returned, his father demanded that he marry Elaine. My father felt trapped and more than a little angry when he heard this news, and he quickly figured out that Elaine had lied. The new baby, Carl, was not Walter's biological child.

Once Walter knew the truth about Carl, his anger began to grow a little bigger each day. The baby was only a few weeks old, but Carl never had a chance. He would be the magnet for Walter's anger. The marriage started with a lie, and a lie can go a long way, especially with Walter Williams.

After Carl was born, the rest of us kids came along, one after another. My sister, Emily, was the second child, followed two years later by Cheryl, then the twins, Bruce and Belinda. I came along one year later. I was born July 10, 1967, the sixth and last of the Williams kids. My mom told me I was a happy baby. I took my first baby steps at eight months. Sometimes I wonder if, even at that age, I somehow knew it would be best to get far away from my dad.

I guess you could say I first left home at the tender age of four. In 1970, I was given to a couple my family knew. "Foster care," I was told. My foster mom was a nurse who had taken care of my mother and me in the hospital when I was born. She and her husband had no children of their own and did their best to make me feel special. My foster dad made me a little go-cart, and there was always plenty of food to eat. The everyday comforts at their home felt like luxuries to me. They told me they wanted to adopt me. I didn't know what that meant, but the hug and smile that came with the words filled me with happiness.

Then a day came that I would always remember. My foster dad and I were riding in his truck when he parked on the side of the road, then reached for me and pulled me on top of him. Pushing on my head, he forced my face down to his lap. His big hands, the same ones that had gently held my hand so many times, pressed into my head like a vise. Fear and repulsion raced through my body, and I struggled, trying to pull away, but he was too strong for me. I had no idea at the time that he was forcing me to do oral sex. At age four, I had no idea what to think about this thing that had happened to me.

This was the day. This was the beginning of the nightmare yet to come.

Chapter Three

While I was staying with the foster family, my dad returned from a trip to Alaska. My mom had been planning to proceed with my adoption, but when Walter returned, he grabbed my mother by her shoulders and growled, "Nobody is gonna adopt a kid of mine! So you better haul your ass over there and tell 'em they'll give my kid back if they know what's good for 'em." Why my father had been in Alaska and what he had done there was a mystery to all of us, but he was back, and so was fear in the eyes of his family. The adoption wasn't final yet, and he insisted that I return home.

I was glad to see my siblings, but they all looked so sad. My parents had no steady work at that time. My dad had worked for Grand Trunk for two years, but since then he'd been unemployed. While Elaine had finished high school, Walter had made it through only the tenth grade. After that, it was the school of life for them.

At one point, my parents opened and ran a bait shop, and that kept us going for a little while. Walter also caught raccoons and sold the pelts. He would roast the carcasses for our supper. On those days, all of us kids were glad to have meat on the table. He was also a master at trapping mink in a barrel and made a pretty penny selling their pelts. But even with these side jobs bringing in some money, the food was pretty slim pickins at our house. It wasn't very long before I missed the good food and the comfortable bed I'd had at my foster home.

After two years, we moved to a different house. Our new address was 666 Harbor Street. My mom made me a cat-shaped cake for my sixth birthday, and I felt like I had a special place as her sixth kid, the baby of the family. *Six must be a lucky number for me*, I thought. We traded smiles as Mom presented me with this special treat. It was better than any gift, knowing that she had taken the time to bake these two round cakes, cutting them into the right shapes and adding licorice whiskers as a final touch.

Food and warmth were at the top of our list as we settled into our new home. Our house became a tad cozier after Dad fashioned a barrel stove for us, and it served us well for heat that winter.

Times were good when Dad started bringing home barrels full of food every once in a while. Corn, squash, even candy lemon drops. We had never seen sweets in our house until that candy showed up, along with a twenty-five-pound bag of brown sugar. A handful of that sugar sure could ward off hunger.

Sometimes quantities of cereal arrived home with Dad too. It took us kids a while to figure out that Walter was probably stealing it from the train cars parked nearby. We all pitched in on the processing of our bulk foods; when we worked together this way, our family really felt like a team.

The bait shop was still going pretty well, too. Many a night, all six of us kids would arm ourselves with empty coffee cans, carrying flashlights with red plastic wrap rubber-banded over the light bulb. We would head out to the golf course that was a mile or two away from our house. Night crawlers run from sunlight, but they didn't run from our special red flashlights. We would dig and then swoop in, filling our cans with the fat, squirmy critters, along with a big scoop of dark, moist soil. As I tagged along behind my siblings, I felt proud that we had something to offer to our family business.

Chapter Four

During this time, all of us kids were sleeping together on a few mattresses spread across rafters in the attic. I remember falling once, between the rafters, and landing with a thud on the floor below. My tears and bruises were met only with the words "Don't be so clumsy. There's nothin' wrong with you."

In some ways, I enjoyed being back with my family again, but a six-year-old doesn't have a word for *stress*. My parents fought, Carl was often beaten, and all of us kids were scared of provoking my father's anger. My oldest sister, Emily, was sweet to me, but the unhappiness in her pretty face was plain to see. It was soon after my return to the family that Emily left us. I don't know why she moved out, but when she looked at Dad, I could see daggers in her eyes. When she slammed the door behind her, I looked at Cheryl and saw that she, too, was sad to see her sister go. After that, it seemed like whenever Dad was around, Cheryl was nowhere to be seen. It was during this time that I started to feel a constant churning feeling in my stomach—kind of a burn—and a tightening in my throat. As time passed, I felt these sensations more and more frequently. Years later, they became such a part of me that I no longer noticed them.

One evening, our dad returned at dusk, tired from a long day of hunting. I saw that he was pulling a wagon heaped full of dead raccoons.

"Go sell these raccoon carcasses," he told Cheryl and me. "Don't come back until every one of them is sold."

Peddling raccoon carcasses was certainly a new experience for my sister and me. We set out, scared and embarrassed at the same time. One neighbor told us, "If you can't sell them, come back and I'll buy them all." Two scared, sweaty little girls had a lot to learn about salesmanship, and we snagged only a few customers. It was late by the time we returned to the one neighbor who either needed a wagon full of dead animals or just felt sorry for us. We arrived home, exhausted, to hear Walter say, "That's *all* the money you got? You two are pitiful."

I do remember some happy times here and there: us kids husking corn on the back steps, or going out together in the neighborhood because it felt better than being at home. Emily, my oldest sister, had already left the family nest, but we were happy to still see her now and then. Cheryl, blonde and cute, was slightly older than the twins, Bruce and Belinda. They were only a year older than me, and the two of them were my built-in playmates.

Belinda was thin and gangly, with long brown hair that framed her face. She always wore glasses, and she usually had a look of concentration on her face, as if she were constantly studying for a test or reading in the library. Belinda's face would light up when she smiled, but she didn't smile very often. I had given her a nickname, "Bennie," when I was younger, and this was what I usually called her.

Her twin, my brother Bruce, was possibly even more somber than Belinda. He was a slim, handsome boy, with a head full of tousled brown hair and thick glasses. His tanned skin and perfect teeth showed off a wonderful smile. But most of the time,

Bruce seemed to carry the weight of the world on his shoulders, finding few silver linings in life. He didn't talk much about the bad treatment he received at the hands of our parents, but I could always see the sadness lurking just under his smooth skin and occasional smile.

I didn't look in the mirror much, but I knew I was short. My green eyes were one of my best features, but I also liked my straight teeth and smile. My hair was brown and thick, and usually messy. Occasionally, I snuck out the pictures my foster mom had taken of me when I was four. I was scrubbed shiny clean and all dolled up in a new dress, my hair combed neat as a pin. Sometimes I wondered if that cute little girl was really me. That girl looked like somebody loved her.

Now, my role in the family was to tag along with the older kids and stay out of trouble. We did our best to look out for each other. I think we all knew we were in the same sad boat. To keep it from sinking, we had to take care of each other. Away from home, we'd band together for protection, because you never knew what might come up. It was harder to protect each other when we came back inside each evening; no matter what adventures we had had during the day, we always had to return to the stress and sadness that lurked in our home.

We did have fun in our own backyard the day Dad brought home a circular display a store had thrown out. Turning trash into treasure, he created a makeshift merry-go-round for us kids to ride. I don't think I ever saw the twins smile as much as they did the first day they got dizzy on that thing.

I started to notice that sometimes Mom would treat the twins differently from me. One day, I overheard her calling from the kitchen, "Belinda, get in here and wash this pot on the stove that you forgot. Bruce, can'tcha see that the trash needs takin' out? Sometimes I wish I woulda left you in that snow bank!"

It's summer, I thought to myself as I listened to Mom yelling. *Why is she talking about a snow bank?* It wasn't long before I heard Walter's footsteps pounding into the kitchen, followed by the familiar sound of my parents arguing. My dad yelled, "You know Cheryl and Lorie are the only two kids in this house that are mine, but you expect me to hunt food for all of 'em. You do all that goddamn whorin' around, and I'm supposed to feed *all* these damn kids?"

I kept listening as my mother snapped back at him, even though I wanted to plug my ears. "You know I couldn't handle caring for twins when I already had three other kids to put up with. That's why I put those two out in the snow. I just couldn't take it anymore. If that neighbor hadn't found them, we wouldn't be having this argument now. And don't go tellin' me Emily ain't your kid, because she is. I oughta know who my own kids are. I lied to you about Carl, but I'm not lying to ya now. Those twins just about did me in when they were babies . . . and they are on my *last* nerve now."

I could feel my throat tighten up again; my stomach churned as I took in my mother's angry words. *I love my brother Bruce and my three sisters, and I don't care who their daddies are!* I thought angrily. *Walter is no prize. Maybe the twins ought to be glad if they aren't his. Besides, it's Carl who causes a rumple in things.*

Carl was treated differently from the rest of us. It was sort of like he never got a fair chance. For a start, my dad was constantly yelling at him. I think my dad blamed Carl for something that wasn't really Carl's fault. He wasn't able to choose who his father was, and it wasn't his fault Mom lied to Dad about him.

I guess Carl was a problem for my parents from the moment they first met, even though he hadn't been born yet. After all, my mom didn't ask to get pregnant by the boy who jilted her, and my dad didn't want to marry my mom when she lied and said the baby was his. Walter probably wouldn't have married Elaine of his own accord, but his father made him do it. So I guess you could say that Elaine married to get away from her father, and Walter married because he was afraid to disobey his. It's no wonder Carl was caught in the crosshairs, and he could sense it. Every day, Carl's anger seemed to grow, and he got meaner, taking his feelings out on the rest of us.

I remember Carl saying, "I take the brunt of Walter's wrath so he will leave you little punks alone. Whenever he beats me, you should be glad that it's me and not you. Ya know how Walter makes me work all the time, diggin' worms for his bait shop or doin' any little job he doesn't wanna do? He works me harder than any of you little brats. You should be happy I'm around because Walter gets so tired beating me that he ain't got any energy left to beat you little brats."

There were very few moments when Carl was actually nice to me. One time, he said, "Come here, let's play a game called 'Snatch Up the Pennies.' So here is how we play it: I throw a handful of pennies, and you see who can snatch up the most." It was sort of fun, except we had to give all of the pennies back to Carl when the game was over.

It sure wasn't fun when I had a brace on my sprained wrist and Carl grabbed hold of my arm and pretended it was a stick shift and he was changing gears. He made car noises while he jerked my wrist around. I saw lights flashing before my eyes, it hurt so much.

The good times didn't happen often, so they are easy for me to remember. One day, my dad took me to Kmart and picked out a new pair of tennis shoes just for me. They were covered with bright yellow smiley faces. It wasn't for my birthday or Christmas. It was for no special reason. That made me feel like I was the special reason, and that was a big deal for me.

I remember another day that made me feel just the same way. I heard my dad's voice calling me from outside. "Lorie, come on out here. I got somethin' to show ya."

I let the back door slam as I darted down the rickety porch stairs, coming to a sudden stop to stand straight and tall in front of my father. I could see what he had for me, and I wanted to jump for joy, but I stayed silent as I looked up at his face, which seemed particularly handsome that day. I waited for him to tell me in his own words.

"I found this here bike and thought I could fix it up for ya. I bet I can make it as good as new."

"Thanks, Dad," I said. My eyes were shining as big as my smile. He reached into his rusty toolbox and pulled out some tools. I tried to help a little here and there as he repaired my very own bike.

Once Dad thought the bike was road ready, he smiled and said, "Okay, kiddo, let's give 'er a try." His white t-shirt had some grease spots on it from his repair work, and his strong arms held the frame steady as I climbed aboard. I wasn't afraid as he held on to the bike to help me balance, one hand on the back of the seat and the other holding one slightly torn handle grip. I rested my hand against his on the handlebar, his skin warm from the afternoon sun. "That's it," he encouraged me, "press down so your feet don't slip from the pedals. Now keep pumping your feet evenly, but remember if ya havta stop, ya push backwards." We had wheeled out to the sidewalk in front of our house. "I'm gonna let go of the steering wheel, and it'll be your job to keep the wheel straight."

When I seemed to have the hang of it, he told me, "I'm gonna let go of the seat for a minute and see if you can keep it balanced." I sailed straight for a few seconds but then started to wobble. "I got ya!" Walter caught the seat in his hand, running along with me as I gained speed. After a few more minutes, he let go again. I was flying along, my heart racing, until I hit a bump in the sidewalk and tipped over into the grass.

"You done good. Hop back on and let's give 'er another try."

I brushed the grass stains off my knees and looked up into Dad's face, tan from the sun. Just a hint of a smile crossed his lips.

"Thanks, Dad. Let's give 'er another try."

I'd become an expert at biking when one day Dad came home with another surprise for me. I saw a swirl of colors in the palm of his hand. "What's that?"

I tried to look closer, burning with curiosity. Dad unspooled a little beaded necklace from his palm. Out of the clear blue, just like that. It wasn't my birthday or anything. The beads were smooth and fun to touch. I felt proud showing off this new treasure. I decided I'd wear that necklace every day as a reminder that my father could act like a real dad sometimes. My fingers wandered to my neck often and caressed those little beads.

Sometimes, when angry words and the sounds of beatings filled the house, I felt as if I might blow away. I would pretend then that the tiny necklace was like an anchor, holding me and sort of keeping me in place. It would give me a little bit of hope that things might be better someday. *That is all I want—for things to get better*, I would think as I ran my fingers over the beads.

CHAPTER FIVE

Things changed that fall and winter. My dad suddenly wasn't around as much as he used to be. During my dad's unexplained absences, we never had much food to eat. Sometimes we got nothing but bird bread. That was stale bread, broken and jumbled together in ripped plastic bags, piled haphazardly in a bin at the store. The sign said that it was for the birds only; it cost just a nickel a bag. *I guess that makes me a hungry sparrow*, I thought as my siblings and I ate the stale, dry bread without complaining. *The Bible says God watches over the sparrows. I hope God is watching me, because it sure doesn't feel like anyone else is. So bird bread it is.* That winter, we lived on water and bird bread alone. We quickly figured out how to have a bit of variety, though. When we wanted a warm supper, all we had to do was toast our bird bread. Voila! Bread for lunch, but toast for supper. God must have been watching, because we all made it through that winter.

We were always glad when the weather warmed and the lakes thawed. We couldn't live on bread alone. Once the ice was gone, fishing in the nearby lake was a must for us, and it turned out to be a skill we'd use for many years to come.

Bruce loved to join me down at the lake. "I don't know how you do it, Lorie. You take that long shoelace and poke a safety pin in the end and pull a couple of kernels of corn you sneaked from last night's supper for bait. It seems like you just throw it out into the river and the fish come a bitin' and latch onto that old safety pin you use as a hook."

One of my first fishing memories was watching Dad smack Carl for not cleaning the fish well enough. "That's all we have for supper tonight!" Walter growled.

I thought that if I could learn how to clean and cook a fish just right, it might please my dad. I carefully watched my mom clean fish, and then I tried it myself one evening. I had watched her so many times that I knew I remembered exactly how to do it, and this gave me the courage to try. I touched my necklace from Dad for luck and took my time. I knew the fish I fixed were done right.

Dad was out for a long time trying to steal some food for us that night, but he came home empty handed. I touched my beaded necklace again, trying to summon up a little courage. I presented the fish to Dad, so proud that I had prepared them just the way my mom had shown me. Dad was drunk and tired. He looked at the plate with a little bit of crazy in his eyes, and I knew instantly this wouldn't turn out the way I'd hoped. He shoved the plate out of my hand. "Get that shit away from me. It ain't even hot. I'm not eatin' it. It's too damn late for you to be up anyway. Git up to your room."

I didn't even put on my pajamas. I just crawled into bed and buried my face in my pillow. I reached for my favorite toy, a stuffed monkey with a banana in his hand. Then, when my hand touched the empty sheet next to me, I remembered, and I started to cry even harder. My dad had thrown my favorite stuffed animal into the fireplace a few days ago, along with some of the other toys we had forgotten to pick up.

After I calmed down, I tried to make myself look at things a bit differently. *Dad didn't really mean what he said,* I told myself. *He was tired from searching for food to feed us, and he was just in a bad mood. Besides that, he was drunk, so he didn't really know what he was saying. The fish was cold. Maybe I should have warmed it up a little bit before giving it to him.*

The next morning, I woke to the sound of my parents arguing again. Lack of trust was my dad's favorite thing to talk about "It takes a long time to build trust, but only a second to destroy it. Don'tcha *never* forget that." Dad's words thundered through our house that morning, and they still echo in my head.

During the summer, I turned seven and we moved again. I started to worry that age seven wouldn't be as lucky for me as the number six had been. We didn't have as much to eat at our new house, because we had moved away from our fishing lake. But my mom always had dinner on the table right at five o'clock. If my dad happened to be around and also sober enough to eat, he expected his dinner right on time. My dad would scream at my mom if she didn't do things just like he expected. When I looked at our mom's tired face after a day full of caring for children and cooking, I couldn't help but feel sorry for her. Mom was just over five feet tall, thin, and beginning to look worn, even at her young age. Her blondish hair didn't show any signs of early gray, but the worry lines on her face were beginning to deepen. I wasn't surprised that sometimes she didn't feel well, as her favorite foods were Frito Lay chips, Hostess apple pies, and Pepsi. Even I knew those were just snack foods and not good for you. Maybe those sugar-loaded snacks were something that Mom thought she needed in order to just get through a day of caring for us kids and a crazy husband.

Even we younger kids could tell that what little romance there once had been between Mom and Dad had left the building. One stormy day, Dad pushed Mom out of the house, right into the mud and rain. She didn't even have on shoes or a coat. We kids spilled out into the rain alongside her, attempting to show our loyalty to Mom. It didn't do much good. It wasn't long before we hung our dripping heads and turned to walk back into the house. Even Mom.

When Mom talked about Dad, her words always remained loyal, but I soon began to question what was really in her heart. How many times could she handle his mean acts toward her? "Lemon tree, very pretty and the lemon flower is sweet. . .." My dad had a really good singing voice, and he loved that song. But each time it came on the radio, he would sing it AT my mom instead of TO her. It was like a big, weird, musical threat. She would cower as if the words were spraying hard against her skin, just like the rain had done that day.

"Where have all the flowers gone? Long time passing." It wasn't long before Dad was at it again with the next song. Dad used it as a weapon as he got up in Mom's face, scaring her with its words. *Why can't Dad act like he did the time he brought the bike home to me? He felt like a real dad that day.*

It was actually a relief when Dad left us again, even though we missed the food that he had been bringing home. My father always enjoyed being in the woods and living off the land. He really loved his trips to Alaska. None of us knew what he did during his time up there, and we certainly knew better than to ask. So without so much as an explanation, he was off to Alaska again. I can't remember him ever checking to see if there was enough food or money in the house before leaving. So, during these absences, my mother would struggle along on welfare and work part time, here and there.

After a few weeks of Dad's absence, Mom began to say, "We'll get that fixed when your dad gets home," after we showed her a couple of broken appliances. "We will do that when Walter gets back," she parroted again and again when we tried to suggest new ways to seek food. "Just wait, it'll be so wonderful when Walter returns to us," she would say. It wasn't my place to remind her that it hadn't been long ago that he had thrown her out in the rain, so I just shrugged and turned away. Yet I hoped that Mom was right. *Things will be better when Dad comes back home.*

This time, after Dad left, Carl assumed the role of "man of the house." Carl was eighteen now, all grown up, and he was meaner than ever. We kids were afraid of him, and Mom was too. Dad picking on him so much hadn't helped Carl's attitude any.

Carl's new role was to steal food so we'd have something to eat. I don't know why we even wasted our time complaining to our mother when Carl would hurt us, because she would stick up for him every time. I didn't know for sure, but I suspected that there was something fishy going on between Mom and Carl.

If Mom needed something from Carl, she was afraid to ask. As the boss of the house in Dad's absence, Carl controlled the use of the beat-up old car we had. One day, when Mom needed the keys, she told me to sneak into Carl's room to get them. I wasn't sure if fearing my brother was a good reason not to mind my mother, so I felt obligated to obey her. I could feel my heart beating right out of my chest as I crept silently into Carl's room to look for those darn car keys. Once I found them, I made a beeline to the door and handed them over to Mom. She didn't even thank me. Later on, when Carl figured out that Mom had used the car, he came looking for me, beating me for stealing his keys. So then I went crying to Mom, who just told me it was *my* fault for making Carl mad. *I'm always caught in the middle*, I thought, wincing from the bruises Carl had given me. *It seems like Mom just gets weaker and weaker as Carl gets meaner and meaner. There's no way out.* I also felt sadder and madder every day, but knew I had to keep it all to myself.

If I wasn't so afraid of Carl, maybe I could have felt sorry for him. I remembered hearing about the day Dad was driving Carl in his truck and plowed the truck right into a tree. Carl's head got lodged in the corner of the door when they crashed. He still had a scar in the exact shape of that metal corner. *Maybe that shook his brain loose or something*, I thought. I could also remember the time that Dad beat him with a flashlight. Carl was Dad's punching bag, sort of a magnet for Dad's anger. So what could Carl do with all that trouble heaped up on him? Sometimes it seemed like Carl's only purpose in life was to pass his anger on to other people. Maybe he had so much anger that he just couldn't hold it all. The rest of us kids weren't like that. We didn't go around hurting other people. We just kept all our hurt inside of us. Locked up tight.

CHAPTER SIX

Our latest house had an upper floor, but we kids were never allowed to go up there. We just lived on the main floor. It was early spring in 1974 when Carl decided he was going to send my sister Belinda to the store for cigarettes. I followed her, calling, "Bennie, you're only nine! No one is going to sell you cigarettes!"

Belinda just stared at me, expressionless, and went straight out the door. After all, she had to mind Carl's orders or expect to get beaten. Once she left, I realized how quiet it was. It was just Carl and me now, alone in the house. Cheryl was hanging out at friends' houses, as usual, and Bruce was off somewhere on his bike.

I watched Carl go and get the key to the top floor of our house.

"Come on up here, Lorie; I wanna show ya something."

I had never been up to this forbidden level of the house before, and, like most seven-year-olds, I was kind of curious about what was up there. But, mostly, I was scared that if I didn't do what Carl said, he'd make me sit in a chair and not move for two hours—a game that only Carl liked to play.

We reached the top step, and Carl unlocked the door. Beyond the doorway, I could see a room with a bed in it. I turned to go back downstairs, but Carl grabbed my arm, dragging me to the bed. My half-brother threw me onto that bed and then started to rip my clothes off of me. His hands felt rough and much too strong for me to ward off. My heart was pounding, and I could hardly breathe. I'd never seen a man's body naked before, and Carl was quickly shedding his own clothes. When I saw Carl's private parts exposed, I began to shake. I had to struggle just to breathe as the shaking spread over my entire body. Then Carl's body came crashing down on me, and he did something to me that I didn't understand, something I didn't even have a name for, other than *pain*. It was something that created a picture in my brain that I could never erase.

When Carl was finished, he told me, "Get back downstairs and don't ya ever tell anyone, do you hear me? You think you're sorry *now*? If you ever tell, your last wish will be that you shoulda kept your mouth shut." I believed him. I didn't tell.

CHAPTER SEVEN

School became my refuge, the one place where I felt safe. I especially liked my second-grade teacher, Mrs. Macon. She told me, "My last name was Williams, before I got married. I had the same name as you!" This made me feel really special. When Mrs. Macon told us all about how she had been a tomboy when she was in second grade, I liked that because I was a tomboy too. During art time, my favorite things to draw were spiders and spider webs. "Those are the best spider webs I've ever seen. You are quite the artist, but I already knew that, because of your beautiful cursive writing." My teacher's words were kind of embarrassing—I wasn't used to compliments—but they made me feel warm all over. Every Friday, I began to dread the weekend and the fact that I wouldn't see my teacher until Monday.

In our neighborhood, there was a train depot with a big, old-fashioned locomotive sitting nearby. This old train engine didn't run anymore, and it sat on blocks, rusting. The weekend right after I drew the artistic spider webs, I walked down there with Bruce and Belinda to play on the train car. I was having so much fun that I told them, "Go on home without me. I still want to play. I'll be home later."

Peeking under the train, I got curious. I noticed that the cinderblocks it sat on would allow enough room for me to crawl underneath and explore its underbelly. I decided to go underneath and look around. A metallic smell filled my nose, and I rubbed my hands across the smooth metal of the huge train car looming close above my head. When I heard voices, I turned my head to see a couple of older boys who went to my school. Lost in the curiosity of being underneath the train, I didn't pay much attention to the boys until they crawled underneath, getting too close to me. One of them grabbed me by my wrists, pinning me down. "I'll hold her while you touch her!" the boy told his friend. When I struggled to get free, he pushed my wrists down even harder. Feeling the gritty sand under my hands, I tried to grab a handful to throw in his face, but he was too strong for me. The other boy, who I thought was named Billy, had captured my legs, but he was having trouble holding them down, and I bucked my body wildly until my legs were free.

"You leave me alone!" I kicked Billy hard, and his yelp caught his friend by surprise. Summoning all my strength, I snapped my wrists free from his sweaty grip. I scrambled from under the train and hightailed it down the street as fast as I could. I didn't even turn around until I reached my back door.

I decided not to tell my mom what had happened because I didn't want to be in trouble. That night, when Belinda and I were both in bed, I turned toward her and told her everything. "Bennie, after you left, something happened at the depot today. Two boys tried to hold me down. One was going to touch me—you know—in a bad way. It was Billy from the fifth grade. Maybe they were going to beat me up. I don't know. Please, don't tell Mom."

"Don't ever stay there by yourself again. It isn't safe." My sister's voice felt cool and comforting in the night air. I was so glad that we shared a bedroom. "We gotta stick together. When I come home, you come home. Promise?"

"Promise." I closed my eyes and smiled to myself. *It's Saturday night; I get to go back to school soon.*

On Monday, about halfway through the school day, Mrs. Macon was showing us some new cursive letters on our shiny black chalkboard. I was just getting into writing these new whirly, twirly capitals when I saw Billy's teacher at our classroom door. Mrs. Macon went out into the hall to talk with her for a few minutes. The other kids were doing their work, not paying any attention, but I could feel my neck get all hot, and my palms were too sweaty to even think about handwriting. *I really hope I'm not in trouble with Mrs. Macon.*

When we went out for recess, I noticed Mrs. Macon ask another teacher to watch us, and when I saw her walk toward me, I thought I was in trouble. But she only said, "Come inside with me, Lorie, so we can talk. You're not in trouble." She took my hand, and we went inside to stand in the hallway, just outside our classroom door.

"Were some older boys bothering you this weekend? Did Billy try to hurt you?" Mrs. Macon asked.

I kept looking down. I didn't know what to say. "Did he try to touch you? It's okay; you're not in trouble here. No boy should make you feel scared and uncomfortable. Billy does not have the right to touch your body."

I stared at the ceiling, not sure of what to say. Then I finally looked up into her face, meeting her eyes. She didn't look mad, just worried. Then she took my hand, asking, "Is there anything you want to tell me?"

For a minute, I thought I could hold it all back, but then the words just came rolling out of me like thunder. "MY BROTHER DOES IT TO ME!"

"What does he do to you, sweetheart?" My teacher's voice stayed calm, but there was a look on her face I'd never seen before.

"He takes my clothes off and hurts me. He hurts me bad."

I knew I wasn't in trouble when I felt my teacher put her arms around me. *She's hugging me; maybe everything will be all right now.* It was a comforting feeling that I hadn't experienced very often in my life. Then Mrs. Macon touched my chin so I had to look up at her. "No one has the right to do that to you. You do not have to put up with that. There are laws to protect you. We can make sure this never happens to you again."

We stayed like that for a few minutes. Then my teacher asked me if I would please tell the principal what I had told her.

"You haven't done anything wrong. This is not your fault. Our principal doesn't want you to be hurt like that either. He just needs to hear it from you. Don't be afraid. Just tell him what happened."

I'd never had to go to the office before. My principal didn't look mad at all, and his eyes were kind, just like when he watched us at breakfast or walking down the hall. It felt a little easier telling the story a second time. Mrs. Macon sat beside me the whole time while I told my story, and while my principal made a phone call. It wasn't long before a pretty lady cop came into the office.

After I repeated my story for the police officer and then a social worker, Mrs. Macon had to go back to class. I stayed in the principal's office for the rest of the afternoon. By the time another stranger came in to join us, my head felt like it was spinning with all the things that were going on. "She's a foster mom," I was told. "You'll go home with her until we get this all figured out."

As I took this stranger's hand and she walked with me down the hall, I looked back to see my teacher watching us. She looked sad.

I wondered if Mrs. Macon would still be my teacher anymore. I didn't have time to feel sad about that right then, though. All I could think was, *I'm finally getting away from Carl.* I didn't know if I'd even miss my mom, because she was such a big fan of Carl. Maybe my dad would come home and make things better. Everything was so confusing; I just didn't know what to think. But the one thing I did know was that I was glad to be far away from my mean half-brother.

It was nice to stay at a different home with my foster mom, but I missed my sisters, Bennie and Cheryl, and I missed Bruce too. I thought about Mrs. Macon and wondered if she thought about me when she looked at my empty desk each day at school. One day, when my foster mom took me to see a doctor, I was delighted to see that my sister Bennie was there in the doctor's waiting room. I rushed to hug her, and then we held hands and waited.

"It's not the same without you at home, Lorie," Belinda told me. "I say a prayer for you every night. Mom won't tell me what happened, but I know Carl did something bad to you. I'm sorry I wasn't there to help you."

I squeezed my sister's hand, trying to smile and be brave. Bennie must have seen how nervous I was. She held my hand tight, trying to reassure me. "I know you haven't been to a doctor before, either, but try not to be scared. I've already had my check-up, and it wasn't too bad. Now that Carl may have to leave our house, maybe you can come back home and everything will be all right."

I didn't have a chance to answer, because the nurse appeared in the doorway and called my name. It was time for me to see the doctor.

The doctor had a kind face, but I hated having to lie still for him in the examining room. I was relieved when he was done poking around and looking at my private parts. It was embarrassing, and it didn't feel very good, either. When the doctor finished with his examination, the social worker joined us in the room. I listened as the doctor told her that I had been abused but Bennie had not.

I learned that my principal went to my house to see my mom. I hoped that she was in big trouble. Maybe this would convince her to take our side on things, instead of Carl's. A few days later, it was time for me to go to court. I felt paralyzed with fear as we entered the courtroom. Everything in there seemed so big. The chair I had to sit in was so large, I felt like it was going to swallow me up. My hands gripped the side of the chair as my knuckles turned white. I looked out over the railing, and all of the adults were staring right back at me. I saw that my mom was out there, too.

It wasn't long before I had to start telling my story to the court. I touched my beaded necklace for courage and began to speak. I told the very same story I'd told to my teacher, the principal, the lady cop, and the social worker. My story never changed, because it was the truth. Only, one thing was different this time. I heard my mother speaking, her words carrying through the quiet, echoing courtroom. In a soft, whining voice, she was repeating the word "LIAR," over and over. *I knew she would stick up for Carl again, and not me! I hope the judge believes me and not my mom.*

The judge must have believed my story, because Carl was sent up north to live with some of our relatives. Soon after he left, my stay in foster care ended, and I was sent back home. My mom was pretty mad at me, but I didn't care. I was just relieved that Carl was gone, and I was happy to be back with my sisters and brother.

Then, a couple of weeks later, the front door swung open with a bang, and who should walk in but Carl. As he tore through the house looking for Mom, I felt my teeth starting to chatter. I tried to calm myself. I hoped the judge would come and make Carl leave again, but he didn't. After that, I felt so scared whenever Carl and I were both in the house at the same time, but he didn't try to hurt me in *that* way again but he still beat up on all of us younger kids, just like before.

Summer arrived too soon. With no more school days to keep me distracted, each day was pretty much like the one before. I had another birthday, but all I remember about that day was how hot it was outside.

Carl liked to play this game where he'd tell me to sit in a chair and not move for an hour. I was so scared of him, so I tried to obey and not wiggle or squirm. But, no matter how hard I tried, Carl would insist that I had moved a finger or a toe, and my hour would have to begin again.

By now, I'd pretty much given up on telling my mom about Carl's games, because I knew she would protect him. With my dad gone so much, Mom was still depending on Carl to be the man of the house. Then, one day, Carl beat both my mom and me with a chain. That day, I knew my mom wouldn't ever save me from Carl, because she was just as afraid of him as I was.

CHAPTER EIGHT

As that summer wore on, I finally began to let myself believe that Carl was not going to hurt me that way again. But then one day, my mother did something that set me on fire with fear. She took me to a house full of men who were strangers to me.

At first, I thought we were just there to visit. The strangers were all black men, and I couldn't figure out how my mom knew them. I realized something else was going on when my mom turned to walk out the door. *She's leaving me here!*

"Mom, please don't go," I begged, but she didn't say a word. She just shrugged and then left me with those strangers.

When I turned back from the door, I noticed two of the men walking toward me. "Hey, sweet thing, come on baby, how 'bout a little drink of beer?"

One of the men held out his beer can to me, beckoning me. *Why are these grown men talking to me like that? I'm only a little kid!* The taller man came closer and tried to touch me. I quickly backed myself into a corner. When the man tried to reach out again, I kicked at him and screamed.

"Don't be like that, baby," the man cooed, pulling me close to him. I let my arms and legs fly, slugging and kicking him until he finally released me. Once I was free, I put up my fists and planted my feet in that corner, ready to fight all four of those men if I had to. The two men seemed to lose interest and just turned away.

They joined their two buddies at a card table, and all of the men ignored me for the rest of the afternoon. I sank down to the floor and clutched my knees to my chest. *I will not let them see me cry.* I couldn't understand why four grown men would want to be bothered with me anyway. So I sat still and waited in that dingy corner, for what felt like forever. I wondered if my mom was ever going to come back and get me. By the time she finally did show up, I was exhausted, all my muscles tight with tension and my stomach clenched from fear.

Mom never explained where she'd been or why she had left me there. The only thing she said as we left was, "We got to get you home."

On the way home, I stared straight ahead; no way was I going to look at my mother. When we got home, I stayed in the car, watching her limp into the house. I didn't touch the car door, just stayed on the scratchy front seat.

As the sun streamed into the car window, warming me, I tried to make sense of it all. Bits and pieces of what I knew about my mom's past came together in my mind. I knew that she limped because she had fallen down the basement stairs when she was young, and her father wouldn't take her to the hospital. Her broken leg had to heal on its own, and that's why Mom always walked crooked.

I knew she was the youngest of eight children and the only girl. She'd told me some stories about the happy times she'd had before my grandmother died, but I knew she'd worked hard caring for her younger siblings and received only beatings in return. Maybe her parents had beaten some of the goodness right out of her. Maybe having to play mom to a bunch of little brothers, when she herself was just a girl, sucked all the feelings of motherhood right out of her.

Even though I could see why my mother's past had made her who she was, there were some things she did that I couldn't forgive, like how she allowed Carl to beat up on us, and what she had done to me that afternoon. I'd never forget how I'd felt huddled in that corner, never knowing whether she'd return.

Finally, I reached for the cool metal handle of the car door. Swinging my feet out, I let the door slam, but only a little bit. *Feet, you might as well head toward our back door, because there's no place else to go.* Inside the house, I was able to slip into my room without my mother seeing me. *I'm not ready to look at her just yet.*

For the rest of the summer, I tried to find as many ways as possible to stay out of the house all day, sticking together with Bruce and Belinda. When we got hot and thirsty, we'd go into our big library downtown. It was always cool in there, and the three of us would take long, cold drinks from the shiny silver drinking fountain. Then sometimes we'd play on the elevators, or head upstairs to put on headphones and watch movies.

"How many times have we seen Burt Reynolds and Sally Field in that movie *Smokey and the Bandit*?" I asked Bruce. He guessed it must have been about a hundred. When we spent the day together that way, the constant knot in my throat almost disappeared because no librarian ever yelled at us there. We stayed as long as we wanted, and Mom never bothered to ask us where we'd been.

Another school year began and fall soon became winter. Even on the coldest days I'd be outside on my sled long after the other kids had gone in for the night.

Carl wasn't the only reason I tried to get out of the house that year. Listening to my mom dwelling on things got old really fast. Without any other adults to talk to, she'd endlessly look back, telling us kids about the few times someone was actually nice to her.

"My mom was so nice to me. I can remember exactly how many days she was in bed before she died, even though I wasn't even old enough to be in school yet! After she passed, I went to live with my aunt and uncle. Uncle Pearl was so kind to me. Why, he'd take me for a walk and buy me a Pepsi. He would listen to me when I would tell him how much I missed my mom. His wife, my Aunt Myrtle, was mean, and she would get drunk and swear at me . . . but I could always count on Uncle Pearl to be gentle. I had a boyfriend before Walter, ya know. He treated me decent. Carl's dad. He loved me too. I know he did." Mom had certainly been through a world of hurt, and maybe that was why taking care of us kids seemed like such a burden to her sometimes.

Dreaming about the past wasn't helping Mom with our situation in the here and now, though. With Dad still gone, she should have been figuring out ways to get us food, but she seemed powerless to even think about it, much less take action. The rumbling of my stomach and the gnawing hunger never went away, just like the tension I felt.

I wished that my dad would return from Alaska. At least we had something more to eat when he was around. I didn't understand what his fascination was with our forty-ninth state.

CHAPTER NINE

This time, when Mom told us we were going to move again, the novelty had definitely worn off for us kids. We'd moved so many times by this point, I didn't know how I could remember so many addresses, but somehow I did.

Our new house didn't have any heat or water. Sometimes there was food, but more often there was not. Mom willingly gave Carl what little money she earned or received from welfare. She even gave him our food stamps, which he'd trade for beer. That left the rest of us mighty hungry. Cheryl would take cans of green beans and hide them in the clothes dryer, so when we'd run out of food, we'd at least have that.

"Mom, do you think there will be any food for dinner tonight?" we asked, one hungry evening.

Mom didn't answer; she just stared off into the distance, her eyes hazy. "My mother was so sweet to me. She would tell me I'm smart and pretty. My brother was good to me too, but he died at such a young age."

"I guess that's a 'no' on dinner then . . ." I said.

Mom's frequent escapes into her dream world made me think about her past, too. Mom used to be lively and pretty, with her blonde hair and a sparkling light in her eyes. Now, she seemed older than her years, and her eyes had dulled along with her hair.

Sometimes, Mom would leave her past behind for a while, and she'd try to be a real mom. When I was younger, she used to sing to me and rub my back until I got sleepy at naptime. "You are my sunshine, my only sunshine. . .." Mom's voice was pretty, and I used to believe she meant the words she'd sing, but when I got older I realized they were just empty words. *I'm nobody's sunshine, and I sure don't make Mom happy.*

I didn't take naps anymore, of course, because I was eight, but sometimes Mom would help me with my hair. She'd take a lock of my hair and swirl it around her finger, and then she'd expertly place two bobby pins so that they formed an X across each coil. She promised me that curls would appear in the morning, like magic. It felt awful to sleep on those pokey bobby pins—and I didn't even like my thick brown hair to be all curly—but I went along with it because Mom seemed to like it.

One day, Mom took a spill down our basement steps, just like she had when she had broken her leg as a little girl. "My knee is a achin' and my head feels funny," Mom told us. She acted kind of weird for a while, but then she came around and was pretty much her old self again. But after that fall, she didn't seem to remember stuff so well, and we kids had to keep reminding her of things.

CHAPTER TEN

Finally, Dad returned from Alaska. I tried to figure out how long he'd been gone this time. I was nine now. *It's been almost a year*, I realized. I wondered what kind of trouble he'd stirred up to make him return to Michigan.

As luck would have it, Dad seemed a bit mellower after his trip. He started providing for us again right away, scavenging dumpsters and landfills for useful objects. One of the first things he did was find a new way to heat our house. He built a wood stove out of a barrel, and then he taught us kids how to cut wood. I'd forgotten how good Dad was at making things with his hands. Some people might call him clever.

With Dad back in the house, Carl stopped being so mean to me. But that didn't mean the house was peaceful. Dad and Carl were always at each other about something. With those two, there could be only one "man of the house," and Carl didn't want to give up that role. Finally, one day, Dad had enough. He told Carl to leave and not to come back. "Get out, you worthless son of a bitch!" Dad yelled at Carl as he scrambled to grab a few of his things and hightailed it out the door.

"Screw you, old man!" Carl hollered as he ran down the street. *I hope it's the last of him I ever see*, I thought as we watched him go.

Not long after Carl left, Mom received a notice of foreclosure on our house. Time for another move, and this time we would have to do it without Dad's help; he'd left for Alaska again. This was the sixth time our family had moved in two years, the eleventh time we'd moved so far in my life. This time, we found a house that was close to Dad's parents so that he could find us when he decided to come back from Alaska.

Mom's plan worked, because when he finally got back, Dad did find us. We noticed that, this time, he was drinking more, and he was meaner, too. He started punishing us for any little thing we'd do. As a punishment, Dad started sending us down into the old basement of our house. It was so dark down there that you couldn't see your hand in front of your face. "You stay down there until you learn to act right, you ungrateful goddamn kids," he'd shout as he shut us into the dark, dank space.

I liked to climb up to the top step and sit by the ribbon of light that seeped in from the crack under the door. I'd stay quiet as a mouse, but Dad always heard me and yelled at me to get back down the steps. Time went by slowly in the dark basement, and there was nothing to look forward to once our time was up.

Somehow, Dad always knew when I was going to creep up to that top basement step. He liked to brag that he had a sixth sense and that he could tell what other people were thinking. Maybe that was how he could know what I was doing even when he couldn't see me. We'd watch Dad use his special powers time and time again. Sometimes, when we were driving down the highway, he'd say, "See that cop over there?" Then, in a kind of mystical voice, he'd stage whisper, *"Don't bother the family in the blue truck."* And the cop wouldn't even look at us as we passed by! Then Dad would boast, "Told you. He knew not to mess with us."

My dad didn't know it, but I was sending the cop my own silent psychic plea: *Notice us! Please notice us!* I wished someone would really *see* us, just once, and stop Walter from doing mean stuff to us kids.

CHAPTER ELEVEN

I guess Mom felt the same way as Emily did; she just couldn't take any more of my dad. With both of them gone, that left Cheryl in charge, and I saw her getting madder every day. She worked so hard to keep food on the table, but all the while she avoided Dad like he was a plague. Cheryl got a job just like Emily had done, and I was worried she was going to leave us too. I had just turned ten and wished I could get a job too. Now Cheryl was the oldest kid at home. That winter, she had gotten a job at the truck stop, but Dad started taking all the money she earned.

One night, we were all surprised when Cheryl came home from work early.

"What are you doin' home? Aren't you supposed to work 'til eleven?" Dad snarled at Cheryl as soon as she walked in the door.

"I quit. I just couldn't do it anymore, so I quit. What's the point? You're just going to take the money anyway." I couldn't believe it when Cheryl said that out loud, right in Dad's face. I was proud of her but scared at the same time.

"You are such an ungrateful little bitch. You got no right, no right at all, to quit that job, ya hear me?"

Dad slapped Cheryl and shoved her into a chair.

"Git your ass outside and git the hell into that truck. I'm driving you back to that truck stop, and you'll take your ass up in there and beg for your job back. If that don't happen, you ain't got no place to live from now on!" Sobbing, Cheryl stumbled her way back to the truck, and Dad got into the driver's seat, filling the quiet street with the sound of screeching tires as he sped away. When Dad came back, he was alone, so I figured that Cheryl must have gotten her job back.

Dad stormed into the house, slamming the door, and Bruce, Belinda, and I immediately scattered. He was hoppin' mad, and we wanted no part of that. Belinda and I were hiding from Dad when we heard him go into Cheryl's bedroom.

Dad stayed in Cheryl's room for a really long time. Belinda and I could hear strange sounds, and a little while later we smelled paint and something burning. We hovered together in our hiding place, almost afraid to breathe. Finally, we heard Dad leave our sister's room.

Belinda retreated to our bedroom right away, but I waited a safe spell, then creeped to the door to Cheryl's room. I touched the lucky beaded necklace Dad had given me, for extra courage, and then I turned that doorknob.

I couldn't believe what I was seeing. Black spray paint covered the walls and the ceiling of Cheryl's bedroom. Even the window had been covered in a thick layer of black paint. Cheryl's clothes were strewn across the room, dumped from her closet and her dresser. When I reached down to pick up a pair of pants, I saw a cigarette burn on them. I picked up more articles of Cheryl's clothing. All of her clothes were scarred with burn marks. Nothing had escaped Dad's wrath. All of Cheryl's books, her stuffed animals, everything my sister owned had been ruined. I snatched up her roller skates. Cheryl loved these; she had worked so hard to earn the money to buy them. Even they were spray painted black. There was nothing left in that room Cheryl could use.

The knot in my stomach was growing bigger than ever, and my throat felt so tight I could barely breathe. The smoky, burned smell of the room was beginning to make my head spin. I wanted to cry, but I couldn't. I knew there was nothing I could do. Anything that wasn't painted black was covered with burn marks.

I wanted to get out of the room as fast as I could . . . but I didn't. I was paralyzed by my thoughts. I couldn't stop thinking of my sister, trying to work after Dad had hit her and forced her to go back to the truck stop. *How can she keep from crying when she waits on customers? Will they notice the slap mark on her face?* I knew when her shift was over she would have to come back here, only because she had nowhere else to go. Cheryl had done her best to make this room look cheery. This bedroom was her getaway from the family, but now her refuge looked more like a haunted house.

I'm going to wait for Cheryl to get home, I decided to myself. I didn't know what I'd say to her when she got there, but I didn't want her to be alone when she saw the horrible sight. So I stayed. After a little while, my knees began to feel weak and my head was spinning from the fumes, so I fell, exhausted, onto Cheryl's bed. The smell of paint and burned cloth right next to my face made my stomach feel queasy. I didn't know how much time had passed, but my eyes started to feel heavy. *Maybe I'll nap for just a little bit,* I thought as I started to drift off.

My eyes snapped open when I felt a hand slap me on my head. I realized I'd fallen asleep on Cheryl's bed. I didn't have any more time to think before I felt two strong hands on my wrists, pinning me down on the bed. I could smell waves of liquor and sweat mingling with the stale paint fumes. *It's Dad.* I shook myself awake, suddenly on high alert. I struggled under my father's grasp until I felt his weight crush down upon my back and I couldn't move anymore. His hands fumbled at the waistband of my pants, and then all I could feel was a horrific pain tearing through my body as he sodomized me. Inside I was screaming, but I knew I couldn't make a sound.

When Walter was through, he grunted and then rolled off of me, quickly falling into a deep sleep on the paint-smeared bed. My father had never done anything like this to me before. *I thought this horrible thing ended with Carl.* I had even believed my dad would stop Carl from hurting me like that if he ever tried to again, but now he had hurt me even worse. Something inside of me was turning, changing, but I wasn't sure what. Everything looked different to me now.

I tried to bring myself to the present, to think clearly through the pain I was feeling. It was commanding all of my attention. *I am in my sister's room, surrounded by black paint everywhere. My father is lying next to me in a deep sleep. There's a strange wetness on my legs.* I touched my skin, and my fingers came back red.

I forced myself to recall why I had come into Cheryl's room in the first place. *I remember now; I didn't want her to face this alone. I wanted to be here for her when she got home.* My thoughts turned back to myself. *My body aches. I know I'm bleeding.* I realized I was hurt, but I couldn't summon the energy to do anything about it. Instead, I cried myself to sleep.

Later, I heard footsteps in the hall, and I woke again to the nightmare of a torn and aching body. I turned my head when I heard the sound of the door opening.

"Oh, my God!" Cheryl moaned. Her knees buckled as she fell into the heap of her treasured possessions, now barely recognizable. My sister didn't even see me where I lay hidden behind Walter's sleeping form. Cheryl's cries didn't stir him from his drunken stupor. Cheryl's wailing was hollow and broken. "I hate him. I gotta get out of here. That bastard. I hope he dies."

Cheryl turned toward the door in disgust, ready to leave. I struggled to call out to her, my voice thin and hoarse. "Cheryl, are you leaving? For good? Will you take me with you?"

Startled to hear my voice, Cheryl turned to look at me. "Please," I begged her. "He came in here and hurt me last night. He hurt me the same way Carl did, that time."

"Hurry up," Cheryl whispered. "We gotta get out of here before he wakes up."

As we tiptoed together down the stairs, my hand reached for the necklace Walter had given me. *How could I have treasured it? Why did I think it meant something?* I twisted it in my fingers and pulled, yanking it off of my neck. The back of my neck stung where the beads had pressed into my skin. The beads glinted in the dim light as they tumbled down the stairs. I dropped the thread, and it fell limply to the floor, damaged and broken. We ran out into the cold night air. *Each step will take me farther from home, farther from the man I will no longer call Dad.*

Cheryl had nothing with her but the clothes she was wearing. *This is all she owns now*, I realized as the cold started to settle in. She wrapped her arms around herself as her silent tears turned cold on her cheeks. We trudged through the snow. We walked and walked, not knowing where to go or whom to call. We still didn't know where Mom had gone when she had moved out of the house, and we knew she wouldn't have been much help anyway.

My sister turned to me, reaching into her pocket. "I know you never wanted to see him again, Lorie, but there is no one else. We have to call Carl."

Cheryl pulled out some change—tips she had earned that night at the truck stop. This handful of change was her first pay that Walter could not steal. We walked toward town, where there was a phone booth.

A drunken voice answered on the fifth ring. "You had it coming to you," Carl's voice slurred through the phone.

As awful as Carl had been to me, he was our only chance of a place to go, and now we knew even *that* wouldn't happen.

The night was getting colder. Finally, Cheryl stopped and turned to face me. Her pretty face looked older, sadder in the moonlight. I knew Walter had stolen something from her too, something she would never get back. The loss of her belongings seemed small in comparison to what he had taken from her, from both of us, really.

"I'm sorry, Lorie," Cheryl said, taking my hands. "I wish I could find a safe place for you. I'm sorry for what he did to you. I know how he is. He will never change. I wish I could make it better . . . but I can't. You're a good sister and I love you, but you have to go home now."

My sister wrapped her arms around me, and we hugged goodbye. I didn't bother asking if she would go with me. I already knew the answer. She could never go home again.

CHAPTER TWELVE

Days later, I discovered that Cheryl did eventually find our mother. It wasn't long before Mom turned up at the door of our house when Walter wasn't home. Cheryl had told Mom how bad things were at home, so she came to get me and my sister Belinda. Mom was living with my oldest sister, Emily. I learned that Emily was now a teenage mother and her husband was named Michael. They let Cheryl crowd into their little house. Bruce ended up having to stay with Walter. Leaving Belinda's twin behind was sad for us. Being Walter's son wasn't any easier than being his daughter.

Emily's house was cramped, but we made do with mattresses on the floor. I remembered Bruce in my prayers each night as I fell asleep.

Mom was using her welfare checks to pay the rent for Bruce and Walter. We sure could have used some of that money at Emily's house now that four people from our family had moved in with the three of them, but Mom was afraid of what Walter would do if she didn't pay his rent. Mom's fear of Walter's vengeful spirit was not unfounded. Once, when Elaine was test driving a used car, Walter had put sugar in the gas tank. It took Carl a whole day just to clean it out.

Running out on Walter had left all of our nerves jangled. There was a heaviness in the air from all of our unspoken thoughts: *There will be payback. It's just a matter of time.* We all knew it wouldn't be long before Walter came looking for us.

The day started out like any other, everyone doing the best she could to keep the tiny house as orderly as possible. Then one by one we froze as we heard the first bizarre rumblings and odd thuds. Walter wasn't sure which house on the street belonged to Emily and Michael, so he just ran up and down the street, randomly throwing rocks at the windows of all of the houses. When Walter finally figured out which house we were all staying in, he got back in a car and drove up and down the street, screaming out the window, "I'll grind up your bones and throw them in the dust!"

Days after the rock throwing and crazy threats, Walter returned. It seemed to me that he'd finally come to kill us. My fear was at an all-time high, twisting my insides into tight knots of panic as I waited for the inevitable. It wasn't long before Walter pulled into the driveway, jumping out of a borrowed car. He was brandishing a baseball bat and a wild look in his eyes. Everyone inside the house scattered immediately, trying to find hiding places. We hid, but Michael, still a teenager, stayed put. None of us dared to peek from our hiding places to see how their encounter was going. When the screeching tires sounded a safe distance away, we each crawled out from our hiding places, too stunned to talk.

Later that night, Michael wouldn't tell us exactly what had happened, but we did learn that a badly bruised Walter drove home in a car with broken windows. He stopped coming around after that.

Michael became a bit of a hero to us. *A teenage boy takes on the man who scares social workers away! The man who puts spells on police officers in their cars, and causes neighbors to hide in their own homes when he hurls rocks at their windows: he's been whooped by Michael.* It was the first time I had ever seen anyone stand up to Walter. It felt so good just knowing that had happened.

For me, our new life in the little house meant that I was allowed go to school every day, not just when Walter decided I could. I was able to eat and sleep in peace, without the fear of Walter coming to hurt me. This meant everything. The constant ball of fear in my stomach and throat began to ease. Some days, it even disappeared.

We weren't rid of Walter for long, though. When he'd see us kids walking home from school, he'd offer us pieces of bubblegum and ask how our mom was doing. Walter started making a point to see Elaine, and his attitude was akin to that of a concerned husband. Once again, Mom gradually started to believe that this time, he had really changed—that he was becoming the man she had always hoped he would be. I could see her falling for his nice-guy act just like I saw strangers do, time after time.

Walter's strategy worked. One day, Mom made the decision that we were going to move back in with him.

"Walter has changed. He needs us. It's time for us to return home."

Her words rang hollow in my ears. Cheryl refused to join us. I didn't want to go home, but I knew I was too young to take care of myself, and so was Belinda. We had no choice in the matter. So we sadly followed Mom back into the house that held so many bad memories. Not long after we left, Emily and Michael took custody of Cheryl. I was happy for her but sad for Belinda, Bruce, and me.

Bruce was so relieved to see us back under the same roof. "Thank God you're back! I've been so worried about you. I wanted to come and look for you, but Walter wouldn't let me out of his sight. You're my sisters. I wanted to do something."

Bruce's voice was full of frustration and regret as he greeted us. He looked more nervous than he had the last time I had seen him, I thought, studying his pale, drawn face. My poor brother had been Walter's only victim during all the time we were gone.

Throughout the years, Bruce had had his own unique experiences with Walter's cruelty. He was treated differently from us girls, but his punishments were sometimes even harsher. Bruce had been beaten with a fan belt and had sat through his own share of lock-ups in the basement. Years ago, Walter had put a live crab down a very young Bruce's pants and then laughed when Bruce screamed. What kind of mind can even think of doing something like that? Another time, Walter told Bruce he was planning on taking his mother out in a boat, tying rocks to her legs, and throwing her overboard. I knew Bruce wanted to be the big brother and protect me and his twin, Bennie, but under Walter's shadow, that just wasn't possible.

Now that we were back in the house, I tried my best to stay away from Walter. That horrible night in my sister's bedroom had left its scars on me. I truly knew what that tyrant was capable of doing.

Sure enough, it wasn't long before Walter started sexually abusing me again, this time on a regular basis. I was sad to learn he was bothering my sister Belinda, too. He'd take one of us up to the attic and have his way with my sister or me, and then we'd have to switch places. It was almost as bad for the sister waiting downstairs as it was for the sister in the attic, just sitting there waiting and thinking, *I'm going to be next.*

Finally, Belinda and I decided to stop these nights of terror. Together, we made a plan. We both went to our counselor at our junior high school, and each of us told her the same story of our nights in the attic. While I was in the counselor's office, I watched her write down exactly what I said. Next, she brought in the principal, and I told her the very same thing. Belinda did, too.

These school officials told Belinda and me that they would inform social services, and they would make Walter stop. We wanted to believe them. We didn't go to a foster home that day, though, like I had when I was in second grade and told on Carl. Instead, we headed home.

Walking home, my shoulder brushing against Belinda's, we told each other different scenarios of what might happen when we reached the house. "I bet we'll see the police taking Walter to the squad car in handcuffs," I suggested.

"Maybe he's already in jail, and it will just be Mom at home."

We were giddy with all of the scenes we imagined. I touched Belinda's hand and felt it trembling as our house came into view. As we drew closer, we could see there was a car parked in front. But our excitement turned to despair when we saw a stranger stumbling out of our house, a red-faced Walter snapping at her heels. Even though we were still several houses away, we could hear his shouting loud and clear.

"You have *no right* to come to my house and tell me how to raise *my* children. Get off my porch. Get the hell outta here. If you *ever* come back, you'll be sorry! Do you hear me? Now *git!*"

Walter screamed the last part at the back of the social worker's head as she jumped into her car. She pulled out of the driveway as quickly as possible, screeching down the street. Lifting his head, Walter noticed us coming up the sidewalk, and the look on his face stopped us cold.

That evening, after Walter beat us, he sent us to the basement for a long time. Belinda and I had thought we had had such a great plan, but once I thought about it (there wasn't much else to do down there but think), I remembered the exact same thing happening a while back when Cheryl had told her school counselor about Walter. Someone came to the house, got chased away by Walter, and never came back. And that night, Cheryl had gone into Walter's cellar lock-up, just like we had. I guess we should have known better than to tell in the first place.

"I wonder if that social worker went to the police after leaving our house," I whispered, still trying to hold on to a shred of hope.

Belinda wasn't so optimistic. Being a little older than me, she remembered all the other times our family had tried to get help. "Maybe the police and social services have decided that it's just too dangerous for anyone to come to our house."

With that, Belinda wrapped her arms around herself and turned away so I wouldn't see her weep.

CHAPTER THIRTEEN

It was April of 1977, and Walter had come up with his biggest plan yet for our family.

"We'll go to Canada and start a new life. Soon as you kids git outta school, we'll take only the things we need and live off the land. Start saving money. We'll buy a van. Canada is a wonderful place, you'll see."

I felt surprised to see my mother's excitement at this plan. Her eyes lit up with hope as Walter described what our new life would be like. I kept losing a little bit of hope every time Walter did something bad to me, and I couldn't understand why Mom still believed in him, time after time.

I wasn't sure what to think about this Canada scheme. I was old enough now to know that it was probably not going to be a good idea. *Something will go wrong, and Walter's temper will get the best of him. Walter will still be Walter, no matter what flag is flown where he is living.* But for the sake of my mom, Bruce, and Belinda, I tried to act excited for this "adventure." I kept my true feelings to myself, as always.

At first we all thought the Canada plan was just talk, but somehow Walter got ahold of a beat-up Volkswagen camper van. Being a skilled mechanic, he soon had it running again after just a few months of repairs.

"Pack up *only* your necessities, everybody, because we're heading to Canada!" These were the instructions we received from Walter, as he crammed an ironing board, iron, motorcycle, canning jars, a pressure cooker, sewing machine, and a bunch of other stuff into the old van. *Why do we need all this stuff just to go camping? These don't seem like necessities to me.*

Bruce, Belinda, and I surveyed the cluttered interior of the van. "Where are we even going to sit?" I whispered to them as we stared at all the stuff.

One thing that I was glad we were bringing along was the three-legged dog who had wandered into our yard one day while Walter was preparing the van for our journey. When we kids paid attention to him, he started to stick around. We decided to call him Tramp. He was a beagle mix with one amputated leg, but somehow he had found us, and I was so glad he had. Tramp needed someone to love him as much as I needed a dog to love me.

The three of us kids were sent inside to pack up our clothes. This was easy because there wasn't much to pack. Mom would usually buy me two pairs of polyester pants at garage sales, and they'd last a long time. We discovered that if polyester pants had cotton thread in the seams, it would always wear out years before the fabric did. So I'd re-sew all my seams with a strong thread. I never had more than two pairs of pants at one time, so I would wear one to school while I washed the other. I think polyester gets a bad rap. It has got to be the most durable fiber on the planet.

Once, a girl at school told me that the tan pants I was wearing were hers. My mom had bought them at her mom's garage sale. I didn't like having her tell me that, but I had a lot bigger things to worry about than my secondhand clothes. So, along with my pants, I packed some cheap new socks and a few shirts I found here and there, and I was good to go.

Our personal items wouldn't take up much space in our van either. I always managed to have a toothbrush, and I could brush with baking soda and water. My fingernails I'd just scrub, peel, and go. I liked to have shampoo for my hair, but most of the time I had to use dishwashing soap. It would get my hair clean, all right, but it was never as shiny as I wanted it to be.

When everything and everybody was ready to go, Walter told us to pile in, and we always did what we were told. Bruce, Belinda, and I sat pressed up against bicycle spokes, pots and pans, a patched-up tent that smelled kind of like tar, and all of the other cargo.

"Let's get the hell out of here," Walter muttered, and away we went.

Twenty miles into the trip, the van stalled. Walter took some time poking around the vehicle, cussing, and glaring at us from outside the van windows before he decided it needed a new battery. He flagged down a man who agreed to give us a jump, and the motor started back up.

For an instant, we glimpsed Walter's charming side as he patted the man on the shoulder and gave him a hearty handshake. But his smile quickly faded as he returned to our van. I hated seeing Walter's fake act. Each time he got away with it only convinced me more to never, ever cross him. *When he's angry, he scares away anyone who'd help us. But when he's nice, no one would ever believe us if we told on him.*

The jump got us as far as Port Huron before our van died again. It looked like we were going to spend our first night away from home in a Kmart parking lot. It was torture sitting still in the hot van while Walter fixed it, but we didn't dare ask to take a walk, or even just get out and stretch our legs a bit.

I let my mind wander as I stared out of the van window, watching the sun set. I could still feel the sting of Walter's abuse the night Cheryl left. At ten years old, I couldn't really wrap my mind around the awful thing that had happened, but it was a pain that didn't seem to go away. I thought of how horrible my life had been in Michigan, but going to Canada wasn't exactly comforting to me, either. It seemed like if I left the things that felt familiar behind, I would never have a chance to get away. *How can I run away in a strange country where I don't know anyone?* The insecurity made the knot in my stomach throb. Looking over at Bruce and Belinda, I wondered how they felt about our trip. It seemed like Belinda was pulling away from the rest of us a little more each day. Bruce just seemed angry about the whole thing, but I noticed that he was still doing whatever he could to appease Walter. Then there was me. I decided that I was going to find something good about what we were doing, in spite of Walter and my fears about this trip. *Maybe there will be a silver lining somewhere in this new country*, I tried to tell myself. Sometimes Bennie complained about me trying to find the bright spots in our bad situations, but somehow that never stopped me. *There has got to be something good that comes out of this new adventure.* I wanted to believe that God was still watching over me.

By the time Walter had finally fixed the van, the sky was dark. Belinda stayed behind to keep Mom company while Walter took Bruce and me on a bike ride all over Port Huron. This was a rare treat.

As we pedaled along the unfamiliar streets, I thought, *Here I am, doing what most kids would love to do with their father. But I can't feel the way other kids do, because so much is not right.* A little part of me was yearning to let go and begin to feel safe, but deep down I knew I wasn't safe. Yet the breeze was in my hair, and the night air felt great after all those hours in the stuffy van. I pedaled hard to catch up to Bruce. My brother and I traded smiles with each other as we coasted down a hill together. I felt a rush of love for my sweet brother; he was really a bright spot in the darkness for me.

The moon was rising as we approached the bridge to Canada. "Look, Bruce, the moon is peeking out at us. It's the very same moon we used to make wishes on from our back porch."

Most of my words were blown away by the night wind before Bruce could hear them, but he gave me a friendly wave anyway. I rode faster, and my excitement grew as we crossed the bridge together. *Presto, we'd changed countries just like that!* My worries were lost in all this beauty.

Walter had told us that Canada was going to be "wonderful," and I wanted to believe him. That night, as we rode under the stars, I allowed myself to get a little bit hopeful, even excited. *Wonderful* had never been a part of my world, but I could still dream that someday it just might be.

Chapter Fourteen

The next morning we pulled up to the Canadian border. "Watch me fool these border guards." Walter was the only one in the hot, crowded van who was excited about this prospect. Seeing Walter con someone to get his way was nothing new to us.

In a low, important-sounding voice, Walter whispered, "Don't question the family in the van. Just let 'em pass on through, 'cause you can't beat a man at his own game." Walter stopped and rolled down the window.

"Good morning, sir. Where are you traveling today, and what is the purpose of your visit?" The attendant scanned the aluminum boat and other items strapped to the roof of our mud-splattered van with the dirty kids peeking out of the grimy windows.

"Just a little family vacation; we're headin' to Sudbury. Gonna see how good the fishin' is here in Canada," Walter said with a smile. The border guard waved us through, and I couldn't help but think, *Walter's con game works in other countries too.*

We passed Sarnia and were heading toward London when the van died again.

"Goddamn piece of shit. Gotta be the alternator. Gonna have to go get one. Gimme the money."

Walter held out his hand to Elaine. She passed him the envelope, which was already growing thin from the other expenses. We watched as Walter walked backward down the highway, holding his thumb up. It wasn't long before a car stopped, and a smiling Walter hopped in. *Maybe he put another one of his spells on the driver.*

While we waited, we threw sticks for Tramp to fetch. He might have been missing a leg, but Tramp was still pretty fast, and he was definitely happy to get some exercise. I was so glad Walter had let us bring him along on our trip, even though there was hardly enough room in the van. Once Tramp got tired, Bruce and I raced each other to a big tree and back.

By the time Walter returned, it was late afternoon. Two hours later, the repairs were done, and Walter ordered us all back into the van. My eyelids quickly grew heavy as the scenery whisked by outside the window. I must have fallen asleep, worn out from all the waiting in the sun. I woke to the sputtering sound of the van as it came to a halt. "Everybody out," Walter snapped. "We're going to camp for a while."

A while turned into more than a week. We set up camp not far from the road, in a sheltered spot surrounded by bedrock and small cliffs. The weathered sandstone gave us a clean floor to live on; no mud got tracked into our raggedy tent. All of us quickly grew to love the beauty of the Canadian countryside. Everything seemed good, but we weren't there long before Tramp ran off. I hoped he'd find our camp again.

Just like at home, finding food was our first activity of the day. Our secluded campsite was next to a lake, and we kids were ordered to fish every day. Along with our catch of the day and some foraged berries, we fried bannocks over the campfire. Bannocks were our campfire bread made from flour, baking soda, and lake water. For breakfast, lunch, and dinner, fish and bannocks were always on the menu.

One day, we were excited to spot Tramp at the edge of the woods near our campsite, but our excitement at his return quickly turned to alarm. Tramp looked different; he was foaming at the mouth and aggressive. My eyes welled with tears as I watched him jump, then back up stiffly, then twist and turn in confusion. I realized Tramp must have rabies. Walter turned on Mom, snarling at her, "See, you old witch, you made this dog sick. You witched him!"

"I didn't. I would *never* do that. I don't know how to witch anything," Elaine cried, burying her head in her hands at this sudden accusation.

"Tramp can't help it; he's sick!" I protested. I looked helplessly at my mom. "What can we do?"

I wanted to go to Tramp and hug him like I had done every day since he had first joined our family. But it was like he wasn't our Tramp anymore.

After a few more herky-jerky movements, Tramp fell down, his tongue hanging out of the side of his mouth. He raised his head and looked up at us one last time, and then he laid his head down and didn't move again. I wept when I saw Walter heading to get the shovel so he could dig a grave for our pet. *I'm not ready to say goodbye to Tramp.* I had just lost my only friend in Canada.

CHAPTER FIFTEEN

On the sixth day of our camping trip, Walter figured out what the latest problem was with the van. It was the crankshaft. Walter was in a rage over his frustration with this vehicle, and his anger would be taken out on us.

Bruce and I were out in the boat, fishing like we were expected to do, when we spotted Walter at the shore yelling at us.

"Get that goddamn boat outta the water."

We were confused, but we knew from the tone of his voice that we had better hurry. We propelled the boat back to the shore as quickly as we could.

"Can't you do anything right? You got work here to do."

Walter grabbed me by the arm, hauling me out of the boat. He spun me around and caught Bruce with the back of his hand. Next, he turned on me again, shouting, "You're supposed to do what I tell ya." Then he hit Bruce in the mouth and shoved us both toward the campsite.

"Your mom has chores for ya to do and you go off fishin'. Goddamn kids. You don't appreciate *nothin'* we do for ya."

We obediently stood in front of Mom, waiting to hear the chores we were to do. When I stole a glance at Bruce, I saw the blood trickling down his chin, and I couldn't keep the tears from filling my eyes. "I don't know what is wrong with you two," our mom barked at us. "You are so stupid. You got no business crossin' your father and me. Go git those buckets and start washin' them clothes."

Bruce and I headed back to the lake to collect the water, and then we heated it over an open fire. Belinda returned now and then to give us more sticks. Her task was to gather firewood from the trees, and she sure took it seriously. She was always out in the woods by herself, gathering sticks and breaking them up. We stirred the clothes around and around in the buckets with a tree branch, and then it was back to the lake again to gather clean water for the rinse cycle. Once the washing was dry, we gathered it from the low tree branches that served as our clothesline. By the time we were done, there were only a few bites of fish and bannocks left for us to eat.

After dinner, Walter had an announcement for us: Elaine and I were going to leave the campsite, hitch a ride, and travel into Sudbury to get the crankshaft fixed. Then we'd be leaving this campsite and moving on.

"That's a long way from here. What if we can't get a ride?" Elaine whined.

"Why do you think Lorie is going with you? People will see you have a kid and give you a lift. Besides, you can always *whore* your way into a ride," Walter retorted. "Now, *git*—and don't come back 'til you get it fixed."

So, without so much as a goodbye, Mom and I set off toward Sudbury. I felt a prickle of excitement about this new adventure; I couldn't wait to see what the town ahead looked like. After we walked about a mile down the road, a man stopped and picked us up. He took us right to the machine shop where they could fix the broken crankshaft for us.

Then, this total stranger drove us to the Salvation Army, where we could spend the night. The kindness he showed us left me with a strange feeling. It was hard to describe, because I couldn't understand it myself. *It's kind of a wanting feeling . . . a longing I don't understand.*

At the Salvation Army shelter, we got to have a real meal and an actual bed to sleep in. Both were a welcome relief to my mother and me. When I crawled into the bed that night, the feel of the cool sheets on my skin was like heaven. I liked camping, but without sleeping bags and a good tent, it was not so fun. The tent we'd been using on our trip had been patched up with a smelly, tar-like substance, and the smell made my head hurt every night when I fell asleep. We did have a piece of plastic and a thin blanket under us, but the ground always felt closer than I wanted it to be. Stretching out my arms and legs as far as I could, I faded comfortably into sleep. *For now, I'm gonna pretend that daylight will never come.*

In the morning, the Salvation Army workers gave Mom and me some emergency cash. We headed straight to the machine shop to pick up the repaired crankshaft, and then we began our return trip. As we walked along the side of the road together, Mom babbled happily to me, suddenly overflowing with things to say.

"Walter will be so pleased that we got the repair fixed and we still have money to spare. Won't he be surprised that we did it in record time, too? We done good! Mission accomplished, I say!"

Listening to Mom talk on and on, I guessed she must have been enjoying this rare moment of freedom, away from Walter, just her and me. But I couldn't help but wonder how anyone could be so foolish. All I could think of was Walter's cruel sendoff to us the day before; he hadn't even said goodbye.

I wondered if I should try to say something to Mom, but I knew by now that I might as well just keep my thoughts to myself, so I just stared straight ahead and kept quiet. Hearing Mom talk about Walter felt like listening to a scratched record that wouldn't stop skipping, over and over. *She always thinks of Walter as the man she hopes he will be, rather than the man he is. Why doesn't she get it? I'm only ten, but I got his number a long time ago. Everyone else in our family understands Walter.* My two oldest sisters had managed to figure it out, and they had left without ever looking back.

And the twins? They still lived with us, but in their own ways, they were already leaving. Belinda already left us behind in her mind, and it seemed like she forgot to take her body with her. Now she was almost like a stranger to me. Bruce was skilled at playing the good soldier, but I could see him looking for ways out of this prison camp.

So to hear Mom bragging about Walter—*blah, blah, blah*— that was something I could do without. *Oh well, why should I ruin her good mood by pointing out that Walter has never given her any credit, so why would he do that now?* As far as telling her how I felt about things—that train had left the station a long time ago. She knew about the cruel things both Carl and Walter had done to me, and each time I had tried to confide in her, my words had fallen on deaf ears. Every time she disappointed me, I would tell myself, *I will never allow her to disappoint me again.* If only that vow actually worked. I couldn't help feeling the sting every time Mom didn't stand up for me.

We were both relieved when we spotted the same man who had taken us into town the day before, and he offered to give us a ride back when we waved him down. Not only did my tired feet get a rest, but my ears got a rest too; Elaine *finally* quit talking. The driver took us to our campsite, and we thanked him and climbed out of his car. Mom's smile quickly faded as Walter approached her. She pulled out the money we had saved, hoping he'd be happy to see it. Just as Mom was opening her mouth to tell Walter her good news, he cut her off. "So you were whorin' to get a ride, *and* this extra money you're givin' me, huh? You are *so* pitiful."

Once the new crankshaft was installed in the van, it was time for us to pack up our things. Walter insisted that we lighten our load, and *he* got to decide what we took and what would be left behind. As our van pulled away from our campsite and I looked back at it one last time, I felt a stab of guilt. Clothes and other household items were left strewn about the once-beautiful area where we'd lived. I was not proud of the mess we left behind.

As the van hummed along over the road, my mind drifted to thoughts of my brother and sister, just as it had yesterday when Mom and I were walking back to the campsite. I sneaked a glance at my brother. Bruce was nervously gnawing on a hangnail, and I caught his eye. I opened my mouth to speak but then closed it again. Walter didn't like to have any chitchat from us kids breaking his concentration while he was driving.

So I imagined myself yelling, *"Hey, Bruce, we sure did have some fun fishing and rocking the boat, didn't we? You're a good brother. Don't look so worried. None of Walter's meanness is ever going to rub off on you. Next time he tries to hit you in the mouth, duck and tell him to go to h-e-double hockey sticks!"*

Next, I turned to look at Bruce's twin, skinny little Belinda. She was sitting scrunched against the door, always trying to get as far away as she could. Belinda could be so much fun if she didn't have to spend most of her time staying out of Walter's way—under the radar, I guess you'd call it. I wished I could tell her, *"I know how badly you want to get away, but don't shut Bruce and me out, too. Remember what you told me when we were little, that we gotta stick together? Stick with us, Belinda!"* But if Bennie and I could have talked whenever we wanted to, what would we really have said? How could we even have begun to put our feelings into words?

Bruce, always so nervous, waiting for the next blow to come from Walter. Belinda, hurt by Walter in terrible ways too, but afraid to even talk about it. My mind raced to thoughts of my other sisters, and now I wondered how Cheryl was doing after losing all of her things in such a sick and brutal way. She would never come home again, but I know she missed us kids. And Emily and her husband, Michael, they must have felt much older than their teenage years as they cared for their new baby and Cheryl too. And what about me? All I wanted was freedom. If only I were just a few years older, I could leave and go off on my own. If I ever got to pick the activity I would want most to do, it would be riding my bike across the whole country. What a feeling of escape that would be, and how wondrous to see all those places I'd only imagined. Then, of course, there was Mom. She was a grownup; why in the world did she stay? *Why can't she see that things are never going to be different? Does Walter not seem so bad to her after life with her mean father and stepmother? Does she just keep kidding herself just so she can go on?* Maybe that's what our lives would always be—just trying to go on. Our only hope was to follow Walter's orders and do what we could to stay alive. *Will the terror in my throat ever ease up? Please, God, look at me!*

My whirling thoughts came to a halt as Walter snapped off the ignition of our wobbly van. We camped outside of Sudbury. Morning came early when Walter's voice woke us just after dawn.

"You kids need to stretch your legs before we leave this morning. Go on. Go for a short bike ride."

He didn't have to tell us twice. Belinda, Bruce, and I stuffed our mouths with handfuls of the berries we had saved from our campsite, and we jumped onto our old bikes. As we pedaled through town, I felt a little sad saying goodbye to this friendly place where Mom and I had been warmed by the comfortable night of sleep and the meal at the Salvation Army. That same wave of longing, of wanting, washed over me again.

When we returned to our campsite, we could see that Walter was brimming with excitement about what he called the "last leg" of the trip.

"Okay, kids, we're heading two hundred miles north, just past Shining Tree, to a place called Grassy Lake. It's the most beautiful place on Earth."

I was sure it would be beautiful, but I knew it would be tarnished by Walter's presence, casting his big, dark shadow on everything.

Bruce, Belinda, and I steered our bikes back to the van and squeezed them into the back. Then we scrunched in around our bikes and the ironing board, which hadn't been used at all. Big surprise there. I imagined myself saying, *"Let me gather the few ragged clothes I own from these tree branches and iron them so I look my best for fishing."*

Soon, I was bumped awake. My eyes opened to miles and miles of trees zipping by us, and oh-so-few houses. I felt a tingle of apprehension, thinking about how we seemed to be heading into more and more remote areas. If this old Volkswagen quit on us now, we were going to wish we had on hiking boots instead of these old, ripped-up tennis shoes that barely fit anymore.

When we stopped at a little gas station, I watched Walter count the cash, and I noticed that gas had taken most of the money we had left. But there was a little left over, and we stared hard, our eyes glued to the door of the general store, hoping to see Walter emerge with a jar of peanut butter in one hand and a loaf of bread in the other. Instead, he tossed a bag containing flour and baking soda onto Mom's lap. She mumbled obediently, "We'll make bannocks tonight."

Walter turned his head to glare at us and growled, "I better not hear any complainin', neither."

Hunger was an everyday thing for us, and disagreeing with Walter was never a choice, so why did he even bother with that remark? Hot and hungry, I fell into a fitful sleep, and then I awakened to hear Walter announcing, "This is Grassy Lake Road. The lake is just down the way."

Bruce, Bennie, and I tried to sit up straight, eyes peeled, looking for our next destination and hoping that, somehow, things would be better.

CHAPTER SIXTEEN

Walter pulled the van into a clearing. We piled out and he began surveying the area, a pleased look on his face. "It's just like I remembered. You girls unpack while Bruce and I build a fire and look for something to eat."

Belinda headed out to the woods right away to gather firewood, her usual chore. Bennie was growing used to making herself as invisible as possible.

Setting up camp was second nature to us now, and we tried our best to make it feel like home, as it was the only home we had at the moment. Soon, we heard Walter returning. He was carrying six walleyes on a string. "The fishin' is just as good as I remember. Get 'em cleaned and cooked; I'm hungry."

I was a pro at cleaning fish now, and everyone was grateful to finally get a meal of sorts.

Walter always enjoyed living off the land, and he certainly didn't mind doing without things from the "outside world," as he liked to call it. The way he could remember a lake or a special spot in the woods was uncanny. His talent for making things with his hands amazed me too. Somewhere along the line, he had learned a lot of good things from Native American culture, and he knew just how to put those things to practical use. He had a respect for nature that rubbed off on me too.

At our new campsite, one of us kids would go fishing with Walter every day. Usually Bennie stayed on shore and helped Mom with the chores. The lake served as our sink, bathtub, and washing machine; the tree branches, our clothes dryer. Both Mom and Walter seemed more content here at Grassy Lake, and I started to feel the tightness in my gut relax a little. On my days to fish, Walter and I sat silently in the boat and caught walleye, pike, or pickerel.

Fishing was my thing at any of our campsites. It made me feel like I was accomplishing something, and it was peaceful. I liked it best when it was Bruce and me in the boat together. Having water between us and Walter's demands made me even more relaxed; I could see the ripples of security stretching between us and the shore. If you didn't see us out rocking the boat, then we were probably treasure hunting over in the dump. But secretly, I always wished I was reeling in a good-sized pike.

The days flowed by at Grassy Lake, and I found that I didn't even know what the date on some faraway calendar might be. One evening, when Mom proudly presented me with a birthday cake she'd cooked over the open fire and wished me a happy birthday, I was so surprised. The day must have been July 10, 1978. I couldn't help but smile because mom remembered I turned eleven. It was a happy surprise because the cake had turned out so well, too. It was the shape of the iron skillet and black on top and on the bottom, but when we cut into it, there was a tasty, white cake inside. That old familiar feeling—the yearning to be a real family and to feel safe and loved—moved like a wave through my whole body. *But cake around the campfire will just have to do for now.*

I gave Mom a grateful hug and cut an extra big piece for Bruce because he loved cake.

A few days after my birthday, Walter had a new idea: "We should build a cabin here."

I liked this idea, and I started to get excited as we began to gather rocks from the area around our campsite. We set them down to form an outline of what would be our little home in the woods. "How about we use the mud and ashes from the fire for the cabin's mortar to hold the stones together?" I suggested while heaving another stone into place.

Walter smiled. "That should work," he said as he ruffled my hair.

I didn't know what other girls my age felt when their dad gave them a little pat; I only knew that what I felt couldn't remotely be the same. I wasn't even sure of how things were "supposed to be" anymore, but I was sure that this wasn't it. Even so, I was glad we were going to build a stone cabin, and whenever I wasn't catching fish, I was gathering rocks.

The walls of our cabin were just beginning to take shape when another family arrived at Grassy Lake. I watched as a happy young couple set up their nice camper, a Coleman stove, and other expensive gear. They were laughing and teasing each other the whole time. I tried to imagine what it would be like to live in their world, even for just a day. Reality came back with a vengeance when I saw Walter waving and smiling at them. Walter was muttering under his breath, and my heart sank when I heard the spell he tried to cast on these two strangers: " Don't pay no attention to the family next to you, and get the hell outta here soon."

Walter loved to show his power over others, and he actually believed the spells he cast could control people. I guess he was right, because the couple didn't stay long. When another family showed up a while later, Walter commanded us to pack up our things: "Let's get the hell out of here." As our van pulled away, I watched the promise of the stone house fade in the distance.

CHAPTER SEVENTEEN

We tried to camp at another lake, but it already had people camping there.

"These people are a buncha mean assholes," Walter announced, and we moved on again. Only this time, our van started to make churning noises as it struggled up a hill.

"There is too goddamn much weight in here," Walter grumbled, as he glared right at Elaine. He pulled the van over to the side of the road, and we all waited silently to see what would happen next. Opening the rear door of the van, Walter hauled out his prized motorcycle. It was a relic he had found at the dump, but had managed to get into excellent working order.

Walter gestured toward us. "You're gonna drive the van and follow me," he commanded Elaine.

"You know I don't know how to drive a stick shift," Elaine whined.

"Just shut up and do it. Bruce will help you."

Walter jumped onto his motorcycle, revved the motor, and drove off without looking back.

Elaine quickly proved she wasn't exaggerating. After many jerks and stops, the van finally lost power.

"I bet the transmission is shot," Bruce said, looking worried. Elaine was hysterical. "What are we going to do? Walter won't leave us here . . . *will* he? Is he coming back? We can't be *left* here!" Her pitch rose higher with each hysterical question.

"Dad will come back," Bruce assured her. "We've got to push the van out of the road, though. Mom, you steer. Lorie and Belinda, help me push."

Bruce's calm words quieted Mom, and the three of us were able to get the van to the side of the road.

"Now we wait," Bruce told us, crossing his arms across his chest. I smiled at my brother. *He is going to be a good man someday. He won't be like Walter; I just know it.* We tried to chill out and relax for a spell, but our apprehension about Walter's return hung heavy in the air. Finally, we heard the whir of Walter's motorcycle approaching, and we all snapped to attention.

"What the hell were you *doin'*? I was almost there when I realized you weren't behind me, so I had to turn all the way around and come back. Why weren't you following me?"

Walter expected his orders to be followed to a "T," even when they included assignments we didn't know how to do. Elaine cowered in silence, and I slipped my hand into Bennie's as we waited for what was to come next. When Bruce told Walter he thought the transmission was gone, Walter went into a rage.

"Whattaya mean? It can't be!"

When Elaine whispered that she couldn't drive a stick shift, Walter shoved her, and she stumbled and fell.

"What did you do, you stupid bitch? I oughta leave you here to die."

Then, turning to Bruce, Walter hissed, "You are *so worthless.*"

I squeezed Belinda's hand as we braced ourselves for Walter's wrath to come our way next. The thought that he might leave us here, stranded in the middle of nowhere, with no food and very little water, chased all other thoughts from my brain. We all sat in silence.

We heard Walter open the rear door to the van. I held my breath in fear. *What is he going to do now?* Then, Walter calmly said, "We're all gonna have to pitch in and carry our stuff the rest of the way. We'll take only what we gotta have to survive. Bruce and I will return later for the van. We'll walk to Fossup Lake. It's a long hike, but we can do it."

As Walter began to haul items from the van that he deemed necessary, we lined up like soldiers, ready to accept whatever Walter plunked into our hands. Elaine grabbed the box of food supplies while Bruce gathered the pots and pans. Belinda and I were left carrying the clothes and a chainsaw. "Let's go," Walter ordered, and we set out on our long hike.

No one dared disturb Walter's mood by voicing a question or complaint. We waded through the grass on the side of the road until General Williams led us into the woods. There wasn't a path, and the brush was deep. No one questioned why we couldn't continue on the road to reach our destination.

I turned to take one last look at the road and screamed silently inside my head, *Why are you dragging us through the woods when the road is the logical way to go when the van isn't working?* We all trudged along in silence, the dense trees blocking the sunlight above us, creating a feeling of twilight.

The mosquitoes and deer flies began as a pesky annoyance. *I can deal with this,* I vowed to myself, trying to stay calm. But the barrage of insects grew more intense as we traveled deeper into the thick woods. We tried to swat and bat at our attackers, then attempted to outrun them, but nothing worked.

The hum in my ears was relentless; the countless bites on my neck, arms, and ankles itched, then burned, then itched again. I shifted the chainsaw back and forth in my arms so that I could rub a sting or scratch an itch, even though I knew I should be saving my energy for the long walk ahead. I tried a second time to outrun the deer flies, but the bumpy roots and sharp branches snapped at my feet, tripping me up. Ahead, I could see the flailing arms of the twins, a grim reminder that they were suffering just as much as I was.

Once Walter decided he couldn't endure the stings any longer, he stopped and offered each of us a few drops of musk oil. *Who knew Walter had squirreled away a bottle of musk oil inside his shirt?* We rubbed it on our sweaty bodies, gathered our loads from the mossy ground, and put one foot in front of the other as we traveled on. The relief was short lived, as our sweat washed the oil away, and the mosquitoes and flies returned in full force.

"Only ten more miles to go!" Walter hollered back to his troops. He offered this nugget of information as if it should be happy news to all of us.

Are you kidding me? I screamed silently. I cringed at the thought and prayed, *Please, God, let us make it another ten miles.* The muscles in my neck and shoulders ached from trying to hold the awkward chainsaw mile after mile, and my legs were beginning to cramp. Most of all, I tried not to think about my feet. No one in our motley group was wearing hiking shoes, that was for sure. Our worn-out tennis shoes weren't meant to travel this far. The menacing bug bites continued, and finally Elaine asked meekly, "Walter, could we have a little more musk oil please?"

"I ain't got enough, and we ain't got that much further to go, so just shut up," Walter snapped back.

I started to cry, being careful not to make a sound, the way I always did. I could tell by the way my sister's shoulders were trembling that she was weeping too. Bruce reached over and grabbed a handful of the clothes Belinda was carrying, adding it to his already-heavy burden. I had no way of counting the hours, but that day seemed endless.

CHAPTER EIGHTEEN

It was late when Walter exclaimed, "We made it! I told you it was here." I could see a small shack in the clearing ahead, in front of a slope leading to the lake. All of us but Walter dropped our loads and collapsed on the ground in exhausted relief. Walter's excitement was almost manic.

"Rest for a minute, and then we'll scout around. This is where we'll stay! Everything we need is right here!" Walter declared, pointing out our surroundings.

After a brief rest, Elaine heaved herself up and ventured inside the tarpaper hunter's cabin. I noticed that she was limping worse on the leg she had broken as a child. *Sometimes, even though I'm only eleven and she's a grownup, I think that I worry more about her than she does about me.* Shaking off that thought for the moment, I stood up on my wobbly legs and followed her into the tiny cabin.

To my surprise, there were real beds inside: two rusty bunks and two cots. They might have been covered with dirty, mildewed mattresses, but they were a welcome sight anyway. We were all sore and weary from our weeks of sleeping on the ground. The tent that Walter had brought for our trip had never lost the chemical smell from the hole he had tried to patch. Our muscles ached constantly from sleeping with only plastic and a scrap of worn blanket between our bodies and the earth.

The thought that this place might work for us crept into my head. *Stay guarded*, I told myself, but my resolve was weak from exhaustion. A little bubble of hope began to grow inside of me.

When I looked closer, I noticed with surprise that every square inch of the cabin walls was covered with writing. I was too tired that night to read the scribbled words, but there were many nights to come when I'd lie awake and read the cryptic messages from previous visitors. Sometimes I even allowed myself the luxury of wondering what their lives were like, these strangers who wrote on cabin walls. For the moment, I sighed and went back outside when I heard Walter calling. I let myself be optimistic for the time being: *Walter is acting decent, and Elaine is catching his enthusiasm. And best of all, there are beds!*

Walter summoned us kids. "Come on, I'll show you around."

Like a proud new homeowner, he took us on a tour of the grounds. We stopped where a bubbling spring ran through the woods near the cabin. "We can drink and wash up here."

I bent to scoop some of the cold, clear water into my hands and take a sip. Milk was always my absolute favorite drink, something I could never get enough of, but the spring water up north in the Canadian wilderness was the most delicious thing I'd ever tasted. It was so clean and refreshing. I was starting to like this place already, and I could tell that my parents did, too.

Maybe this really is why they packed our van with everything we own. Perhaps we will make this our home and never go back to Michigan. I turned my attention to the nearby bushes, just dripping with berries.

"We'll catch fish for supper and make jam and maybe some juice too. It's perfect, isn't it?" Walter beamed.

I smiled and nodded my head. Bennie was staring off into the distance; she didn't look so sure. "We can live here," Walter added. "We have food, water, and shelter. We got a lot to do tomorrow, so we gotta get some sleep. You kids go decide which bunk you want."

Bruce ran off toward the cabin, and Belinda and I followed close behind. I stopped at the doorway, letting the twins pick first. When I turned back to look at my parents, I saw that they were gazing out at the lake, side by side. Walter put his arm around Elaine, and she rested her head on his shoulder. It was a small thing, but something I didn't remember ever seeing before. Seeing the two of them like that made me think about the stories I had heard from them about how they had met.

I tried to imagine my parents as teenagers as my mind went back to the story I remembered so well. My father was only sixteen the day he sat nursing a cup of coffee at Barry's Drive-In. My mother was the carhop who gave it to him. It was 1957. Mom was still grieving over her recent breakup with Carl's father. I could almost picture her gazing at my father, a handsome teenager in fatigues, waiting to be deployed to Korea. With his slim build, dark hair, and smooth features, I suppose Walter could be classified as handsome. I'm sure in Elaine's eyes he looked pretty good. Elaine may have caught his eye too. She was pretty, thin, and blonde, and she had a friendly nature. Maybe she decided to go on her first date with Walter just to escape from the drudgery of her life.

My dad had always been small for his age when he was growing up. As a kid, he was bullied a lot. Those bullies sure taught him well, because he became a master bully himself.

Both of my parents had such sad lives, years before I was born. I felt sorry for all the cruel things my grandparents had done to them, but I wished it would have made them want to do better for us kids. Shaking my head, I brought myself back to the present. I tried to fit the pieces together in my mind. It was disorienting to see them looking like a contented couple, gazing at the lake together as we tried to create yet another new home. I wasn't sure where to put all of this in my thoughts. It was all too much to think about at the moment, so I tucked my thoughts away and turned toward the task at hand—settling in to our new, so-called "home."

As I explored the cabin and prepared my bunk for bedtime, I felt curious and confused, with a little bit of happiness mixed in about this new move. Mom had seemed about ready to lose it these last couple of days, but now relief was washing over her, like ripples from our little lake. Our lake. I liked the sound of that. I tumbled into my bunk with a hopeful exhaustion, watching the puff of dust that rose from the dirty mattress vanish into the air. *Maybe Walter's dream place will work out after all.*

When morning came, I could truly see what a dump the cabin was, but I wouldn't let that get me down. My bones felt better from just one night spent on that dingy mattress, and I was curious to start reading some of the writing on the walls. *I wonder if I could sign my name here too. Maybe I'm the youngest person to ever stay here.* I'd have to think more about that later, because it was time to start my first day at Grassy Lake.

Elaine was already cooking breakfast (bannocks and berries *again!*) over the campfire. Walter started doling out jobs as soon as we sat down next to the fire.

"Fishing every day is a must. If the money holds out, we'll be able to get a few supplies from town. We need to pick berries every day, and make sure we have drinking water near the cabin at all times."

Bruce and I were excited to begin fishing, but our boat was still tied on top of the van, miles away on the side of the road where we'd left it. Belinda's job would be the same as before, finding sticks for the fire.

As the days drifted into weeks, everything felt a little bit easier at our new campsite.

Walter showed us how to make plates and dishes out of birch bark from the trees around the cabin. We learned that we could also brew tea from the birch bark, and it tasted pretty good. Looking at the forest around us, we could tell that the lumber companies had felled several kinds of trees, but, fortunately for us, the birch trees had not been as useful to them.

Finally, it was time to fetch our other belongings. We especially needed the fishing boat. Walter and Bruce were going to hike back to the van and get our stuff. So off they went—only, this time, they took the road. They planned to walk and hitchhike along the way. This reminded me: *Why did Walter have to drag us through that mosquito-infested forest to get here, when we could have used the road?* Then I remembered that Walter was *always* suspicious of the outside world. *He doesn't want anyone to mess with us or know our business. It's kind of like getting here was a secret.*

After the menfolk left, I couldn't help missing my brother and worrying about his safe return. To distract me from my worries, I helped my mom and sister make our shack in the woods as homey as possible.

On the day that Walter and Bruce returned, what a sight we saw! Walter was driving his motorcycle, which had been left behind in our broken van. Behind him trudged a weary Bruce. The motorcycle was pulling the aluminum boat with a rope, right across dry land, thumping and bumping over roots and rocks. The boat was packed with all of the stuff we'd left behind. After we unloaded all of our supplies, we discovered that the trip across land had worn a hole in the boat. Walter patched the hole, and soon Bruce and I were off on a long-awaited fishing expedition.

The fishing went great for a while until one day, when Bruce and I were way out on the lake and the patched-up hole became unplugged. We looked down between our feet in horror. The hole was as big as a baseball, and the boat was filling up fast. When we tried to start the motor, nothing happened. It was probably out of gas, and of course we didn't have life vests. Through the hole in the floor, I could see murky weeds swaying underneath us. *What if they pull us under?* I thought, panicking. Together, Bruce and I paddled as hard as we could, but within minutes we were sitting in water up to our waists. I searched the shoreline, so far away, to see if either of our parents was looking out for us. Just as I'd expected, no one was watching. Bruce and I were both good swimmers, but the sinking boat was so awkward.

"We can't go back without the boat," Bruce shouted, his voice thick with dread.

What would Walter do to us if we lost the boat? The thought of drowning filled my head as Bruce and I desperately paddled toward shore. The boat became harder to move by the minute as the water continued to rush in. By this point, I was praying just as frantically as I was paddling: *Please, God, just let us make it to shore!* My arms were on fire with the effort, and my wet legs were beginning to feel numb, but I could see that we were making progress. Finally, we neared the shore. When it was shallow enough to stand in the water, Bruce and I jumped out and pushed the boat to shore. Then we both fell to the ground in exhaustion. I remembered to offer a prayer of thanks as I felt my eyes close.

Chapter Nineteen

Now that our boat was unreliable, Walter began gathering birch bark to build a canoe. What little free time I had was spent watching this challenging feat. When Walter finally completed the canoe he'd been building, I could see that it was a beauty. It floated well, but we didn't use it for fishing. It served as kind of a monument to Walter's ingenuity, resting in a place of honor just outside the cabin. So, our old boat with the patched-up hole was still in use. Our newfound belief in Walter's craftsmanship took another dive when he taught us to fashion bows and arrows. The weapons looked good, but the arrows never shot straight. So fish was the only meat we ate while in Canada. The fishing lures Walter created proved to be much more useful than his arrows.

We'd started making jam from the berries we picked around the cabin. It turned out really well, so next we decided to try to make juice. Walter sent us to a small dump a ways off from our little cabin, to see if we could find bottles. We gathered as many unbroken bottles as we could to contain the berry juice, and then we used sand to clean them. There were also some old tires down there. One day, Walter decided he needed three of those tires and instructed Bennie, Bruce, and me to each bring a tire back to camp for safekeeping.

When we arrived back at camp with our tires in tow, our parents were watching us with their heads together, talking in low voices. When we got closer, we saw that they were both chuckling.

"You're each carrying your tire just the way we predicted," Walter laughed.

Bennie had been lugging hers with her arms wrapped around it, making her job quite difficult. Bruce had been kicking his tire like he was angry, just like they'd guessed he would do. I was rolling mine through the woods, trying to make a game out of it.

"We *knew* you'd find a way to get some fun out of it, Lorie," my parents said.

I marveled at the thought that Walter and Elaine actually noticed our individual personalities. It surprised me, as most of the time they seemed to pay no attention to our physical needs or our happiness. *If only they could get to the next step and DO something about their observations,* I wished to myself. *Couldn't they see that Belinda was depressed and pulling away from all of us? Life was so hard for her that she didn't bother to even try to make transporting a tire as easy as possible. It doesn't take a psychologist to see that Bruce was kicking the tire because he couldn't kick Walter. And God knows he sure would like to kick him, and kick him hard.*

By mid-August, our family knew that with fall approaching, living off the land would become more challenging. We kids picked berries daily, and we noticed that each day we spent more time searching and less time harvesting. The fish weren't biting as much now, and we saw smaller catches as the days went by. All we ate for the whole summer was fish and berries, fish and berries.

I knew those weren't balanced meals, and sure enough, our strange diet had been causing us some problems. Elaine suffered the most. The huge amount of seeds we ate with our berry diet had her plugged up and miserable. She spent a lot of time in our makeshift outhouse. For some reason, I was always the one she called. "Lorie, I need warm water and some Ivory soap!" she moaned from behind the cabin. I'd run to help her, of course, all the while knowing this was not much of a substitute for a balanced diet or laxatives from a drug store. Her calls for help were happening more and more lately. Walter thought it was hilarious to hear her voice calling me from our crapper. Sometimes I'd hear him mimicking Mom in a high, shrill voice: "Lorie, I need some warm water and Ivory soap!" Then his laugh would echo through the woods, sounding a bit like a loon. *I could laugh at his little joke too if I didn't know how miserable Mom was. If I make it out of this place alive, I'm going to read everything I can on proper diet and nutrition.*

Because our food supply from Mother Nature had grown thinner, Walter decided to hike to the nearest town, which was almost a hundred miles away. While he was there, he made a little business deal. He managed to sell our broken-down van, which was still abandoned on the side of the road, for a hundred dollars.

When Walter returned, he gave Elaine a few of the Canadian bills he had made from his little bargain and told her to take me and walk into town. "There's a church there that will help you out," he explained.

We headed out obediently, but our shoes were already worn thin. My tight tennies didn't even have soles anymore; there was only a thin, rough layer between my feet and the road. I could feel each pebble on the ground as we walked. Yet our hunger was more pressing than our feet. With each step, I gave God a word of thanks that Walter had not forced himself on Belinda and me while we were camping in Canada. As unpleasant as hunger could be, it still beat the terror I'd felt each time Walter had had his way with me back at home. Of course, it had been a huge relief to be alone at night, but being in survival mode out in the wilderness, unsure of where our next meal was coming from, had stolen some of the calm I felt.

We were relieved and grateful when a truck driver picked us up for the majority of the long trip. Knowing that we were out of everything, Elaine was protective of the forty dollars Walter had given her and was determined to stretch every penny. She decided that we'd try the Salvation Army first. The attendant told us, "We give money only to Canadian citizens, but we will give you some supper and a few staples to take with you. We have no beds left here, but we'll arrange for you to go to the shelter nearby to sleep."

After a shower and a good night's sleep, we returned to the Salvation Army the following morning. Mom thanked the woman there who gave us a food voucher, a box of flour, sugar, a few cans of soup, some vegetables, and bread. Next, we went to the grocery store to top off our supplies. After our meager purchases, we set off again for "home sweet home." We walked to the road, turned in the direction of our campsite, and started hoofing it. When a police cruiser pulled up next to us, I was surprised that the officer offered to give us a ride. He even insisted on driving us right to our destination.

As we pulled up to our hunter's-cabin home, I was dismayed to see what it looked like from afar. After being away, everything appeared differently to me: the cabin was a rundown shanty, and our hand-washed clothes were dingy rags fluttering from the branches of the surrounding trees. Our necessities and household supplies looked crude and messy scattered about our campsite.

An idea crept into my head as Mom and I climbed out of the police car: *Maybe this officer will see that things here aren't right for us three skinny kids, dressed in such ragged clothes. Maybe he'll investigate our strange situation. If only this cop could read my mind.*

As Walter approached, the hostile look on his face quickly changed to one of sincere gratitude when he saw the cruiser parked on the dirt path. He shook the officer's hand and thanked him for the ride in a jolly, hearty voice. The polite look on Walter's face transformed back to dark and menacing as soon as he turned his back on the cop. My heart sank as I watched the taillights of the officer's car grow smaller, finally disappearing into the dim forest. I turned to help Mom unpack the supplies. *At least our meal won't be fish and berries tonight.*

When fall arrived, our staples and all of our money were gone, along with the supply of fish and berries that had sustained us all summer. One day, a partridge wandered into our camp. Walter attempted to shoot her, but his homemade arrows were too crooked and the bird ran away. Shortly after that, she returned, followed by her flock of chicks. We had no food to eat that day, but Walter only sat watching the partridge and her little brood, making no attempt to shoot her or catch any of her young. Somehow, for him, killing them was too cruel. It was confusing to me, his strange twist of right and wrong.

Days later, as I was getting ready for bed, I overheard my parents discussing how long we might be able to survive on water alone. "Forty-two days," Walter said. Elaine nodded in agreement. *Is that how it will all end?* I went to sleep wondering if tomorrow would be Day One of our starvation countdown.

The next day, I was so relieved when I woke up to see Walter and Bruce mounting their bikes to ride the hundred miles into town for help.

"That way I won't have to worry about *you* whorin' around to get a ride and food," Walter said to Elaine—his classic parting words.

"We can do at least fifty miles a day, right?" Walter asked Bruce.

Bruce nodded and glanced back to reassure me, a determined look on his face. But I could see the fear lurking underneath his brave smile.

As the two of them disappeared down the road on their rickety bikes, I sensed how frightened Mom was, alone in the woods with her two girls and no food for any of us. I thought about how the twins both insisted they'd seen wolves in the woods while hunting for berries, and one time even a bear. I wondered if that was what Mom was thinking about, too.

Mom, Belinda, and I persevered during the absence of our menfolk, though. No bears or wolves entered our campsite. The gnawing hunger was our worst intruder. We were able to scrounge a few remaining berries, but we sadly found the fish were no longer biting on these hot August days. Mostly, we filled up on water and waited, day after day, for Bruce and Walter to return. My thoughts turned often to my brother, alone on the road with Walter. Bruce was twelve now, and I could see glimpses of the fine young man he would become. He was such a sharp contrast to his father. I hoped that this time alone with Walter wouldn't snuff out the light that I still saw faintly glimmering in my brother's eyes. *Be strong, Bruce,* I prayed night after night.

CHAPTER TWENTY

Two weeks later, father and son returned. I was hungry and attempting to fish when, in the distance, I heard the crunch of tires on dirt, and, to my surprise, I saw a big rental truck pulling into our camp. Mom was tending the fire. I watched Walter approach her with a rare smile on his face. "Guess what, Elaine? We're goin' home."

I paddled to shore and called out into the woods to summon Belinda, who was attempting to snatch the very last of the berries. There was excitement in the air as we all gathered around Walter to hear the news about his plans for our homecoming. I was relieved to see Bruce standing beside him, looking relatively intact. We exchanged a smile that said, *We'll find time away from our parents and talk about these last two weeks soon.*

The marvel of an actual rental truck wasn't missed by anyone. We were all thrilled to see it there, gleaming and new. Walter chuckled, "Once I drop off the title to the van to this guy in Sudbury, I'll have more cash."

We all looked at each other, confused. *Didn't Walter already sell our van to someone else?*

Walter, looking pleased with himself, was happy to explain. "One guy has the key, and the other sucker will have the title. I hope they both show up at the same time to get that piece of shit on the side of the road. Sure wish I could see *that* fight."

He was the only one laughing at this bit of news. We all knew better than to protest his double cross. I found myself being further repelled by Walter, avoiding his menacing eyes and speaking to him only when I had to.

While Walter was bragging to Elaine about his escapades in town, Bruce and I decided to sneak off so that I could hear all about their trip from him. "We're going to look for more berries," we told our parents.

We found a comfortable spot in the woods, and Bruce settled in to tell me the story.

"We started out and I was really nervous about where we were going to sleep. We didn't even bring the tent with us. But along the way, Dad remembered another hunter's cabin he'd seen hidden in the woods. We stopped and hid our bikes in the place where he thought it was, and I thought, *Here we go, we're going to be searching for this cabin for hours.* But we actually found it really fast! Then Dad found a can of tomato soup and some coffee hidden in a corner. He was shouting all about how he 'hit the jackpot!' We got really lucky because he managed to find an old coffee pot, too. 'Go find some water, boy; we're gonna have us a feast!'"

Bruce's imitation of Walter shouting orders was pretty good, and I couldn't help but giggle. He explained that Walter taught him a new way to make coffee: "You put the coffee grounds right in the pot. Then, once the coffee boils, you set the pot on a cold stone. That way the grounds will sink to the bottom. Then you pour and enjoy. That soup and coffee really did taste like a feast, we were so hungry. At least it stopped my stomach from growling for a while."

My brother was intrigued by the little cabin Walter had some-how re-located. He assumed they would sleep there that night. "But Walter said we had to sleep outside. It was raining! But he told me we'd both just get spoiled if we slept inside. He said it was important to get used to sleeping outside, and that there were plenty of trees to shelter us from the rain. Well, it was far from comfortable, but I was so exhausted from biking the whole day that it didn't take me long to fall asleep. But, guess what. First thing in the morning when I woke up, Dad was nowhere to be found. When I went into the cabin, there he was, sitting on one of the cots. I think he waited until I fell asleep, and then went inside and bedded down for the night."

I nodded in agreement when my brother told me this. I was not surprised at all, knowing how strange Walter's ways could be at times.

"Next, he told me to grab a cup of coffee, and 'get ready to cover a lot of miles.' The bikes were falling apart, but we made it down the road a good piece until Walter got a flat tire. After that, it was slow going. We each had to take turns riding the good bike while the other one walked the old three-speed with the flat tire flapping along. Then he suggested that we should split up."

Bruce's face grew pale at the memory, and he told me that he had to slip to the side of the road and throw up at the thought of this. Bruce was always leery of Walter, but his fear of being totally alone on that isolated road was even worse.

"We kept going, trying to hitch," Bruce continued. "But nobody wanted to stop and pick up a couple of filthy hitchhikers with broken bikes."

The trip became more and more tedious. It was downright boring until Walter decided to provide a little entertainment. Each time a car passed them, Walter would hurl an insult at the driver:

"I hope your mama croaks from syphilis."

"You're a son of a bitch."

"I hope your big, shiny hood ornament gets shoved up your ass."

Bruce, bored and lightheaded from lack of food, couldn't help but laugh at Walter's crazy antics and creative insults. That seemed to please Walter.

"Finally, someone stopped and offered us a ride. Of course, by that point, we were only a few miles outside of town! Walter shouted at the guy, 'Go to hell. We're *here, now!*' It took us nine days to get to Sudbury. I was about to pass out by the time we got to town. All we had to eat after the tomato soup was wild plants and whatever berries we found."

When they arrived in town, Walter was turned down by the Salvation Army, which was full for the night. "He did one of his tricks," Bruce said, shaking his head in amazement. "He left, circled around the building, then went back in and tried again. Somehow, he convinced them to let us stay the night."

For a week, Bruce and Walter stayed at the Canadian Salvation Army, getting a small complimentary breakfast each morning if they would listen to a minister's sermon that day. Then, armed with a sack lunch in hand, they'd head into town to find work. Odd jobs were hard to come by, and they didn't have much luck. Finally, Walter told Bruce, "There's nothin' left to do but call that goddamn grandmother of yours and have her wire us some money. She will hex us for sure, but we have no choice."

"You should have seen him on that pay phone asking for money," Bruce confided. He launched into an impression of Walter's phone conversation, clenching his jaw and balling up his fist. "'Your grandchildren are stranded here because the van broke down. You *need* to do it—for *them*.'" She agreed to send us two hundred bucks. Then Dad started in on his 'witch' talk: 'She'll witch us now. *Never* take somethin' from a witch, 'cause she'll *hex* you for it.' We got the rental truck once the money came through. He was pretty impressed with himself, coming up with that surprise for you guys."

Bruce had done his very best storytelling, and I felt like I could picture every step of their journey. Shaking our heads and laughing, we got up to leave. By the time Bruce and I returned to the campsite, Mom had dinner ready. That night, we had our first good meal in a long time: fried potatoes and bannocks that were topped with blueberry jam. Full of food, we basked in the glow of the rental truck. Everyone was excited about the prospect of no more travel on foot. A little blip of hope filled me with calm as I fell asleep and dreamed of home.

The next morning, we all pitched in to pack up any belongings worth keeping into the rental truck. It was a big box truck with orange letters on the side that spelled *Ryder*. Walter strapped the birch bark canoe onto the roof of the truck. We did our best to clean up the campsite that had been home to us for months. It was a hot September day when I turned to say goodbye to our latest home. Bruce, Belinda, and I crawled into the back of the truck willingly enough, but the reality of our surroundings slapped me in the face once the rear door of the truck slammed shut. It took only a minute to feel how poor the ventilation was in our windowless prison, and I was shocked to discover that I couldn't see a darn thing. There was nothing I could do but sit down among our camping equipment and try to calm myself. I felt like I was drowning in the darkness. The knowledge that only Walter had the key to the back of the truck terrified me.

"Bruce, Belinda, are you there?"

They answered me in shaky voices, and I reached out to touch them. I felt Belinda's hand shaking and wondered if she felt the same tremor in my touch.

"It'll be all right. You'll see," Bruce whispered into the darkness, but I knew he didn't believe it, and neither did I.

As the motor fired up and our long journey began, it was easy to lose all sense of time and direction. Everything felt unreal in the rumbling blackness. All sorts of questions began to fill my head, and I couldn't tell if I was just thinking them or speaking them aloud into the darkness. *Are we really going home? If we stay with our grandmother, will she really put a hex on us?* Then, for the millionth time, the thought that refused to go away: *Will things ever get better?*

The floor of the truck felt gritty and rough under my hands and legs. It grew more uncomfortable with each bumpy mile. The truck shifting bumped us now and then, but I tried to lie down and fall asleep. I told myself, *You made it through three months in Canada; you can make it through this trip, and then you'll be home. Home . . .*

The truck lurched to a stop, and I awakened suddenly. I had no idea how long I'd been asleep.

"Get out and stretch your legs. I gotta get the money for the van," Walter ordered us as he flung open the back door.

We shaded our eyes from the bright light as we picked our way through the motorcycle, old camper stove, pots and pans, bikes, outboard motor, chainsaw, and other possessions. Bruce hopped down first and then offered a hand to my sister and me.

We watched Walter make the exchange: a title to our van for a handful of bills. Then Walter returned to the truck with a wicked grin on his face, talking to himself. "Wish I could see those two bastards fight over that van. They'll *both* get what they deserve: *nothin'*!"

By now, we were all used to Walter's strange behavior. He hated people he had never met, people who'd never done a thing to him. He thought everyone was out to get him. I knew this wasn't normal, and I just couldn't understand how he could be this way. With Walter in this kind of mood, it was hard to say what would happen next, but I was sure it wouldn't be anything good.

We clambered back into the truck for the long ride to the Michigan border. My throat was so dry, but I knew better than to ask for a drink of water. I just tried to focus on the thought of going home. The darkness swallowed us again, and time became an idea that worked only in the light.

Finally, the door was opening again, and the dazzling light flooded in. We had reached the border. Mom told us to empty the truck while Walter went to make arrangements to switch from this Canadian truck. When the rental agent saw the rest of us, he blinked in surprise. I looked down to see that my ragged clothes were covered with dirt, and my shoes looked like they should have been thrown away months ago. I reached up to touch my hair, and I could feel how oily it was. Lake water can only do so much. I wished I had something to wipe the smudges from my face. "We can set you up with a U.S. truck just like this one for two hundred fifty," the rental agent told Walter. When I heard that price, I held my breath and braced myself.

Walter was shocked that there was a cost to trade the trucks at the border. Two hundred and fifty dollars? It might as well have been a million. I was relieved when Walter contained his rage, speaking in an even, reasonable tone.

"I was told by the fellah at the Ryder exchange that we could just swap trucks at the border for no extra cost." Walter even offered one of his best smiles.

"I'm sorry, but that is not the case. Our policy states that there is an additional fee when you switch trucks," the agent explained.

Walter's rage was starting to boil to the surface, but he forced his face into a placid expression.

"Perhaps you can unload your things and get a friend to come and help you take them home," the man offered. He took a step back as Walter's face began to contort. The thought that Walter would have friends was suddenly comical to me. *Yeah, why doesn't he put in a call to one of his golfing buddies, or friends from the Lions Club?* This tidbit of humor didn't entertain me long, because I could feel the storm clouds gathering around us. So I tucked this thought away for later and held on tight for whatever was going to happen next.

"I'll unload this truck myself, you stupid son of a bitch!" Walter declared, stalking away. First, he calmly unloaded the few things he planned on saving to continue the journey with us; the outboard motor and the chainsaw were spared. Then, he began hurling the rest of our stuff out of the back of the truck while screaming at the frightened man: "You lyin' son of a bitch! You can take this stuff and shove it up your ass. I'll take what I need—AND I WON'T LEAVE NOTHIN' FOR THE ENEMY!"

When the truck was empty, Walter pulled the cord on the chainsaw and approached the rest of our stuff. Everyone was stone silent. We could only look on helplessly as Walter began systematically destroying everything we owned.

Mom was crying, Bruce and Belinda clutched each other, and I stared in disbelief. When the chainsaw had nothing left to shred, Walter took his sledgehammer and slammed it against the frames of the bikes. They fell into a twisted heap. The pressure cooker we had used to can jam at our campsite folded like paper under Walter's brutal blow. As it collapsed, the dozens of jars of raspberry and blueberry jam inside—which took us countless hours to can—oozed out in rivers of red and purple, coating our crushed belongings like a strange lava.

Finally, Walter turned to his motorcycle, which he had spent so many hours rebuilding. He raised the sledgehammer over his head and gave it a crushing blow, then another, and another. Finally, he pulled down the birch bark canoe. It crumbled with the first swing of his hammer. The rental dealer was speechless and looked more than a little afraid as Walter shouted his parting words: "You can go to hell and take this truck with you!"

Walter turned away, scooped up the outboard motor and shoved it into Bruce's hands, and then passed the chainsaw to me. Mom scooped up a brown paper bag that contained a few ragged clothes.

"We'll walk from here," he calmly told us.

Now that Walter's thunderstorm had passed, I noticed all of the onlookers who were staring and suddenly felt exposed and embarrassed. As our bedraggled group walked by the diners sitting at the windows of the nearby restaurant, I could see the strangers turning their heads to look at this odd parade of ragtag people passing by: a maniac, followed by a sniffling woman, and three skinny, dirty kids who carried, of all things, a boat motor and a chainsaw. *They don't know that these two things, along with the clothes on our backs, are all we own now.* No one seated inside the comfortable restaurant could resist staring out the windows at this strange floor show. As the people we passed turned to look with curiosity and disgust, Walter returned their stares, snarling, "I ain't *never* gonna leave *nothin'* for the enemy!"

We trudged in the direction of the bridge, and still countless heads turned our way. I could feel my face go hot at what a sight we must have been. The day was dark and damp, without a ray of sunshine, and it suited my mood just fine. I looked at the four people walking in front of me, as if I were seeing them for the first time: *Walter—who just showed the world the same kind of violence he inflicts on his family. His wife—so beaten down by life that she can't even care for herself or her children. The twins—both damaged by this three-month survival trip, but just trying to hold on.*

As we kept walking, the chainsaw growing heavier in my arms, I began to feel so tired that I stopped caring what we looked like. Feeling embarrassed was the least of my worries now. I tried to hang on to hope, trusting that God would get me through this somehow. My thoughts wandered as we walked mile after mile and dusk set in. I could still see the expressions on the faces of the border patrol guards, the rental truck dealer, even the police officer who gave my mom and me a ride back to camp. Then there was the attendant at the Salvation Army, the volunteer at the women's shelter . . . *didn't anyone notice that something wasn't right? Am I invisible?* I could only assume that Walter's nice-guy act was convincing to everyone he charmed, and his mean-guy side scared everyone else so much that they would never cross him. *Good or bad, Walter always wins.* I could only pray that we would survive this. I reminded myself to hang on to the hope that someday, maybe, I would be free.

Many miles later, Walter stopped at a party store just short of the bridge. I couldn't help but smile when he walked out with a cold soda pop for each of us. Knowing it most likely took the last of our money didn't stop me from enjoying every sip. We found a grassy spot outside of the store to rest. Getting off of my feet and sitting down with my family felt good. Our exhausted silence was interrupted only when Walter patted Bruce on the head and told him, "We're survivors. It won't be long before we're outta this goddamn place and back to the U S of A. We've looked death in the face, and we *won*. We didn't let *nothin'* stop us!"

Then he turned to look at Belinda and me. "You girls are survivors too."

Belinda mumbled a thank you, but I turned my head away. I couldn't look this man in the eye when all I could see was him destroying all of our belongings in a rage. The thought that he had brought us into the woods to die would not stop swirling around in my brain. The thought only fanned the fire of the hurt from the times he had invaded my body. No, I could not look at this man. I felt my mom's disapproving stare, though I wouldn't look her in the eye either, but I didn't care. I had no choice but to obey Walter, but I could no longer pretend he was the greatest thing since sliced bread. I'd use as few words with him as possible. *The wrath we all had to witness just a few hours ago, and now these encouraging words . . . I just can't make sense of it all.* I was ready to leave these thoughts behind and go home.

The awkward weight of the chainsaw felt lighter in my hands as we approached the bridge. Walter put on a pleasant smile for the border officials as he made his pitch: "I understand that you don't want folks crossin' this bridge on foot, but our vehicle broke down and we lost everything we own. We're down on our luck. It isn't easy putting my wife and kids through this, but we havta git home."

"One of our officers will drive you and your family across the bridge," the guard explained.

"Thanks, much obliged," Walter replied, and then he crowded into the car with us. After a few more pleasantries from Walter, the attendant parked and let us out in the United States.

Chapter Twenty-One

Home sweet home—back in the USA! We found a rest area in Sault Ste. Marie where we'd bed down for the night. Mom, Belinda, and I decided to seek refuge in the women's restroom. We sat down on the cement floor and leaned against a wall, close to the heat register. The heat felt good after our long walk in the damp weather, but there was no way of shading our faces from the bright lights in this public place. I tried to lie down, but the cold cement floor felt as uncomfortable as it looked, so we just sat in silence for a while. Then Mom said, "You know, girl, you should go apologize to your father. He worked real hard to get us out of this god-forsaken place, and you haven't been very nice to him."

Because I didn't thank him for buying me a pop and saying we were brave, after walking for miles all day, after he destroyed all of our stuff and scared everyone? Really? I couldn't believe this accusation, but my mother kept on going, telling me I had to talk to him, and I knew I didn't have a choice.

"Your dad did the best he could do to get us out of there, and *you* ain't even been talkin' to him. You've been acting like a little brat. You oughta say you're sorry. Now git."

I turned away and reluctantly went outside to find Walter. My chest was burning with the unfairness of Elaine's request. *I know I haven't been mean to Walter. Who in their right mind would even dare? My mother has never said a word about all the mean things*

Walter has done to me, and now she tells me I'm *the one who should apologize?*

I found Walter and Bruce lying beneath a picnic table. A misty rain was starting to fall. I leaned over the bench and forced myself to whisper a painful word—one I hadn't uttered ever since the night in Cheryl's bedroom when Walter had raped me in the most violent way yet.

"Dad." I choked, the word catching in my throat. My stomach flinched. "I'm sorry, Dad, if I've been mean. I know you got us out of Canada. I'm sorry."

Walter climbed out from under the table and put his arm around me, looking down at me with a tender expression. I knew better than to believe that look in his eyes.

"It's okay. You done the best you could. There'll be plenty of time for you to make it up to me. You can sleep under this here picnic table with Bruce and me for now."

I don't know why he accepted my apology. He knew as well as I did that I hadn't done anything wrong. I wiped the tear from my cheek before he could see it, and then I climbed under the table and squeezed in next to Walter. When I began to hear his snoring and Bruce's even breathing, I let the tears flow.

In the morning, I could see in everyone's faces that it hadn't been a restful night. Shaking off the fatigue, I went into the women's restroom to wash up the best that I could, while Bruce followed Walter into the men's room. I returned to see Walter eyeing a diner across the street.

"Wait for me here," he told us. "I'll go see about somethin' to eat."

A minute later, we could see Walter through the restaurant window, talking to a man and gesturing to us. After this exchange, Walter left the restaurant and waved us across the street, looking pleased.

"Come on. We're gonna have breakfast," he called.

We stashed the chainsaw and boat motor in the shrubs and turned in the direction of the diner. Our steps felt light with anticipation as we crossed the street to join him.

"I told the owner that my wife and kids are hungry. Told him we lost everything we own and are just trying to get back home. He says to bring you all over and he'll feed us. Said we can order whatever we want. I told him we'd send him the money as soon as we get back home. I *will* send him the money, too. Ya get out of Canada, and people know how to treat you right."

There had been little aroma to the bannocks, the flat bread made from flour and soda, that we'd lived on every day during our time in Canada. So when Bruce pulled the restaurant door open for me, I stepped into a whole new world.

After our months spent outdoors, the enclosed air inside the restaurant even felt different. I loved the way the delicious smells stayed captured within the restaurant's walls. The scent of "panny cakes," as we called them, and sweet syrup intermingled with sausage, bacon, and fried potatoes greeted my nose first. Then subtler smells like toast and fried eggs joined the aroma party. I thought I could even sense the tingle of fresh-squeezed orange juice beneath everything else.

After I got over the amazing aromas inside the restaurant, I noticed how the shiny chrome bases of the stools reflected the sunlight streaming in through the windows. The novelty of seeing people other than my family invaded my senses too. The squeak of the waitresses' shoes, the back-and-forth of the swinging door to the kitchen, the clink of spoons stirring coffee, the laughter of the customers—happy people who looked like a breakfast like this was nothing unusual for them—all these things reminded me of the past. *I know I've heard these sounds before, but I can't recall when that might have been.*

Bruce and Bennie were looking over the menu with wide eyes, and I'm pretty sure my eyes were popping out just the same. The glass of milk the waitress placed in front of me tasted so fresh and wonderful after three months of doing without. Then we actually ordered eggs, bacon, hash, and toast. The first bite was amazing. I shoveled more eggs onto my fork while I was still chewing the buttery toast. I smiled at Bruce, who was busy slathering grape jam on his toast. I noticed that Bennie was avoiding the red jams too; they were too similar to the berry jam we had eaten every day during our camping experience. Even Mom looked relaxed as she sipped her coffee. Walter seemed sincere as he thanked the manager, slipping the address of the restaurant into his pocket. Walter *did* send this man a check once we were home.

With our bellies full, it was a bit easier to obey the orders Walter began barking at us after we left the diner. The kindness of the manager and the good food revived us all. The day was misty, cold, and dark, but we willingly gathered around for our instructions, rubbing our hands to ward off the cold. We stood at attention as Walter gave us our final traveling orders.

"If anyone can get a ride, go ahead and take it. Have the driver drop you off at the rest stop on I-75, just before the Mackinac Bridge. That way, we'll all know where to meet."

We scooped up the chainsaw and the outboard motor from their hiding place and strolled along the highway, thumbs up. After a few miles with no sign of a willing driver, Walter returned to the same antics he had performed while hitchhiking with Bruce.

"You're a son of a bitch," he shouted at a passing car.

"Your old lady's gonna die of V.D.," he yelled at another.

I could tell Walter enjoyed putting on this little show for his family. Each salutation Walter created was an original. It was a cruel gift he seemed to have. Bruce was the one who found it funniest. I could hear him chuckling appreciatively as we walked.

Finally, a man with a pickup stopped to offer us a ride, and that got us down the road a piece. Next, an elderly couple offered a ride to just two of us. Walter insisted that Bruce and Belinda should be the ones to get in the car. I could hear the quiver of fear in their voices: "We don't mind walking."

"Don't argue with me," Walter hissed. "We'll catch up with you," he said in a louder voice, giving the couple an encouraging wave.

I watched the car disappear down the road with my brother and sister inside. *At least they'll get a break from this cold*, I thought. The damp, misty day wasn't going to get any warmer. I could tell that Walter was keeping me with him to increase his chances of getting a ride. I traipsed along behind Elaine's heels as we journeyed on. She and Walter were talking to each other in low voices, and I overheard a little bit of what they said.

"Maybe Bruce and Belinda won't be at the rest stop when we get there. . . . Well, it would be two less mouths to feed when we get home," Mom confessed.

My mouth dropped open. I knew from the tone of her voice that she wasn't kidding. She actually sounded hopeful.

"Ain't gonna happen," Walter responded. "No one is gonna keep *those* two. It'd be too much of a pain. But it would be way too good for us if someone *would* keep them."

My throat tightened, and my eyes stung with tears. *If both of my parents feel this way about the twins, then of course they feel that way about me too.* Walter's voice interrupted my thoughts when he growled, "Move faster, girl. Can't you do *nothin'* right?" I shifted the weight of the chainsaw to my other side and started to move faster. I stared down at my aching feet, marveling that my tennis shoes hadn't turned to crumbles. When I saw that a car ahead was pulling to a stop, I began to run. The tone Walter had used on me was long gone as he thanked the driver warmly for picking us up.

The driver dropped us off at the rest stop in St. Ignace, and my eyes began searching for Bruce and Bennie before my feet even hit the ground. I scanned the whole area and felt a stab of panic in my chest when I didn't see them anywhere. I watched every car that drove by, hoping one would stop and let my sister and brother out.

It turned out that the soda pop Walter had bought us hadn't used up the very last of our money after all. For a moment, I forgot my worries when I saw that Walter had purchased a loaf of bread, peanut butter, and a jar of pickles. We combined the three ingredients, and the sandwiches tasted delicious.

My parents were joking about someone not returning the twins when I saw a car pull up, and Bennie and Bruce stepped out. I ran quickly to hug them both. I couldn't imagine what life would be like with just Walter and Elaine. Bruce and Belinda were my real family, and they made each day bearable. My arms refused to drop from my sister's neck, and the hug she returned was exactly what I needed at that moment.

"The driver made a wrong turn after getting gas," Bruce explained. "We had to back track. The people were nice. We thanked them for the ride."

"Make your own sandwiches and hurry up about it. We gotta get going," Walter snapped in an annoyed tone. Elaine had no words of welcome for the twins.

Walter rushed off when he spotted a man with a large van pull up to the rest area and returned a few minutes later with the news that we had another ride. It was getting dark when the driver dropped us off where I-75 and U.S. 27 split.

"We need some rest," Elaine complained, but Walter ignored her.

He secured one more ride with a man named Bill. He explained that he was a former sheep herder who'd held many odd jobs over the years. It seemed to me that he was an old hippy who seemed happy to be driving an old bread truck. He and Walter swapped stories as the rest of us listened from the crowded backseat.

Bill shared his thermos of chicken noodle soup with us when we stopped at a gas station. We were all thirsty, but we didn't have a dime left. Walter went inside to ask if we could get a drink of water, and the attendant just laughed.

"We have a lot of drinks for sale, but no water, and you've gotta pay for any of these."

"You got a spring out back where we can drink?" Walter suggested.

"Huh?" The clerk gave him a puzzled expression, confused at the question. I supposed he didn't even know how great the spring water was up there. We left, still thirsty, and disappointed.

"Time to saddle up!" Bill called to us, and we piled back into his bread truck and continued toward home.

CHAPTER TWENTY-TWO

It was early morning when Bill dropped us off. Sleepily, we muttered our thanks to him and climbed out. We stumbled onto grass at a county park, almost home. Walter instructed Belinda and me to cross the highway and take some corn and apples from the farm over there, while he'd look for some plastic for us to sleep on. Elaine said, "This is disappointing; why don't we just walk to your mother's house from here? It's not far. I'm sure she'd take us in."

"What are you talkin' about, woman? She'd jinx us for sure—just like she did when we lost that Ryder truck."

Bennie and I ran off together to the nearby farm. When we were out of earshot, Bennie turned to me. "Do you believe that Dad is actually asking us to steal? I know it's not right, but we don't dare question him. It was a long time ago that I ate that sandwich. I'm hungry. How about you, Lorie?"

I studied my sister. I could see the change in her now that we were out of the woods. *I think Canada might have been the hardest on her, out of all of us.* This was such a rare chance for us to have a moment to talk.

"Let's hope the farmer doesn't mind us taking his crops. Let's pretend he knows how hungry we are—*and* he knows how mean Walter is. Here, I'll stretch out my sweater, and you fill it up with these apples, and then we'll grab a few ears of corn. . . . I've missed you, Bennie."

"Missed me? Where have I been?"

I didn't tell her how far away she'd seemed these last few months. Instead, I just shifted the apples to one side and gave her an awkward hug.

We got back to the park in time to see Walter returning with a piece of plastic and an old mattress. He'd also spotted some Lasso Herbicide cans and tossed them down in front of Bruce and me.

"Wash these out, and we can fill them with water. One's for cooking, and the other's for our drinking water."

I knew that herbicide was poison; it didn't seem like it should be holding our drinking water. But I knew I would keep my thoughts to myself.

Walter told us that bathing was to be done in the river. Next, he fashioned a tent out of the plastic he had found, propping it up with some tree branches.

"We should be able to stay here for a while," Walter announced, looking over our makeshift campsite.

Why had I been so anxious to get home if we're just going to live outdoors again in a county park? I couldn't help feeling disappointed, but unlike my mom, I didn't voice my thought aloud—just like all the other thoughts bottled up inside me. *I wonder if there will be a time that my brain just can't hold back any more thoughts and they'll all come pouring out like Niagara Falls.*

I was so weary that the dirty, discarded mattress looked pretty inviting after dark, so Bruce, Bennie, and I piled on. I guessed it must have been a king size. Elaine took her place on the other side, and somehow the four of us managed to fit. But as tired as I was, sleep didn't come. I lay awake listening to the sounds of animals in the nearby woods. I was trying to put an animal name to each sound when I felt a hand clamp over my mouth. The hand was rough and had a familiar smell I knew too well.

"Don't move, and don't say nothin'." With his other hand, Walter yanked my pants down. Seconds later, he was forcing himself inside of me.

He hissed in my ear, "You don't get *nothin'* for free. I got you back home safely, and *now* you're gonna pay."

After a few more painful thrusts, he rolled off of me. I felt the hot tears running down my face, but I held back my sobs. Next to me, I could hear my sister crying too. She and I didn't talk about this business with each other. *I know he has done the same to her. What could we say?* We both cried ourselves to sleep, careful not to make a sound. The camping trip had provided a welcome relief from Walter's rapes. Now I felt smothered with fear.

Our days in the county park turned into weeks. Each day, we ate the same things: field corn, apples, applesauce that we cooked in one of the herbicide cans, and coffee with powdered creamer. Our diet had the opposite effect of eating tons of seedy berries. We had no outhouse and had to make do ducking behind a tree or bush.

I tried to focus on doing exactly what I was told to do, so I could keep Walter's wrath at bay as much as possible. My days were filled with chores such as stealing food from neighboring farms. My nights had become nightmares where I endured abusive visits from Walter.

Facing him the next morning was the second stage of each nightmare. He behaved as if the horrendous events of the night before had never happened. My emotions became like a wheel that tumbled from terror, to despair, to the hope that someday soon I could, maybe, just go numb and stop feeling altogether.

There was one bright spot for me; I enjoyed tagging along with Elaine and Bruce on their errands. These little trips were rare, but I looked forward to the escape from Walter and the park.

One day, when we took a trip into a neighborhood that bordered the park, I spotted a "for rent" sign in the grimy front window of a house on James Street. When we got back to our camping spot, I told Walter about it, and he and Elaine started to make plans.

After four months of living outdoors, we were finally able to move into the house I had found. Now, my mother took the necessary steps to reconnect with the welfare system. The food stamps arrived, and the gnawing hunger in my stomach eased up a bit. Bread, peanut butter, beans, cornmeal, and flour were a wonderful sight to see in our kitchen cupboard. I'd been hoping things would improve for all of us now that we had a roof over our heads. But now that Walter wasn't living off the land, I could see him turning darker. He didn't have any plans, or projects, or wide open spaces now. He seemed like a caged tiger.

Elaine received $312 in welfare assistance every two weeks, and Walter insisted she give him $100 of that money each time. Now, his abusive words were accompanied by slaps and punches. Mom was more afraid of him than she had been before, so she didn't hesitate to hand the money over to him. We didn't know what he was doing with that money, and no one dared to ask.

Our home sweet home turned out to be not so sweet after all. That fall, it was always cold. The food from our food stamps could stop the rumble in our bellies for a while, but we were still hungry most of the time. I started coughing and having trouble breathing, but no one paid attention to me for a long time. As my condition worsened, my parents began to take notice, but their reaction was irritation at the fact that I was going to require a doctor's visit. After giving me a brief exam, the doctor told my mom that I had pneumonia and a trip to the hospital was necessary. Obviously annoyed, my mom checked me into the hospital. Once the paperwork was signed and a nurse tucked me into bed, my mother turned and left without a word.

My stay in the hospital was a bit of a holiday for me: there was plenty of food, a nice warm bed, and no fear of abuse. I wasn't surprised that no one came to visit me, but it was also a relief. After a few days, I overheard a hushed conversation between two nurses about me being left on my own.

On the fourth day of my stay, a social worker appeared in my room. The fear rushed back, tying my stomach in a knot as she asked me questions that I was not sure how to answer: "Do you know why your parents have not been in to see you? Has something like this happened before? Is there anything you want to tell me?"

I told her as little as possible. *If I tell her what is really going on, she will go to the house, Walter will shove her out the door, and I will get a beating and a lock-up.* Next, she asked, "I would like to sign your release papers; do you think that would be all right with your parents?"

I nodded.

As she steered her little Honda toward my home, I could feel the fear come back in full force, like a wave washing over me. *I know Walter will be angry to see this stranger at his door.* We arrived to see Walter working on a motor, its parts spread out across the dining room table.

"I'm concerned that no one from Lorie's family came to the hospital to visit her while she was sick," the social worker began.

Walter immediately cut her off. "We'll take care of her now. She's *our* kid. There's the door, so *use* it. Go on, now."

The social worker tried again. "She had pneumonia, and there was a prescription that required an adult to pick it up . . ."

Now, Walter's tone was more menacing as he snapped, "Get the hell *out*, I said."

The worker dropped the release papers and medications on the counter and then rushed to the door. Before leaving, she handed me a small card with her phone number on it and then hurried out to her car.

Walter snatched the card from my hand as the door closed. "You won't be needing this. Now, *git* in the kitchen and help your mother."

After that day, everything seemed to get darker. As 1979 turned into 1980, we all felt the pangs of hunger; no one was able to get warm enough, and there was the endless tension caused by the constant arguments between my parents.

Walter kept getting his cut of Elaine's welfare money, and there was less and less available for Mom to continue paying the rent on our grimy little house. Still, no one had figured out what he was doing with this money until he pulled up to the front of our house one day in a rusty old 1955 International school bus. Walter summoned us outside, his face bright with manic energy.

"I'm gonna fix it up into a motor home," he proudly told us, opening the big back door and showing us inside. "I'll tear out these old seats and put in a heater, a table, and a bench. There ain't nothin' wrong with this motor that *I* can't get into workin' order."

We all nodded our approval, and I wondered if Bruce and Belinda felt heat rising in their chests as I did. In the silence, it was clear that another trip would be in our future. *Would we ever just stay in one place?*

CHAPTER TWENTY-THREE

By May, Walter had indeed created a makeshift motor home out of the old school bus. The engine was now in working order, and he had painted the exterior a slate gray. For a final touch, Walter signed his name on the driver's door. Fold-out beds, benches, and a water pump now filled the interior. There was even a wood-burning stove with a metal plate on top for cooking. The electrical sockets he'd installed were another feature Walter bragged about to us. *He feels right proud,* I realized, *and he has no idea of the dread that the rest of us feel.* I tried to imagine the bus as it had been years ago, new and shiny yellow, full of kids riding to school, laughing and talking. I wished I could stay on that bus instead of this one, and just go to school and never come back.

"We ain't never gonna havta sleep on the ground again. We'll take 'er to the lake and see how she does. It won't be nothin' like Canada . . . just a little test run," he reassured Elaine.

I could tell that my mom was not on board with Walter's latest plan. Her downcast eyes had lost what little light they had once possessed, and her mouth was turned down into a permanent frown of hopelessness. Her body had become more lopsided as she walked, and fear never left her eyes. *She looks like she just can't take it anymore.*

The next day, I knew I was right. That morning, Mom just up and left, without even so much as a goodbye. Walter didn't seem to mind, and he continued to act as if nothing had changed. He kept talking about taking a trip as soon as school was out.

Now that the school bus motor home was completed, Walter turned his energy toward other projects. While we were in school, he'd spend much of his time scavenging in dumps and exploring the land around our home for thrown-away treasures.

One day, he found an old Ford pickup truck. It was a Michigan Bell Telephone truck, and he painted it the same color as our school bus, a grayish color. After repeated trips to the dump with his toolbox, he was able to repair the motor enough so that he could drive it home. Then he returned to the dump to find replacement metal for the rusted-out body. Panels of metal from washing machines and refrigerators served him well as he cut out rusted sections and filled them in with his new finds. Walter got lucky again when he decided to stop and chat with a farmer who lived near the dump. Sure enough, the old truck belonged to the farmer, and he gladly gave Walter the title.

Now that the truck was road worthy, Walter decided that it was time for Belinda, Bruce, and me to learn how to drive. He decided one weekend to take us for driving lessons. Our mistakes were met with hits and slaps. Fear was a good motivator, and by the time the weekend was over and it was time to go back to school, we were all adequate drivers.

Walter's next project turned into a place of terror for me. One day, he found a run-down little building in the wooded area near our home. He fashioned it into a shack for himself, adding a wood stove and a chimney to his little hovel. He piled discarded quilts on the cement slab inside the hut to create a makeshift bed.

Walter created another weekend mission for my sister and me. He'd spotted some windows along the side of the highway, and Belinda and I were told to go pick them up and bring them back so he could install them in his shack. It was a long hike, but I was glad to have the rare time alone with Belinda.

"How's school going for you?" I asked.

"My teachers are all pretty nice, I guess. I'm doing all right in all my classes. I haven't missed any homework assignments either." Bennie shrugged and looked off into the distance.

"I haven't made many friends, though," she admitted. "I guess I'm just too tired and sad about all the stuff going on at home to worry about that very much. Still, it *would* be nice to have a close friend."

Neither of us had ever had the experience of having a best friend. Sometimes I wondered what that must be like, but most of the time I tried not to think about it. I tried to stay positive, giving her hand a reassuring squeeze.

"Well, you'll always have me," I told her. "I'm glad you're doing well. I guess I'm doing my best too, but it is hard to keep my mind on what's going on in class when I'm so worried about going home. I dread hearing that bell ring at the end of the day."

"Yeah, me too . . . *hey!* Look, there are the windows we're supposed to drag home."

Belinda walked around the windows, looking them over. "They look pretty good. None of the glass is broken."

I picked one of them up. It was heavy, but not too heavy. Bennie lifted her window and began the awkward task of walking home with it, and I followed behind her with mine. Behind us, we heard tires crunching on gravel.

"Oh boy, that cop car is stopping for us. Walter will be so mad if we take too long or if he finds out we said one word to that officer." My sister's shoulders stiffened, and we both held our breath.

"What are you young ladies doing with those windows? You shouldn't be out here in this traffic on foot anyway," the officer added with a bit of a smile.

"We were just moving them off the highway, sir. We'll just leave them here and head home now."

He didn't look too convinced by our explanation, but he got back in the car and drove off. We waited a spell, and then we each picked up our window and continued on home.

When we reached our yard, Walter stormed out the front door, slamming it. "Why in hell did it take you so long?"

We hung our heads, mute, as Walter snatched the windows and headed off into the woods to finish off his precious little shack. Bennie and I scrambled off to bed, not worrying about dinner. "Hopefully that's the last we see of him tonight."

Walter had finished his getaway in the woods, and he had some plans for it. "From now on, after school you ride your bike straight there, nowhere else, and you wait for me," he told me.

That afternoon, I looked down at my feet pedaling the little bike—the same one Walter had fixed up for me years ago. Remembering that day he had taught me to ride, I choked back a sob, knowing that a moment like that could never happen between us again. As I got closer, I began to shake, my teeth chattering together. The late spring weather was warm, but I couldn't stop shaking. When I arrived, I saw that Walter was already there, waiting for me. My shaking was uncontrollable, but I endured his rapes without making a sound, other than the sound of my teeth banging together.

The visits to this shed became routine, every afternoon after school. Each time I walked or rode my bike there, the trembling began. *Run and hide!* a voice inside of me screamed, but I always followed Walter's orders to be there when he told me I had to. *My life depends on it.*

I'd try to let go, to float away and allow my mind to wander during these ordeals. Sometimes I'd think about other girls at school. What were other eleven-year-old girls doing today? *Homework? Maybe telling their moms about their day?* I couldn't imagine what that must be like. I'd just clench my teeth, trying to silence their endless chatter, and try to pretend I was somewhere else— anywhere else but under my grunting father.

One day, Walter came home in a rage: someone had broken into his one-room house. Revenge was always such a good motivator for Walter. He devised traps for this intruder at each of the two doors of his hut. One such trap was a piece of plywood that held a small collection of large rocks above the door. Opening the door would release the rocks, sending them cascading upon the head of any would-be trespasser. The other door was set up with spikes that could swing down upon any trespasser who entered.

It was a relief to me when we eventually discovered that the rightful owner of this property had discovered the shack and then had it demolished. The terror of this place came to a blessed end for me.

As the school year neared a close, Belinda and I could feel the shadow of another trip with Walter looming over us. I was twelve, and she was thirteen. Together, we decided to try one more time to try to escape. We went to our school counselor and told our story again, trying to describe the rapes and abuse that were common in our home. Both of us also reported the information to a school nurse and our principal. It was so hard to put it into words, but they did listen. Separate reports were filed.

Everything happened just the same way as before. Bennie and I returned from school, and again we saw Walter cussing out the social worker and sending her on her way.

Belinda and I did try to seek help together one last time. A few weeks after the social worker's visit, Walter beat Belinda and me over some unwashed dishes he had found in the sink. When he finally stopped beating us, he left the house. This time, we decided to call the police. An officer soon appeared at our door, and Belinda and I told him what had happened. For once, Belinda really let go and poured out her feelings about Walter and our nights of terror.

He informed us that because Walter wasn't present, there was nothing he could do. Then he added, "Aren't you girls just mad at your dad because he made you do the dishes? Have you tried telling your father how you feel when he's upset with you? Think about that. You girls have a good day now."

The officer slipped his notebook into his pocket and pulled away from our house in his squad car. Walter rounded the corner just in time to see the police car leaving. He stormed into the house just as Belinda and I hid in Elaine's closet.

"Was that a police car I just saw? You think you can sneak around and tell on me? Don't *think* you can hide from me! I'll find you and I'll show you. *There* you are, you goddamn ungrateful little bitches . . ."

Soon after that tirade from Walter, Belinda followed in the footsteps of the other women in our family. One day, she just left. I really didn't miss my mom that much when she left, but my heart sank as I watched Bennie walk out the door one day when Walter wasn't at home. Now it was just Bruce and me left.

I couldn't help but wonder how much longer Bruce would stay at home. He was all I had now. Bruce didn't have to undergo trips to the attic with Walter, but he had taken his share of abuse and was often the victim of Walter's bizarre whims. After one brutal incident, in a moment of desperation, Bruce stabbed himself in the head. He was taken to the hospital but released soon afterward, and the school and hospital authorities didn't bother to investigate into why a schoolboy would do such a thing to himself. Bruce's cry for help was left unanswered.

Now that the shack in the woods was gone, and Belinda was gone too, every night became a real-life nightmare again. It was summer, so I didn't even have school to bring some reality to my days. Walter would creep into my room, slap his hand over my mouth, and rape me. Sometimes he'd sodomize me. The nightmare always ended in the exact same way: before Walter left, his parting words hissed in my ear: "If you tell anyone, I will kill you."

Chapter Twenty-Four

Bruce and I were far from excited when Walter told us it was time to take the "motor home" to a nearby lake for a test run. "Time to make sure this is road worthy," he told us.

His nightly assaults on me continued while we were at the lake. On the return trip, we stopped at a rest area. I hadn't been feeling well, and I ran to the ladies' room, making it to the toilet just in time to be sick. When I came out, pale and shaky, Walter pulled me aside and said to me in a low voice, "I think you're pregnant. That's why you're getting sick. If anyone asks you about it, you tell them you were raped. You tell 'em you were raped by a stranger at this rest stop, and you were afraid to tell anyone about it. That's *all* you say."

"I don't know . . ." I began, but Walter cut me off in an evil tone.

"Yes, you *do* know. You listen, and you listen *good*. You were raped by a stranger at the rest stop. Do you hear me, girl?"

I tried to understand this foreign concept: *I'm pregnant?* I was as confused as I was scared.

We returned home to our house and a few weeks later, my mom showed up, walking back into the house as if she'd never been gone. Walter waved off her hello and didn't let her explain why she had been gone for two months. "We gotta talk," Walter told her. "I think Lorie's pregnant."

"I don't understand. How can that possibly be?" Elaine asked.

"She was raped at the rest stop by the lake. She didn't tell anybody until she started getting sick every morning. That's what happened. You tell her, Lorie—*isn't* that what happened?" Walter gave me a meaningful look.

"I was raped at the rest stop." I felt like a robot, the phrase coming out of me in a flat, monotone voice. My voice sounded like it was coming from somewhere else, not from me.

"Mmm, mmm . . . only twelve years old, and pregnant!" Elaine turned her disapproving look away from me, saying to Walter, "She's too young to be havin' a baby. We'll have to get her an abortion somehow."

Two weeks later, I found myself on the way to an abortion clinic. Walter made me rehearse my story in the car. "I was raped by a stranger at the rest stop in St. Johns." I parroted the line several times until Walter seemed satisfied.

On the way home from the clinic, the only thing Walter said was, "We can't have that happen again. We gotta be more careful." I stared straight ahead, squeezing back the tears that were stinging my eyes. My stomach felt sick, and my brain was so confused about what the words *pregnant* and *abortion* really meant that I had no words.

Soon after this ordeal, I overheard Bruce ask Walter for permission to do something. I can't remember what, but it was something that shouldn't have been a big deal. Walter beat Bruce, and he kept on beating him until he was too exhausted to hit him again. Later that night, Bruce ran away. I was so worried about him, but I also thought, *Wherever he is, it must be better than here.*

I found out later that Bruce was staying in a nearby park. I also heard that he had gotten in touch with Cheryl, but I wasn't sure where they had ended up. Elaine was gone again as usual, so now it was just me and Walter, alone in the house. My days were spent trying to stay out of Walter's way, trying not to make him angry, just trying to survive.

One day, out of the blue, I got an unpleasant surprise from the past. Who should show up at our front door, but Carl! I hadn't forgotten the abuse my half brother had liked to send my way when he had been living with us before. Now I had to try to stay out of his way as well as Walter's. I guessed that Carl's homecoming happened only because he was desperate and had nowhere else to go.

One night, I overheard Walter and Carl having a hushed conversation. They were talking about going out West, maybe to Wyoming. *I wish they'd both just go and never come back. It would be my worst nightmare to go anywhere with both of them. They are my tormenters. I want no part of this.* I couldn't sleep the rest of that night. All I could do was pray.

Two weeks later, my nightmare came true. I found myself loading up the bus for a trip out West. I was almost thirteen. I was too scared to run away, and I had no idea where my mother and sisters were anyway. I didn't know what else to do, so I continued to follow Walter's orders and pack things up.

I was hauling a stack of plastic pails out of the house and into the bus. Weeks ago, Walter had found a potato chip factory that had closed down. He brought home all of the chips that had been stored in the factory, truckload by truckload, and re-baked each batch of them to get the moisture out. Then, he stored them in these pails with lids. As I loaded the buckets into the bus, I realized, *This is what we will be eating for the next month.* I stacked them inside along with a few other foods Walter had found. I'd had lots of experience packing because we never stayed anywhere very long, so I was good at making everything fit. I could hear bits of the hushed conversations between Walter and Carl. "There are plenty of jobs out West in the oil mining business. We'll have no trouble getting hired. We could get rich off this trip."

The fact that Carl was back, and that I'd be brushing shoulders with him inside this crowded bus, was not a reassuring thought. At first, all the fear within me was ratcheted up as we began our road trip. Being caught in the dark chemistry between Walter and Carl could be the end of me. As I watched our house on James Street recede into the distance, I felt like everything was closing in and there was no way out. I didn't know what would happen between the two of them, but as we traveled on, I noticed that they were actually trying to be civil to each other. Carl must have been really desperate for a place to stay, and Walter must have needed his help for them to pretend to make nice like that. *Maybe I will survive this trip after all*, I thought as we crossed the Michigan border, heading west.

Walter took his time along the way on our trip. He let me visit Pioneer Village in Lincoln, Nebraska. I was fascinated with the museum visit and soaked up everything I read about inventions and history. Sometimes the trip almost felt kind of normal. There were some good moments. The bus-turned-motor home was actually pretty comfortable to travel in, a far cry from our crowded van or being locked in the back of a rental truck like in Canada. I tried to ease the ball of fear in my stomach and let myself enjoy some of the sites we passed.

CHAPTER TWENTY-FIVE

Nine days later, we arrived in Wyoming. First, we stayed at a small campground near a town called Evanston. Wyoming felt like a whole new world to me. Even stranger was how things were going for me with Carl. It was weird, but with Carl around, I actually began to feel a bit safer around Walter. Now Carl was kind of a buffer between me and Walter. Carl might have been the only one in the family who didn't know about the bad things Walter did to me. Maybe Walter wanted to keep it that way. I noticed that like before, Carl was the one who took the brunt of Walter's anger. I guessed that was the only nice thing my brother had ever done for me.

My relief over this new situation didn't last long. I was by myself one day cleaning the kitchen area of our bus, when I bumped a plastic paper towel holder and it broke. I felt my heart sink as I tried desperately to fix it, even though I knew that it was impossible to fix broken plastic. I was so afraid of Walter's anger that I set the piece down and fled from the bus into the woods, where I tried to focus on picking berries. Later on, when I heard Walter's angry shouts, I returned with the berries I had collected. Walter demanded to know what had happened. I felt my face flush as I said the words that I knew were lies, hoping they would protect me from Walter's wrath. "I was in the woods picking berries." I avoided his eyes, knowing that it was dishonest not to admit I was the one who had broken the thing.

As soon as Carl returned home, Walter confronted him about the broken paper towel holder. Carl replied, "I don't know nothin' about it. I've been out tryin' to find me a job. Ain't got time to worry about a goddamn paper towel holder. What in hell's the big deal, anyway?"

I saw that Carl's civility toward Walter was gone. *It was just a matter of time. I know that Carl always hated Walter, who isn't even his biological father. I also know that this is not going to end well, and it's my fault.* My stomach burned with the guilt of knowing I hadn't been truthful in this sad scenario.

Walter stepped toward Carl. "You lousy bastard. You come along for a free ride. You eat my food. You don't do *shit* around here, and then you break stuff that I worked *hard* to fix up. Get out! Don't come back! You hear me? When you find out you can't take care of yourself, don't even think of coming back here. I'm done with you."

My stomach knotted up as Carl gathered his few belongings and headed out the door. I stepped outside and watched his silhouette growing smaller as he disappeared into the woods. I had always thought of Carl as my abuser, but now I could see him a bit differently. He was the first kid in the family, and, being the oldest, he had had the most years of Walter's bad treatment. It was true that he often had taken the brunt of Walter's anger, leaving Walter too exhausted to raise a hand to the rest of us. Now I wondered what kind of man Carl might have been if Elaine had given him to his real father instead of to Walter. The thought of me running into the woods, following in Carl's footsteps, flashed through my mind for a second before I turned the handle of the door to the bus, returning to Walter and his broken paper towel holder.

Later that same night, Walter told me, "We gotta go where there is work. Get our stuff packed up. I don't want to be here in case that little bastard comes back. I'll get a job, and then you gotta get in school or there will be nothin' for you to do all day." I could see now that Walter was looking for any excuse to put Carl out.

I blinked in surprise when I realized that it was already September. Other kids my age were back in school now. That seemed like another world to me. I shook myself back to my grim reality and began packing up our things for the trip, but I felt a little more optimistic. *School.* The word alone made me feel happy.

"This must be it," Walter mumbled the next afternoon as he turned the bus into a wooded area, following a road that was so bumpy I felt scared our bus might actually tip over. We were still in the town of Evanston but just at a different location. The mountains were beautiful. I could see tents ahead, so I figured Walter must have already gotten directions to a campground where we could stay. "There are oil rigs not far from here. This is gonna be home—for I don't know how long—so you might as well get used to it," he told me as he steered the bus into our campsite.

I started to gather a few things to unpack when Walter grabbed my arm and snarled, "Forget unpackin' that stuff just now. I got somethin' I need to get unloaded first."

I made sure not to move a facial muscle because I knew how the least change in an expression on my face could anger Walter, but I guess I must have flinched a little because I heard Walter say,

"Don't give me that look. You know you gotta do what I tell ya." He slapped my face as I struggled from his grasp. Then he dropped his pants and raped me. When he was through with me, this time I couldn't stop the tears. Now, the reality began to set in for me: *Carl is gone for good; it's just Walter and me now. He is the only person I know in the state of Wyoming.*

As we settled into our Wyoming home, the weather grew cooler. I was thankful that our bus home had a lot more conveniences than we'd had at our hunter's cabin up in Canada. We had a wood stove for cooking and four bunk beds. We could pass logs through a small door to feed the wood stove. We could go in the front door of the bus or out the back double doors. Walter found two old pillars at an abandoned gas station and made a back porch for us. Of course, we also needed to have curtains. I bought an animal print that I liked for the inside of the bus. Next, I attached a thin blanket to the backside of the material to make it sturdier. That way you couldn't see through the material, and it would help block out the sun on hot days. For curtain rods, Walter snared some free banding at a lumber yard. I covered it with duct tape so it wouldn't tear the material, and Walter attached it around the whole perimeter of the inside of the bus, leaving only the front windows uncovered. Walter came across some sponge rubber cushions, and I made covers for them to go on the benches he built. Finding more room for storage was always a challenge. Walter solved that by hanging cupboards up high. The bunk beds had hinges and opened like trap doors, so we could store canned goods under them, too.

A couple of times, Walter even managed to hook the bus up with illegal electricity. It was ungrounded, and he didn't warn me when it was hooked up. The few times we had this convenience I would touch something in the bus and then be thrown down by a powerful shock. Walter got a real kick out of that too, of course, and I would hear his gleeful laughter before I even knew what hit me.

CHAPTER TWENTY-SIX

Always on the run, I thought as Walter moved our bus again to a new location. This time, we settled in Green River, near a town called LaBarge, just outside of Big Piney.

"Guess it's time we get you enrolled in school so you can keep yourself out of trouble," Walter mumbled one evening as we ate our meager supper. A week later, Walter took me to enroll in school. The principal was polite to me as we entered his office at the high school. He gave me a welcoming smile and gestured for me to sit in the comfy chair across from his desk.

"Can you tell me a little bit about what your education has been like and what you've learned, Lorie?"

I was careful to reply with only the words that Walter had coached me to say. I could see that Walter was on his best behavior, but the principal was not so welcoming to him. I was surprised at the realization that Walter's nice-guy act might not be working on this man. The principal told him, "You will have to get Lorie to the main road for the bus to pick her up each morning. We can't get our buses down to where you people camp." Now I could see that this man was no stranger to the lifestyle of the people who came to work long hours in the oil fields. *Yes, Walter's good manners don't seem to fool him at all.*

"I'll do my best to do that, sir." I was astonished that Walter could hold back his anger, continuing his little charade of politeness. Of course, on the way home, I had to listen to him rant about the way we had been treated. "I'll havta get you to that main road in the morning, but you're gonna *walk* home when that bus drops you off, damn it."

I kept looking straight ahead and didn't move a muscle. *Walter doesn't know that I'd walk many a mile just to spend a day at school.* I was so relieved when Walter worked out his arrival time with his supervisor, and he really did get me to the bus stop every morning, at least for the first few weeks.

Being back at school, I could feel the tightness in my stomach finally ease up a bit. My new school was a friendly place, and there was one girl I did become friends with, but I found that I always had to dodge her questions about my family and where I lived. When she invited me to her house, I had to make up an excuse. I wished I could be more honest with her, but I knew that wasn't possible. Even so, I was glad to have a friend.

All of my teachers at this school were good, but I especially liked my shop teacher, Mr. Randall. He was soft spoken, which felt like heaven to me. He taught me how to use a lathe, and I was really proud of the wooden bowl that I made for my class project. Sometimes I'd wonder what it would be like to have a kind and gentle father like Mr. Randall.

That fall was such a welcome relief to me, with time away from Walter, a new friend, and a kind teacher. But like the autumn leaves, the events in my life were about to change too. One afternoon in late November, the other students and I were left standing in the cold, wondering where our after-school bus might be. It was already a half hour late.

A teacher came out and explained that the bus had broken down and we should come inside and call our parents for a ride home.

"I'll just wait here for my dad to come and get me," I replied, turning my thin collar up against the cold night air. A few minutes after 6 p.m., I saw Walter's truck pull up to the school bus stop.

"The bus broke down. I didn't know what else to do but wait," I began, holding up my hands defensively as I watched Walter jump out of the truck and charge toward me.

"You lyin' little bitch!" he hissed. He grabbed my arm, shaking me, and the books I was holding spilled onto the ground. "You were probably doin' somethin' *stupid* and missed the bus, didn't you? *Didn't* you!" He shoved me against the side of his truck.

"Is there a problem here?"

Walter whirled around to see the school principal standing behind us.

"Yes, there is. Suppose you tell me why my daughter didn't get on the bus today. I'd like to know why I had to come all this way to get her."

"We had a mechanical problem. I apologize if it caused an inconvenience," the principal answered.

"Goddamn *right* it caused an inconvenience! I was afraid she'd run away or gotten kidnapped or somethin'. This better be the *last* time this happens. Now *git* in the truck, girl."

I apologized all the way home, trying to soothe Walter's rage, but nothing I could say did any good. As we entered our bus motor home, he was screaming at me: "Don't you *ever* do that to me again! You won't go to school if *this* is the kind of shit you're gonna put me through." Then the punches rained down on me, again and again. Once I could no longer find the strength to move, Walter unzipped his pants and the brutality continued.

After the bus incident, I spent less and less time going to school. On the days that Walter didn't allow me to attend, I'd do my chores and then spend the afternoon reading my schoolbooks.

I did have one companion to spend my days with: a lady named Ethel had given Walter a dog before we left. He was a cute corgi and terrier mix. I had named him Scrapper, and I was glad he was on this trip with us.

One day in March, I returned from school and played with Scrapper for a while, and then I turned to my science homework. I don't know why I loved studying the planets and the solar system so much. I became so absorbed in the assignment that I lost track of time. I was horrified when I heard the rumble of Walter's truck approaching the campsite. *I haven't started supper yet!* I realized in a panic.

I quickly grabbed some potatoes, chopping them and tossing them in a pan just as Walter stormed in the door.

"Why in *hell* ain't my dinner ready? Can't you see that I'm *home*?"

"It'll be ready soon," I reassured him. I began frying the white fish I'd caught in the Green River the day before.

"It damn well *better* be," he snarled.

Stoking the fire in the wood stove, I tried to rush the cooking and quickly dished up two plates and poured two glasses of water, setting them in front of Walter.

Walter bit into a piece of potato and yelled, "*Goddamn* it. This is raw. Can't you do *nothin'* right? I ask so little of you, and this is the crap you do. And this fish is full of bones. Don't you know there's more to cookin' fish than just cleanin' and scalin' 'em?"

Then he threw the full plates out the door and shoved me outside as well. Out in the darkness, I heard him yell, "You can go join those plates of garbage you tried to serve me. Then you can sit out there with your goddamn little dog and figure out what your job is around here. Don't come back until you're ready to tell me you're sorry!"

I huddled close to Scrapper in the cold night air. My tears fell on his furry back. It was so dark in these woods, and it was getting colder. I knew there was nothing I could do except apologize to Walter. An hour later, I tapped on the door of the rusty bus, and like a robot, I recited the words that I knew Walter had to hear before he'd let me in out of the cold.

"It damn well better not happen again," Walter hissed, pulling me back inside. "And now, it's time for you to make up for it." His eyes were fierce. He ripped the buttons on my sweater, yanking it apart. I didn't even try to fight him. He made me wish I were still outside in the cold.

CHAPTER TWENTY-SEVEN

The next morning, I woke up to find Walter gone. Looking around the bus in the dim light, I saw my homework papers ripped to shreds—my report on the solar system I'd put so much work into. I couldn't bear the sight of it, and I rushed outside. The day was unseasonably warm for mid-March in Wyoming. After the previous night, and seeing my homework destroyed in the morning, all I could think was that I just had to get away from this wretched bus and all thoughts of Walter for a while. *No, that's not enough. I want to get away forever.*

I knew it wasn't safe to flee in such an untamed area. The threat of cougars, bears, or other wild animals was very real, and there were few people around. If I screamed for help, no one would come. Even the terrain itself was dangerous. Running off by myself could mean the death of me. *Would an attack by a cougar be any worse than what Walter does to me?*

Not sure of where to go, I jumped on Walter's old bike, just pedaling away from everything. *At least being eaten by a wild animal would be faster than Walter chewing me up, bit by bit, each day. I'm not gonna turn back, no matter what.* When I reached the main road, I kept on riding and crying. I felt like I couldn't stop pedaling, nor could I stop the tears from flowing. I didn't hear a truck pull up beside me. "Are you all right, little girl? You shouldn't be out here by yourself. This is dangerous. Where are you going?"

"I don't know . . . I'm just trying to get away from my dad."

"Your dad?" the man asked. "Where is he now?"

"He works in the oil field for Mr. Nelson."

"I work for him too. Let's go see what he has to say about this."

The man had a kind face, and best of all, he wasn't Walter. After this stranger hoisted my bike into the back of his truck, I climbed into the cab. It wasn't long before we pulled up to a large trailer that said "Nelson and Company." The man went inside and soon returned with a man who said, "Hello, young lady. My name is Mr. Nelson. You say your father works for me? What is his name?"

"Walter Williams."

"I'm going to call my wife to come and talk to you. Then I'll check my books to see if we have a Walter Williams working here. Let me get you a glass of water, and you can sit here while I make that call."

Mr. Nelson was a big man, and he chewed tobacco. There was something funny about one of his eyes. But I wasn't afraid of him, so I thanked him for the water and sat down.

It wasn't very long before a nice-looking car pulled up to the trailer. A woman wearing clothes that looked expensive to me got out. She had a kind face.

"Are you all right?" the woman asked me.

I couldn't even answer, so she asked again. All at once, the words and tears started spewing out of me like hot lava out of an angry volcano. "I just can't do anything *right* for him!" I cried.

"For who, dear?" The woman's words were kind and gentle, and that was so strange to me. It made me cry even harder.

"For my dad. I mess up all the time, and he beats me and screams at me. I try, I try hard, really I do, but I *still* get in trouble.

He won't let me go to school now because he thinks that makes me mess up my chores at home. Now he's ripped up my science homework. There's nothing I can do right. Nothing! I don't know what to do or where to go . . . I just don't know." The words poured out of me like a hard rain.

The woman stepped forward and gently brushed the hair from my dirt- and tear-streaked face. "Where is your father now, dear?" she asked me.

"He's working . . . in the oil fields . . . and . . ."

"My husband is the manager of one of the oil companies out here. He's making a call about your father right now. Why don't you and I go see him and ask what he has to say about all of this?"

I looked at this woman, this stranger. *How can I trust her? I'm so afraid of what Walter will do when he finds out I talked to her.* "You already met my husband. His name is Don Nelson. He's pretty certain your father works for his company, and he is checking to be sure."

When Mr. Nelson opened the door of his trailer, I studied him again. I think some people might call him burly, but his eyes were kind. At least the one eye was. The other eye looked like it was made of glass and was just trying to look at me. I stared up at him, unblinking, as he said to me, "If it's okay with you, Lorie, my wife will take you to our place for a bit. We need to get to the bottom of this. You can stay with us or with my mother while we straighten this out. Is that all right with you?"

I just nodded. My thoughts were jumbled together. *I want to get away from Walter, but I'm so afraid. I've tried before, but there is no stopping Walter. He may kill me when he finds out what I'm doing. He may kill me or somebody else. What if he hurts the Nelsons?*

Mrs. Nelson drove me back to our bus to get a few belongings. The old gray bus looked so shabby as we pulled up to it. The rusty door we used to supply the burner with firewood added to the dilapidated look of our so-called "RV." The patch of dirt at the doorstep was a far cry from a welcome mat. I cringed to have Mrs. Nelson step inside the bus with me, but once inside all she did was remark that I was a good housekeeper—and that was worth something. I gave Scrapper a hug and food and water and said a quick prayer that Walter would feed him that night. We knew that Walter wouldn't be home for quite some time, but I didn't want to waste a minute.

Back in Mrs. Nelson's car, I was silent. My head was filled with so many questions as we drove up the road, speeding away from the campground I'd called home for so many months now. We drove up a hill, through a gate, to a house that was surrounded by a fence. The Grand Tetons were in the distance, and Mr. Nelson's mother's house was close by. The sandy cliffs behind this brick one-story made the home look even prettier to me. Two Doberman dogs in the yard ran up happily to welcome us, but I suspected that would not have been the case if I hadn't been with Mrs. Nelson. Holding very still, I let them sniff my hand, and within seconds the dogs were friendly to me. I liked them right away. Mrs. Nelson led me inside, and I marveled at how nice the Nelson family's house was.

I hadn't seen many fully equipped kitchens before, and I imagined that cooking a meal in this spacious room would be a breeze. Mrs. Nelson fixed us soup and sandwiches, and as we ate lunch together she asked me more questions.

"Does your father hit you every day?"

Now, I could only nod. It was as if Walter had paralyzed the words from coming out of my mouth. All I could think was, *I know he is going to kill me*, but something in me was stronger than that thought. I planted my feet in that kind woman's kitchen, and I didn't run out the door. A glimmer of hope was starting to swell within me. I was holding my breath, wondering what would happen next.

In the evening, Mr. Nelson arrived home with the news that Walter Williams did indeed work for his company. That night, when I climbed between the clean, fresh sheets in the guest room, I let the flood of tears come, and this time I didn't try to stop them. It had been so long since I'd had the luxury of crying out loud, and for as long as I wanted.

My sleep was invaded by a dream. In my dream, I was in some kind of a fight. I'm not sure where I was, maybe a boxing ring. My dream took a frightening twist. I couldn't fight back. I couldn't lift my arms to protect myself. I tried to open my mouth, but I couldn't scream. I awakened, breathing hard and covered in sweat, and tried to calm myself. Eventually I fell asleep again, but the same unwelcome dream returned. Morning came as a relief.

I found Mrs. Nelson in the early morning light of her tidy kitchen. It was so peaceful, and everything smelled wonderful, but seeing a kind face at the breakfast table was the best thing of all. She had cooked warm oatmeal and poured chilled orange juice—just for me. Having someone prepare breakfast for me was certainly something new. The cereal was flavored with a hint of brown sugar, and it tasted delicious. It was served in such a lovely bowl, and the hot cereal had warmed the milk just right. *I guess you would call this comfort food.* The fresh orange juice was such a change from the glass of water I usually had with each meal.

Mrs. Nelson told me, "My husband will find your father and tell him you are safe, but you will not be returning home. We are going to take you to school and meet with a social worker there."

This woman's words were kind, but my heart sank when I heard the words "social worker." *They have only brought me more abuse from Walter for telling on him. They can never stop him; no one can.*

"Walter is so mean. I'm afraid he will hurt someone." *Maybe you. Maybe your husband*, I thought to myself. *I know Walter is capable of anything.*

"We'll let the authorities handle that if it happens. Don't you worry. Let us take care of this for you."

The concern in her voice sounded genuine. I so wanted to believe her, but I could feel the fear bubbling up inside of me. *She doesn't know who she is up against.*

As we drove to school, Mrs. Nelson told me it was my choice if I wanted her to sit with me while I spoke with Mrs. Jacobs, the social worker. I asked her to stay with me even though she had heard it all before. For an hour, I talked to them. I told them all about my time in Wyoming and some of the mean things Walter had done while we'd been here. I talked about Carl, the broken paper towel holder, and how angry Walter had been on the day the bus didn't pick me up after school. I described the supper of half-cooked potatoes and the beatings. But I did not tell them about the rapes. Walter's words were not wasted on me. I could still hear his whispered threat echoing in my ears: *"If you ever tell anyone, I'll kill you. I'll kill you, I tell ya, do you hear me?"*

I hear you, Walter. You aren't even in the room, but I hear you. I believe you. I know you would kill me. I couldn't shake Walter's voice from my head. I couldn't tell Mrs. Jacobs and Mrs. Nelson the whole story, the worst part of the story. I hated the things Walter did to me more than anything, but I couldn't bring myself to tell. *My life is far from what I wish it would be, but even so . . . I don't want to die. God help me.*

I avoided the social worker's gaze when she asked me if I had told her everything. I just nodded. It didn't feel good to be dishonest. These women were acting like they really cared about me, and that felt so good. Yet I knew neither of these women could be a match for Walter, nor was burly Mr. Nelson. My head was reeling with fear from what I'd already revealed to these women. *Yes, I am done talking.*

Being able to focus in school became easier for me now that I was staying with the Nelsons. School officials had been alerted to keep an eye out for Walter, and he never showed up at school. The weeks began to flow by, and I could feel my fear ebbing a bit, the dark knot inside me loosening. Uncertainty about the future tugged at my mind, but I didn't dare ask the Nelsons what they would do with me next. It wouldn't be fair to expect them to take on the likes of Walter Williams, but at the same time, I sure didn't want to go back. I tried to take it day by day, thanking God that I could go to bed and feel safe, and wake up to what some people must call a normal day. I didn't want this peaceful feeling to end.

Walter's beat-up truck did start to show up at the Nelsons' home occasionally, but their big security gate blocked him from getting into the driveway, and Mr. Nelson, or one of their workers, always alerted us, so Walter would get sent on his way. His attempts to see me became fewer and farther between, and finally stopped completely.

One afternoon, I was in my room, which was starting to feel like home to me, doing my homework. When I heard Mr. Nelson come home earlier than usual, my curiosity got the best of me. I moved closer to the door of my bedroom and overheard Mr. Nelson say Walter's name. "The police are looking for Walter Williams. An officer stopped by my site today and told me Williams cleared out of town suddenly. It's possible that a deputy tried to stop him and ask some questions based on the reports made by the school social worker. I don't know exactly what happened. Apparently, when the deputy tried to stop him, Williams may have gotten in his truck and run off or possibly something worse. There is a concern because the officer is missing at this point. We are unsure if that has anything to do with Williams. It is just speculation at this point."

"Are they sure it was Walter Williams?" Mrs. Nelson asked her husband.

"No, they're not sure, and at this point, there's no proof. There was a witness that said the truck matched the description of the one Williams drives, but as far as I know there is no concrete proof. Whatever happened, they can't find the son of a bitch now. Looks like he packed up and headed out of town. The fact that he left looks pretty suspicious."

I clutched my stomach at the thought of someone possibly getting hurt by a man I once called my father. My head was spinning as I entered the kitchen in time to see Mr. Nelson sink into a kitchen chair.

"He's gone? Are they *sure* he left?"

Chapter Twenty-Seven

Mrs. Nelson put her arm on my shoulder. "Oh my dear, did you hear all of this?"

I nodded, but hoarsely asked again, "Are you sure he's gone?"

"The campsite where he was staying was empty, other than a few things that were left lying around. Looks like he cleared out in a hurry. The police are aware that he may be heading back to Michigan. His bus is gone, and no one has seen his truck. Officers are trying to find out if there is a connection between the missing truck and the missing officer. He could be a person of interest at this point, that's all. The investigation has just begun. There are a lot of unanswered questions."

I crumpled into a kitchen chair, my legs too wobbly to hold me. This was so much to take in all at once. All the times I feared he would hurt someone, the times I thought he'd kill me, this made his threats to me feel even more real now. *Walter gone? Will he really disappear? Will I always see him behind every corner? Lurking behind trees and bushes? They say he's gone, but they don't know Walter. This won't stop him. It will just make him madder and meaner.*

"We'll work this out, Lorie," Mrs. Nelson told me, patting my hand, which felt more than a little clammy.

I stood to face her. "I *knew* he was capable of anything. I hope the deputy is unharmed."

I turned and retreated to my bedroom, closing the door behind me. I crumpled onto the bed and cried until there were no more tears.

I attended school every day, but the fear of Walter was still with me. My heart leapt into my throat whenever someone would enter my classroom unexpectedly. When I was at home with the

Nelsons and I'd hear a truck motor, I'd run to the window, think-ing, *Walter is coming after me.* My sleep continued to be interrupted by my recurring dream. I was still fighting that faceless creature in my nightmares, but my arms couldn't move to stop the blows he inflicted on me. I awakened with the thought that it wouldn't take a psychiatrist to know who my faceless opponent was. This dream was easy to figure out, because it used to be real.

CHAPTER TWENTY-EIGHT

By May of 1981, I knew something had to change soon. The Nelsons had been so kind to me, but I could see the strain in their faces from the unintended consequences of helping me. The tangled web of Walter and me had become much more than what they had bargained for when they had taken me in. They probably never thought that helping a crying girl on the side of a road would lead to a possible police investigation. Mrs. Nelson's voice was gentle when she finally asked, "With Walter gone, do you think it is safe for you to return to your family now? Is there someone we can call?" I saw the relief in their faces when I told them my family would want me to come home now. With the police on the lookout for Walter, we agreed that it would be safe for me to return to my mother and Bruce and Belinda. I heard a catch in Mrs. Nelson's voice when she told me, "We will make the necessary arrangements."

When they told me my mother had wired money for me to return home, I couldn't help but wonder if it was actually the Nelsons who had paid for my train ticket. Elaine informed them that she hadn't heard from Walter in months. I reassured them that it was safe for me to return home now. Even though I wasn't so sure about this, I knew my time here was up, and I didn't want to impose any longer on these kind people.

"I'm grateful for all you have done for me. Your kindness to me has meant more than you can ever know. I'm going to miss you."

"I'm going to miss you too," Mrs. Nelson said as she hugged me goodbye at the train station. I looked into Mr. Nelson's face, and I could see concern and even fear for me in his expression. As his wife helped me get my things situated, I noticed that Mr. Nelson actually had tears shining in his eyes. Big, burly Mr. Nelson might actually care about me. *He must know that Walter might return to Michigan and find me.* I knew that the Nelsons were probably ready to have me and my complicated life out of their home, but I also knew that they were worried about what might happen to me. Perhaps God had sent an angel named Mrs. Nelson to help me escape after all these years of waiting for the right moment. *These two strangers from the West who saved me from Walter . . . it's all too much to take in.* My gratitude overwhelmed me. As I stepped up the stairs of my Amtrak train, I turned and gave them a big smile, saving the tears for when I'd be out of their view. The Nelsons arranged a convoluted route for me to get home, taking me north before I'd head east. I was well aware of why they did this, knowing that Walter could be nearby after all.

As I watched the telephone poles and trees whiz by my window, my thoughts turned to what was left of my family and how much better things would be for all of us with Walter on the run, or better still, in jail. What a luxury it would be to return from school and find a home that was not in turmoil. Best of all would be falling asleep on my own, knowing that Walter couldn't enter my room and turn my dreams into living nightmares. *Who knows, maybe the police have caught up with him already, or perhaps he's hiding in Alaska or Canada. Who cares, as long as he's far away from me and my family?* Walter had always cast such a dark shadow on all of us that in some ways I had never gotten to know my mom and sisters and brother the way I would have liked to. *Now we can all have a new start.* I let the feeling of hope well up within me as I fell asleep to the soothing sound of the train.

Several days after leaving Wyoming, the view from my train window began to take on a familiar shape. As I started to recognize the landmarks and the names of the towns, I stretched my legs and made sure my things were all packed up and ready to go. I was thinking, *A hot bath is going to feel so good when I finally get home. I wonder what Bruce and Belinda will say when I tell them Walter may be on the run and probably is as far from us as he can get.*

When the conductor announced that the next stop was my hometown, I pulled my bag from under my seat and sat up straight, eyes on every detail moving past my window. *This is it—my new beginning.*

As the train crept into the station, I had my eyes and hands glued to the window. I scanned the crowd of people who were waiting for their friends or family to arrive. *I don't see my mom. Did she forget to come and pick me up?* Then I spotted her. *She didn't forget after all.* A huge smile spread across my face when I saw that she had brought Bruce, Belinda, and even Cheryl with her. I breathed a sigh of relief. *Things are going to be all right after all.*

I tried to keep my family in sight as I quickly made my way down the aisle toward the door. I glanced out the window again, hoping to wave back at my sister, when I noticed that someone behind my mother was stepping into view. *No . . . it can't be!*

My hope turned to terror as, frozen in place, I watched Walter push forward, nudging his body beside Elaine. A huge grin was spreading across his face, a grin that said: *"Just wait 'til I get my hands on you!"*

This cannot be! I must be imagining this. The Nelsons had convinced me that Walter's entanglement with the law had finally stopped him, forced him to run away for good. I felt this thought pushed aside as my fight-or-flight instinct kicked in. My heart was racing, my cheeks burning. My hands clenched at my sides as all of the dark fear came rushing back, twisting my insides into a knot.

I turned to look for another way out, charging down the aisle in the opposite direction, bumping into other passengers as I raced away from the train's door. "Can I get out on the other side?" I asked the conductor, my voice cracking. I knew the answer before he said it. I don't know which thought terrified me more: knowing how angry Walter must have been that I ran away from him, or my knowledge that Walter had possibly caused a deputy to come up missing. *I can never tell him that I know he is a possible suspect of a crime.* My shaking hands dropped my bag with a thud as I slipped back into my seat, not knowing what else to do.

I closed my eyes for a moment and tried to just breathe. I managed to corral my racing thoughts; I had only a few minutes to figure out what to do. I knew I couldn't hide, because Walter had already seen me. I couldn't expect my mother or my siblings to help me. I was sure they wished Walter wasn't standing there with them at this moment as well. There was only one door out of the train, and dropping my bag and running through the station would only inflame Walter more. The train jolted to a full stop, and my heart sank as I watched each passenger, one by one, exit the door. I knew there was no escape.

I was the last person off the train. I walked slowly to this group that I called my family, dragging my feet, dragging my bag. All the excitement I'd felt about returning home had turned to a sadness too deep for tears. I couldn't summon the strength to return my sisters' hugs. "Welcome home," Walter greeted me, in a voice that only I could interpret. He stared at me with seething hatred. He put on an artificial smile when Elaine turned his way, and then his eyes flashed back to that look that threatened me to my core. *Walter may have killed once, and I could easily be his next victim.*

It was after nine o'clock, and the sun was setting in the western sky. The day was still very warm. As we piled into Elaine's old car, my siblings hounded me with eager questions. "How was your trip? Did you like Wyoming? Why didn't you write us? Are you glad to be home?" I couldn't understand what they were saying. It was as if they were speaking another language. I stared straight ahead as the shock of my homecoming began to settle in, along with the thought that, this time, there was truly *nothing* that could stop Walter.

CHAPTER TWENTY-NINE

My family drove me to yet another home. As the story unfolded, I learned that Elaine had managed to find another house on North Avenue, and that she and the twins had been living there peacefully. Then Walter showed up. Could it be possible that the Wyoming police could not find a crazy man driving a painted school bus to the state border? Or perhaps they had never looked for him at all. *Maybe Walter didn't actually commit a hit-and-run and didn't even flee from the deputy who wanted to question him. Maybe Mr. Nelson's story didn't pan out. Or maybe Walter outfoxed them and the law officials in all the states in between*, I thought. *Walter wins again!* The crushing pain I felt in my chest told me I would never be free of this man. Pushing the swirling thoughts out of my mind, I tried to focus on getting through the next minute, the next hour. Walter was the angriest I had ever seen him. I could tell he was putting on an act for Elaine now, but when he managed to get me alone . . . I might not survive his brutality this time.

I dropped my suitcase by the front door, and we all found a chair in the living room of this house that was new to me. I could tell it was story time. "I came home after a hard day's work, and Lorie was nowhere to be found," Walter explained. "I called to her as I searched, but no Lorie. I reported it to the police, who said they would begin looking for her once she was missing for twenty-four hours. The days turned into weeks, and then months.

Every *day*, I checked with the police. I was frantic. I realized she must have been kidnapped—and I swore I wouldn't stop looking until I found her. And here it is, my lucky day. You have returned to me, Lorie," Walter declared, sweeping his arms in a grand gesture.

Everyone looked at me to see what I could add to the story. Staying silent, I stepped to the window and gazed out to see that the old school bus was parked behind the house. I guessed Walter probably found a clever way to get rid of the possible murder weapon, his truck with the tow bar in front. *Perhaps he pushed it off a hillside in Wyoming. Maybe it was not really a murder weapon after all.* I was beginning to wonder if I had only dreamed the story Mr. Nelson came home and told us. *Only Walter knows what really happened.*

Walter had found his strongest way yet to keep me in check. I had used to feel a little hint of doubt when Walter said he would kill me if I ever told what he did to me. That doubt no longer existed.

This was all beginning to feel like a bad dream. As Walter liked to say, you can't fool a man at his own game. *If Walter really did something terrible in Wyoming and got away with it, how easy would it be for him to get away with killing me?* I'd left for Wyoming believing that Walter always wins, and I'd started my return trip thinking this would be the one time he lost. *I should have known better.*

Shortly after my homecoming, Walter took me to a park near downtown. "Sit next to me here," he told me, patting the park bench next to him. "You know I can never trust you again. What you did back in Wyoming, running away from me, I can't ever forgive that, you realize that, dontcha?"

Walter was staring me down with that dark anger burning in his eyes. I nodded mutely.

"You're lower than dirt to me now. Awful. You're worthless—a liar and a runaway."

Maybe he is right. Maybe I am a terrible person.

Next, Walter made me promise that I would never tell anyone that I hadn't really been kidnapped. Then he made it clear to me that if I ever told, I would be very, very sorry. I believed him.

In Wyoming, Mrs. Nelson had given me a calculator to use in math class. I'd brought it home with me in hopes of continuing in school. When Walter saw it in the pocket of my backpack, he made me throw it in the bushes as we were walking home from our little talk.

"There might be a tracking device in that contraption. Don't you forget. I know lots of ways of disposing of bodies. A wood chipper or a sinkhole are great ways to get rid of a corpse."

In the days that followed, stories from various family members helped me piece together how Walter had made it back to Michigan. After his quick exit from Wyoming, he went to his sister's house in Michigan. His brother-in-law ran a foster care home there. Walter stayed there for a while and did chores in exchange for an old car, a Chrysler New Yorker. In time, he found out where Elaine was staying. He called her, telling her some of his same old lines, and Elaine took him back.

I wasn't surprised that Elaine had fallen for Walter's act yet again, but I wondered what Walter's sister must have been thinking. Did she hide Walter at her home out of fear? The situation reminded me of an old family story I remembered hearing when I was younger. Years ago, Walter's other sister, Esther, asked Walter for a ride to California. Walter took her there. Shortly after that, she was reported missing, and her body was never found. Now, after Walter's threatening words to me, I couldn't help but wonder, *Am I the only one in the family who suspects Walter may be responsible for Esther's disappearance?*

I soon learned that our family's housing situation was as unstable as ever. Shortly after my return to Michigan, Elaine found yet another house and moved again. This turned out to be bad news for me. The house was small and cramped. Walter suggested that he and I could return to living in the school bus again. I knew that if that happened, Walter would have complete control over me again, and this time there wouldn't be any Mr. and Mrs. Nelson to help me escape. Elaine didn't protest, but I was relieved when she moved again a few months later, this time to a house just outside of town, and Walter and I soon rejoined her and the twins.

In the new house, Walter acted more like a husband to Elaine, but this only meant that he saved his harsh words and beatings for us three kids. Walter didn't know that I knew he had said some things to Bruce and Elaine about a deputy sheriff. Yet he never mentioned it to me. Whether the story was true or not, it was one more thing that kept me in check.

One good part of my return to Michigan was that I got to enroll in school again. In spite of all the bad things in my life, I still liked school. I could find slivers of happiness during my days there. Not being beaten or yelled at during the day felt like a breath of fresh air, and the meals were decent. My love of learning had not been snuffed out. I looked forward to school every day, yet I stayed very guarded, not letting my hopes get too high. All the good things in my life never lasted long, and soon I began to fear that my days in school were numbered. By October, my fear turned into a certainty: I was pregnant.

Each day when I went to school, the halls were crowded with students greeting each other as they passed by, slamming locker doors, finding their way to various classrooms. I disappeared in that crowd. I was alone. I hid my nausea and my growing stomach, wearing big t-shirts and a down-filled vest long after the weather was too warm for a jacket.

Belinda and Walter were the only ones who knew my secret. When a girl in class accused me of being pregnant, I denied it. At home, Walter told me, "Keep your goddamn mouth shut. Don't tell *no* one about it, ya hear?" My mom acted like she didn't know, even though I heard Walter tell her I was pregnant. I was fifteen.

There were several attempts to get me an appointment for an abortion. I barely understood what the word meant. Once, Walter tried to use Belinda's ID to get funds, but that attempt failed. Of course, he had no money of his own to buy one. I had no say in the matter. My body was changing, and it was all so confusing. There was no one I could talk with about what was happening to me. To Belinda, I was an embarrassment. When she would see me in the halls of the school, she would turn the other way. If I spoke to her, she wouldn't return my greeting. I knew she was hurting too, and just trying to survive the reality of being a member of our family. I felt sorry for her as well as for myself, but I sure could have used a friend to talk to once in a while.

At home, it was just Walter and me now. The others were able to escape in various ways. In January of 1983, my mother checked into a hospital with a nervous breakdown. Walter was happy to have her out of the way. The twins were done with Walter taking his anger out on them. Bruce took to the streets, and Belinda moved in with her boyfriend. They were the lucky ones. Being pregnant, I knew I couldn't just take to the streets like Bruce did. Walter would find me anyway, so what would be the point?

While I was in school, Walter did a few odd jobs, which added to the meager unemployment he managed to draw. As usual, there was little food in the house, so I was careful about eating everything in my free lunch at school. I never got a chance to learn that much about pregnancy, but I did know it was important to eat a balanced meal, and to get enough food for myself and the child growing inside me.

CHAPTER THIRTY

One morning in April, I awoke to a pain in my abdomen. I barely understood what was happening to me, but I rushed to wake up Walter. When I felt a gush of water run down my legs, I had no clue what that meant. All Walter said was, "Put some of those cloth diapers on the seat of the car and get in."

Walter didn't say anything about going to the hospital, but as the pains grew worse, I hoped that was where he would take me. Walter didn't drive toward the local hospital but instead began driving aimlessly around town. I hoped he was debating about checking me into the hospital. *He must be worried that someone might find out about us.* Walter headed out toward the country and found a cemetery. He parked the truck. He waited. He got out and stalked back and forth, his brow furrowed and his lips appearing like he was mumbling to himself. He came back inside, started the engine again, and drove some more.

The labor pains were screaming inside my body, but I didn't say a word the whole time. I was not allowed to talk unless spoken to, and I assumed that included screaming and crying. Finally, after what seemed like forever, he pointed the truck in the direction of town. The sun was low in the sky now. It had been a full day of labor pains and Walter's strange behavior. By the time we reached the hospital, I was doubled over in the front seat. Walter gave me my instructions: "You listen to me, and you listen good.

I'm the grandpa to this baby, and that's what you tell anyone at the hospital that asks. If they wanna know who the daddy is, you tell 'em you don't know. You got that? If you say *anything*, you'll be sorry. Do you hear me?"

I could only nod as I prayed, *God, please get me through this.* Then Walter yanked me out of the car, pulling me into the hospital.

A hospital orderly brought out a wheelchair when she saw us enter. "This here is my daughter. She has been in labor since this mornin'," Walter explained. He smiled and agreed to fill out papers at the desk. "You take care now. I'll be right here if you need me," he called to me as they whisked my wheelchair down the hall.

I was slipped into a gown and hooked up to a monitor. It wasn't long before a smiling Walter turned up at the door to my room. Walter told the nurse, "I want to stay with her. Her mother left us, and I'm all she has now. I know she wants me to stay with her."

I nodded my permission, knowing Walter was really more interested in what I might say if he left the room. He stayed in the room for the labor and was there for the delivery. Afterward, when the nurse placed my daughter in my arms, I was overwhelmed. *This is a new beginning that will change everything.*

"She's a beautiful baby. She's perfect, just perfect." Walter's happiness seemed genuine. When we were alone, he told me, "We'll call her Tammy. I always liked that name. It's the name of an auctioneer I once knew in Alaska. You know, she couldn't be perfect if you was really *my* daughter. This proves it. I always figured that witch of a mother of yours cheated on me. You *ain't* my real daughter. That's why this baby turned out so good. This is all gonna work out. There's nothin' wrong here. Nothin' at all."

As Walter talked, I realized that he was using the baby to convince himself that what he had been doing to me wasn't actually wrong. *This baby is only minutes old, and he's already using her! He knows he's the grandfather and the father.* The only thing that *wasn't* wrong here was the love I could already feel for my daughter. I had not asked to be in this situation, but when I looked into my baby's face, a powerful emotion I'd never known before rose up in me, and my eyes brimmed over with tears. *I know I will do anything for this child. I will find a way to protect her.*

"You go on and sleep now." Walter's voice brought me back to the moment. "You better remember what you're supposed to say if anyone asks you."

I watched him walk out the door, and then I turned my face to the window and let myself cry. *It's all too much.* The exhaustion, the pain, the overwhelming love I felt for my daughter, a child I didn't ask for—*but now that she is here, there is so much I want for her.* I touched her velvet skin and felt her fingers curl around mine. I put my face close to hers and breathed in her smell. Walter was right about one thing: she *was* perfect, her dark hair and brown eyes, her dainty little elf-like nose. She let out a tiny squeaking noise, and it stirred happy butterflies in my stomach. *This is Tammy's first day on Earth, but already I know two things about her life. I will always love her, and I will never let Walter hurt her. She will have something I never had, a mother's love and protection that will stop at nothing.* Now I could sleep.

My time of rest in the hospital didn't last long. After two days, Walter brought us home. My routine of cleaning, washing, cooking, and other chores remained the same as before—only now, I had my baby to take care of, and my days as a schoolgirl had ended. Exhausted and overwhelmed, I felt much older than my fifteen and a half years.

I nursed Tammy on demand and did the best I could dealing with her colic. She wasn't a happy baby, and evenings were especially difficult. By June, I had regained my strength and was able to find creative ways to keep Tammy close to me while I did my chores. I kept her basket inches from me, or I'd cradle her papoose-style when I was on the move.

One warm summer day, I was busy folding clothes when I was suddenly interrupted by Walter, angry and red faced, rushing into the living room.

"You take Tammy, and go hide in the bedroom!" Walter barked.

He shoved me through the bedroom door as I grabbed the homemade bassinet.

"Your mother just pulled into the driveway, and she's got some woman with her. Don't make a sound, and keep that baby quiet while I get them out of here."

Tammy was sleeping soundly, so I crept near the closed bedroom door where I could hear bits and pieces of the conversation from the living room.

"Walter, I've been in the hospital," Elaine began. "I was awful sick. Just *terrible*, I tell ya. The doctor said it was a nervous breakdown, and that I'd better rest and watch my stress . . ." The rest was muffled, but I did hear something about a social worker named Catherine being there.

Now Walter was speaking in his calm voice: "There was no need to bring anyone with you, Elaine. We've been managin' just *fine* since you left us. I'm sorry, ma'am, that Elaine bothered you.

There's nothin' wrong here, and there's *nothin'* we need. This visit is just a waste of your time." Walter's words sounded like he had poured syrup all over them.

Now I heard a strange woman's voice. This must have been Catherine, the social worker. "So please tell me, where is your daughter now, Mr. Williams? I'd like to talk with her."

"She's sleeping right now," Walter objected. "She has a bit of a cold and decided to take a nap. What do you want to talk to her about?"

At this point, I cracked the door ever so slightly. A gray-haired woman wearing a navy dress was standing with her back to the door. With a jolt of alarm, I noticed that one of Tammy's half-filled baby bottles had been left on the table nearby. *There is no way Elaine or Catherine could miss that.* Then I heard Walter saying something about coming in to see if I was awake, so I sat back on the bed just as Walter opened the door, charged in, and quickly closed the door behind him.

"Your mother brought some social worker here who wantsta talk with you. If you know what's good for you, you'll tell 'em everything is fine here."

The anger in his eyes was alarming. I brushed past him and entered the living room.

"Oh, Lorie, how are you, honey? Oh *my*, I've been thinking about you so much. I woulda been here sooner but seems I had me a nervous breakdown!" Elaine rushed to embrace me, but I shrank away from her attempt. I couldn't even make eye contact with this woman I had once called Mom. "I really *do* love you. You know that, don't you?"

"I don't think you do." My words sounded hollow to my ears, but I knew they were true. Elaine could have been a safety net, a protector for me, but she never tried to help. *Now that I have my own daughter, I understand how she failed me.*

My rebuke startled my mother, and she took a step backwards as the social worker approached me.

"I'm Catherine. Your mother wanted me to come with her and make sure that you are all right. Do you have everything you need?"

"I'm fine," I said, holding Walter's menacing gaze for a second.

When Catherine asked again if I needed anything, Walter was quick to say, "I have money in the bank for anything she might need. We don't take charity."

As Walter tried to rush Catherine out the door, it reminded me of all the other times social workers had fled from our house, never to return. This one was putting up more resistance than some of our previous ones. When Catherine insisted that she had more questions for me and was concerned about my welfare, Walter lost his patience and let his true colors show. "You got *no* goddamn right to come to my house and bother me and my kid. This stupid whore *left* me and her daughter, so she's got no goddamn right to ask any questions either. You can just leave us the hell alone. If you come back, you'll be very sorry."

Catherine made one last attempt. "I hope you understand, we may need to investigate further," she said, but I could hear the quiver of fear in her voice.

"There ain't gonna *be* no further investigatin'. Now get off my property."

With that, Walter shoved both of them out the door. Elaine whimpered as she landed on the sidewalk. "Don't you ever come back here!" Walter yelled as both of the women rushed to Catherine's car.

As I watched my mother leave, I vowed to myself that from that day forward I would never call her "Mom" again. Her passiveness and neglect had ended up hurting me just as much as Walter's violence had. I had always thought someday she'd really stick up for me, but I saw then that that was just a pipe dream.

Once the women had driven away, Walter turned toward me, on fire with anger. "You know this is your fault! You're the one that left the damn bottle out."

He slapped me, hard. "If you weren't so goddamn *stupid*! Now we haveta worry about them coming back."

Walter started pacing back and forth as he continued his tirade. "We gotta get outta here. *Fast*. We can't have that witch comin' back here and bringin' that goddamn bitch with her. We'll head up north. . . . Yes, that's what we'll do. We'll load the bus, pack up Tammy, and get outta here before they come back. Goddamn *witch*, that's what Elaine is."

Walter took off around the house, picking things up here and there. I realized he was gathering up anything that he associated with Elaine. He tossed a blanket, a wooden bowl, some clothes, and some knickknacks in a pile on the floor.

"We'll burn all this shit. Ain't no way we're takin' *anything* that belonged to her, or else she'll keep witchin' us. And there ain't no way we're gonna leave a damn thing for her to come back and get."

Childhood pictures of Elaine and those of her relatives were added to the demolition pile. My mother's old watch, her jewelry, even her birth certificate were not spared. It felt like Walter was erasing her from my life.

Walter hauled the items outside and began to build a fire in the backyard. Clothes, dishes, bottles, pillows, anything of ours that Elaine might have touched were piled in a heap and set ablaze. The sight and smell of everything going up in smoke brought back nauseating memories of that horrible night in Cheryl's spray-painted room, and the drone of the chainsaw when Walter had destroyed all of our things at the Canadian border. "Never leave *nothin'* for the enemy!" Walter howled into the smoke-filled night air. It was two o'clock in the morning, and there was nothing left that Elaine had touched.

With the stench of the fire still in my nose, I began to help pack the rest of our things, moving stiffly and automatically like a robot. *Here we go again.* I had packed things into the bus so many times that I didn't even have to pay attention.

Walter gathered the quilts I'd made from old upholstery fabric and stuffed with batting we had gotten from the mattresses at the dump. He snatched the things the baby would need and shoved them into the bus. "Go get the baby, and let's get the hell outta here," Walter commanded.

I was so exhausted that I spoke before I had time to think. "I'm *so* tired; please can we wait until morning?"

Walter grabbed me by both forearms, squeezing hard. "Do you gotta argue with me *all* the time? We're leavin' *now*, so shut up and get Tammy—and make it quick."

As I rushed through the house to get the baby, I paused at the window. I saw Walter hitching the old rusted Lincoln Continental behind the bus. Wild thoughts ran through my head: *How much time will that take him, three minutes, maybe four? I could scoop up Tammy and run out the front door. . . . Where would I go? How far would I get before Walter would catch me and beat me? One block, maybe two? Would he beat me so long and hard that I could no longer take care of Tammy?* If Walter killed me, my last thought would be of my child. *How could I leave her with Walter?*

There was no way to run now, not with a baby who needed me, so I had to ignore those thoughts. I gathered up my child and climbed into the bus with Walter.

"We're gonna go to the lake and hide out for a while," he explained as the bus roared to life, taking us away once again.

CHAPTER THIRTY-ONE

When we arrived at the lake, I got to work arranging the things that were spared from the fire, trying to make everything nice for my baby.

Walter had been hoarding some cash from his unemployment. He'd told me in the past that I could use it if Tammy needed anything, but I knew better than to touch it. Now, we used that cash to buy gas for the bus and the car once we set up camp. It wasn't long before his stash ran out.

Again, Walter had to rely on his talent of making something out of nothing. He began to craft some handmade lamps. He used diamond willow branches to make the base and birch bark for the shades. They actually were quite remarkable.

After Walter stopped by with his good-guy act, the hardware store in town let him run a credit for the electrical cords and sockets to put inside the lamps. Now Walter was ready for business. That was where I came in. It was my job to take one of the lamps into the bars around town and try to sell it, or get the would-be customers to come outside and see Walter's collection that was for sale. Walter was pretty convincing at pointing out how unique these handmade creations were, and he managed to pocket ten dollars here and there. It kept us going for a while.

Once again, the birch tree became the means for our survival. We knew how to use the two main layers for making tea, and it contained a healthy ingredient that was good for teeth. I thanked God for that. My teeth were in good shape in spite of never seeing a dentist. Even if it was just with water, I brushed regularly. Walter was a man of many contradictions. His respect for nature was evident, but there was no carryover to a respect for humans, especially his family.

The ten dollars we got for selling a lamp here or there was helpful, but our sales method made little sense to me. We were driving an old Lincoln Continental, a gas guzzler at eight miles per gallon. We'd spend more on gas just getting to places where there were customers than we'd earn from our sales. Gasoline was an ongoing problem. Once, Walter drove away from the station without paying. I hated stealing but couldn't help but hope that maybe it would lead the police to Walter one day. Another time, he found an old abandoned gas station. Walter was able to locate the lids to the underground tanks, and he'd lower a jar on a rope into the tank. The jar returned filled with dirty gasoline, which we then had to filter before it could be used in our car's tank. It was a slow process, but Walter was patient with this liquid treasure he had found.

It sure wasn't an exact science, but I was learning some tools to use when dealing with Walter. Most important was to keep him from boiling into a rage. I had to know just what to say and how to say it. I had to keep my tone of voice a certain way and watch all body language when he was around. Facial expressions were especially important. By not provoking him, I was protecting my little girl. He was still forcing himself on me regularly, but I was getting better at keeping my body neutral, while letting my mind drift away to another place. I knew there was no way for me to win this game or get away from Walter. For my survival I did the best I could, considering I was up against a madman.

It was easy to keep busy and distract myself with household chores, especially knowing how upset Walter would be if things weren't done exactly to his liking, but I felt isolated and lonely. Walter wouldn't stop ranting and raving that it was my fault we had had to move. In spite of him, I did my best to make our bus home pleasant for Tammy. I could cook a healthy meal out of very little and still make it taste good. Organizing and sewing were no problem for me either, and I managed to keep our space tidy without spending money on expensive cleaning supplies.

Once he was out the door, I'd hug Tammy close to my heart and twirl her around. "Hush little baby, don't say a word, mama's gonna buy you a mockingbird." I'd sing and laugh, and Tammy would giggle and bury her sweet head in my chest. Singing Mother Goose rhymes became a special time for my baby and me, and I made sure she would see me smile, so that she would learn to smile too. We made the most of that precious time when Walter was away. I wanted to indulge Tammy as my only child and make her feel important. I knew I was pregnant again.

When I told Walter about it, he was so mad. He told me I should be more careful. He continued to rape me and wouldn't buy me any type of birth control, and then he'd insist that it was my fault.

I could feel my mind falling prey to Walter's control more and more every day. He already owned my body, but now I was losing my hope, too, and maybe even a little bit of my sanity. Living in fear every minute of every day took away much of who I was as a person. I barely thought about running away anymore. If anyone did speak to me when I was outside of the bus, I would begin to shake with fear, knowing I was not allowed to communicate with anyone except Walter and my baby. Walter spoke for me, and he'd tell people I was his daughter. He once versed me on what to say to sell a lamb to a would-be customer. My words were to be no more or no less than what was commanded. I felt like a circus performer, and Walter was the cruelest of ring leaders.

Once, in explaining Tammy and my pregnancy, he told some people, "My pitiful daughter is too stupid to know better, and she got herself pregnant again. It's my burden to take care of her. I'll make sure she and the baby are cared for, since she isn't capable of doing it herself."

After being forbidden to speak, I wondered if I could carry on a conversation with an adult if I had been allowed to do so. All of my human interactions were with my daughter, and she wasn't even one year old yet. *If I ever get out of this prison I'm in, I wonder if anyone will ever believe me.*

I looked at my beautiful daughter and knew I had to keep going for her sake. *It's all for her.* All I had left was faith. If I ever got out of this situation, it would be through God's hand. Through it all, I had managed to hold on to my belief in God. I still prayed every day. For me to be free would take a miracle, but I feared that miracle might take the form of something disastrous.

As usual, money was tight. Walter had been passing a series of bad checks. We kept on the move, and he hadn't been caught yet. The dishonesty was just another thing about my situation that sickened me, one of so many I had no power to change.

CHAPTER THIRTY-TWO

Pausing for a moment with a felled tree at my feet, I lifted my head to feel the wind on my face. I could smell spring in the air. For me, the winter of 1984 was filled with countless snowy trips into the woods to chop down small trees. I would saw them into logs and then haul them to the wood-burning stove in our bus. It was back-breaking work sometimes, but I had to keep my home warm.

May of 1984 brought with it more than a promise of warm weather. Tammy had a little brother now. We named him Jimmy. Walter allowed me to go to a hospital for Jimmy's birth. My baby boy arrived fifteen minutes after we got to the birthing wing. Social workers began asking me questions immediately after the birth. I didn't tell them we were living in a school bus. I didn't tell them Walter was actually my father, not my husband. I figured Walter didn't put down an address for us when he filled out the paperwork. I hoped and prayed someone there would actually see through Walter's act. During my time there, it seemed like the hospital staff was on to us, and Walter was more than suspicious when he was asked questions. So, we left the hospital without checking out, not knowing if social services would be sending someone out to investigate us or not.

I was back in the primitive school bus again, parked in a vacant area in the woods, and now there were four of us living inside. I was still exhausted from the birth in May. Walter expected me to keep up with every pioneer chore I'd been doing before I had two children, and to still have the energy left over to meet all of his other needs.

Most of the time, I felt like I was in a trance. My whole world was bordered by the cluster of trees I could see through the screen door. My only joy came in attending to my son and daughter. I loved my baby boy, who was still nursing. Tammy was now two, and she was curious about *everything*.

One day in the spring while I was inside tending to the children, Walter was just outside the bus in the woods. A state police officer stopped by and told Walter he needed a camping permit to be there. Days later, Walter found an abandoned cabin nearby. He decided to move in. I got to enjoy a new luxury for a while when Walter found a way to hook up electricity for the cabin without running it through a meter. This arrangement lasted through the summer, and then we were forced to return to our bus.

Walter found only a little work here and there, and our food was running out. He decided to move again.

As we drove away, I kept the children as comfortable as possible, giving them a reassuring smile, but I quickly changed back to my expressionless robot face when Walter addressed me.

"If you hadn't been nuts on gettin' back to the south of the state, we could have been just fine where we were."

Let it slide, don't talk, look straight ahead, I told myself. Of course, he was now going to blame me for his inability to get along with a boss.

I tried to remain quiet, but this time I just couldn't. I could feel it bubbling up inside, and there was no more room to contain it. I had to say something.

"But . . . *you* didn't like it up there. So it wasn't my fault."

Okay, stop now, look how angry he is. I knew I'd pay for this, but I just kept talking.

"Those lamps were not going to make enough money for us to survive, and you know it. We could have starved to death. Don't keep saying it's my fault—because it is *not*."

Okay, no more. You've said way too much already. Gotta move the baby out of the way before he begins slapping me. I can't believe I just did that!

"Well, don't you got some nerve?" I heard anger in Walter's voice, and I braced myself for what was to come next. But the next thing I knew, he was laughing and slapping his hand against the steering wheel.

"The *nerve* of you, gal. Ain't you somethin'?"

We drove on in silence for the rest of the trip. I wasn't sure if I felt better or worse after my little outburst. A wave of dread washed over me—the all-too-familiar feeling of waiting for Walter's revenge.

We turned down a dirt road that was overgrown with weeds and continued on until we found an old, unused campground.

"We'll set up camp here for a spell," Walter told me.

I settled Jimmy into his crib and then reached for Tammy, who'd just woken up. "I'll take Tammy for a walk. We'll see if we can find some water while you're getting things set up," Walter said.

Before he left, Walter picked up the folded newspaper he'd been studying before we left our old campsite. He threw it at me, calling, "See what ya think of what I got marked there."

As I picked the paper up from the floor, I saw that Walter had circled something, a classified ad in the real estate section:

House for sale. Land contract. $500 down. There was an address listed, in a small town close to where we were parked. I looked out the window to see Tammy and Walter, jug in hand, walking down a path in the woods. I shrugged the idea off: *Just another one of Walter's grand schemes.* Forgetting about the ad, I checked on Jimmy and then continued settling our things for our stay.

When Walter and Tammy returned, Tammy rushed back with a hug for me. Walter had a full jug of water. "There's a stream nearby where we can fetch as much as we need," he said.

Tammy pulled on Walter's leg, pointing at something nearby. "You run along and play now," Walter told her. "I gotta talk to your mama about somethin'."

I turned my eyes toward her to make sure she stayed in sight. I was tying a clothesline between two trees when Walter asked, "So . . . whatta ya think, huh?"

"Uh, about the house in the paper?" I asked.

"Yes, about the house in the paper. I think we oughta go look at it."

I just nodded. I knew Walter's history. Even if it did work out, it wouldn't last long. He'd find fault with it and get mad, and we'd move on again, just like always. But I tried to keep my face expressionless, hoping the nod was the right move.

Walter was quiet for a long moment. Then he suddenly grabbed my arm from behind, twisting it ferociously behind my back while he hissed, "How come you're so goddamn quiet now? You wasn't so quiet back in the bus, *were* ya? You didn't have no goddamn problem talkin' then, *did* ya?"

He let go of my arm and gave me a shove. I felt a sharp pain in my spine as I hit the tree, the one I'd selected for a clothesline pole. I grabbed onto it to keep from falling.

Walter shoved his fist under my chin, lodging me between him and the tree. "Just don't wanna give me no credit when I have a good plan, do ya?" he screamed, his face reddening.

My neck was wrenched around in an awkward position, but I didn't try to move. I could see the fury in his eyes. "Who do ya think you are, crossin' me?" He slapped me as he let me go. "You ungrateful little bitch. I try to get us a *real* house. Somethin' *nice*. And *this* is how you thank me?" Giving me a final hateful stare, he stomped inside the bus.

I rubbed my neck and head, checking for injuries. I turned to look for Tammy and found her playing in the flowers, oblivious. *Thank God she didn't hear any of that.* Jimmy was still napping. Through the windows, I could see Walter pacing back and forth in the bus like a caged tiger. My eyes caught on the two bikes strapped to the side of the bus. A fleeting thought of me pedaling away while holding an infant and a toddler passed through my mind for a second. I dismissed it immediately, tightened the clothesline, and turned to other chores that were waiting for me. Walter's anger would pass. I realized that my thoughts of escaping came less and less frequently every year.

We had been dragging the old Lincoln Continental behind our ragged school bus. The next day, Walter unhitched it and told me to gather up the children because we were driving to town.

"We're gonna look at that house whether you like it or not."

I settled the children into the backseat.

"That's fine. A house would be nice." I held my breath: *Did I say just enough, or too much?*

"So you finally found the right way to talk to me. *Finally.* That's more like it." Walter reached over and patted my thigh after I got settled into the front seat. My stomach contracted when his hand went higher. In a lower voice, Walter whispered, "Now that you're talkin' to me the way you should, I'll be *real* nice to you later."

Walter had called the owner of the house from a pay phone and was told we could drop by any time. Before we arrived, he had instructions for me. "You make sure you tell them just what I told you, in case they ask. You tell 'em you're my wife and *nothin'* else. That's all. *I'll* do the talking."

I've heard that little speech for two and a half years now. Only now I've been upgraded to wife. This arrangement could prove interesting if anyone from our past happened upon us. *So now I'm the wife rather than the "daughter who is so stupid she continues to get pregnant by God knows who." Okay, Walter, whatever you say.* Walter rarely let me out in public anyway, but when he did, he always stayed close enough to me to guarantee that I wouldn't talk.

The dismal little town seemed to be about five blocks long, with just one sad main street. My observations were interrupted by Walter's voice.

"There it is. That's the one."

He drove by slowly, his eyes focused on a run-down old house nestled in a neighborhood of other dilapidated houses. He passed it right by, though.

"Are we going to stop?" I asked.

"Gotta get the *feel* for this place first. Gotta make sure I don't get a bad feelin'. I can't be somewhere that don't feel right."

After a closer examination, Walter mumbled, "I guess it's okay." He turned the car back around, and we parked in front of a large general store, which was right next to the house. He sat and stared at the house and its surroundings for a while. I took it all in, too.

I saw dingy gray shutters hanging loosely beside the dirty windows of a house that was in bad need of paint. There was a tiny dirt patch that served as a yard, a driveway that was two tracks worn in the ground, and a crumbling sidewalk. I was more interested in the tall, barn-like building that was a store. It was so close to the house that its walls stood about six inches from it. Its dirty window displayed a sign reading Grocery and Goods. It was too dark and dirty to see anything inside, other than the light from a single bulb suspended from the high ceiling. A small group of teenagers, laughing and grabbing each other, lounged on the steps of the store. *It's curious: a house almost connected to a store.*

Many of the houses looked like they were once stores, and maybe that is why they were settled so close to the road. What a peculiar place this was. My home-and-garden review was cut short by Walter. "Let's go," he said suddenly.

I took Tammy by the hand while balancing Jimmy on my hip. We caught up with Walter in time to hear him say, "It ain't so bad for $1,400."

The door swung open, and a man extended his hand. "I'm Hal. You must be the guy that called."

"That's me, all right, Walter Williams. And this here is my wife."

Walter shook Hal's hand. As Hal extended his hand toward me, I was sure I could see something in his eyes, like he sensed something wasn't right. We followed him into the house.

It didn't take long to see that the dilapidated exterior was probably the best feature of this place. The porch floor and wallboards were warped from water damage. The kitchen area was separated from another area by a soiled blanket hanging from the ceiling. It would be hard to even define the room as a kitchen. One plywood cabinet on the wall was the only kitchen feature in the dingy room. There were some pipes hung on the walls, but no evidence of water or electricity. Hal sensed my silent surprise and laughed, "I suppose this here place is what you might call a fixer upper. This building used to be a blacksmith shop, then a beauty shop. Years ago, they used to hold wrestling matches in the living room. Quite a history this ol' house has. It could use some fixin' up, but you sound like you're a real handyman, and I respect that."

Hal then hurried us out of the so-called "kitchen." *No sink or appliances, no water, or electricity to power anything . . . we might as well keep camping outdoors*, I thought.

The dining room, although tiny, looked better than the kitchen. So did the living room, but it was a very low bar I was comparing it to. The walls in there were also made of cheap fiberboard. The paint color choice was an unfortunate mauve pink. The floors were filthy. A propane heater in the living room served as a grim reminder that the house had no furnace. The windows on the west side of the house featured a view into the side of the store next door, a wall of ugly brown asphalt shingles.

When Hal asked if we wanted to see the upstairs, Walter only nodded. I noticed he'd been pretty quiet on this little home tour.

Holding the baby in one arm, I helped Tammy up the stairs. At the top, we could see a hallway and four doors leading off of it. Hal saw me looking up at the ceiling, trying to figure out what it was about it that just wasn't right. "Tornado hit about five years ago and lifted the roof right off the house," Hal chuckled. I turned only to notice the floors were slanted too.

Following Walter and Hal into another ugly pink room, I noted the cracked and warped walls, supported by an uneven, sloping floor. As Tammy tugged on me in hopes of going back downstairs, I turned to Walter for permission. With his nod of approval, I assisted Tammy back down the stairs while Jimmy clung to me. As I let the children play in the living room, I was left with a sinking feeling. *Whatever Walter wants to do with this house, I don't care. A van, a bus, a handmade tent of plastic in a county park, it's all the same. I'm stuck, and so are my children.* I tried to swallow the lump of melancholy I felt swelling inside of me.

So Walter paid Hal the five hundred dollars he had saved from his truck driving job, and we agreed to a house payment of ninety dollars a month. *Hal sure got the best on this deal.*

We were driving back to the campground when Walter said, "We'll finally have our own place. That old witch Elaine can't take *this* away." I couldn't imagine where that comment had even come from. We hadn't seen Elaine in three years.

The next day, Walter decided that he would watch the kids at our campsite while I went into town to clean the house. Walter didn't abuse the children like he did me, and I knew he could care for their basic needs in my absence. I would have rather brought them along with me, but I didn't really have a choice. The work would be hard, but time away from Walter was always a bonus. He knew I'd return to him at the end of the day. Tammy and Jimmy would be watching for me.

It didn't take long to see that this house was worse than I had thought. There was no bathroom, just an old outhouse in the back. I found a chamber pot in the solitary kitchen cupboard. A bathroom would be out of the question anyway: there was no well or septic system, a minor detail Walter must have missed in his enthusiasm about this great bargain.

I told Walter about this when I arrived back to the bus, and he decided to return to the house himself. *I guess he thinks I'm lying to him or something.* Later, he came back to the bus and grumbled, "Don't worry about it. We'll dig a well ourselves." I could tell he was mad. For once, Walter was the one who had gotten screwed over in a deal. I would have found this quite funny, if I hadn't been aware of the mountain of work that awaited me.

CHAPTER THIRTY-THREE

Soon after we agreed to buy the dilapidated little house, Walter got a job as a hot oiler. His job sounded like dangerous work—heating up oil and then pumping it into a well to clean away the paraffin build-up. Days later, he got rid of the Continental and bought an old Datsun truck. While Walter was gone, he didn't worry about me running. I had no friends and no means of communication. I was stuck in a deserted area with an old bus I couldn't drive.

The new job meant that we could pay the ninety dollars a month for this house, but Walter had less time to watch the kids. So I took them with me when I went to clean the dump of a house he had just bought. I found that the old building was more than just a challenge to clean. As I pulled down rotted walls, I found dusty hornets' nests behind them and discovered that the cardboard walls were rotting and there was no insulation anywhere in the house. But I continued to clean that dark, miserable place as best I could, using water I'd brought along from the campsite.

In late July, shortly after I turned eighteen, we moved into the first home we'd ever owned. I had to give Walter some credit for throwing himself into the job of making the place livable. He got to work right away on home renovations. Drilling a hole in the living room, he was able to tap his own well. Then he purchased an old pump at an auction for a dollar. Now we had a water source. Next, he got an old bathroom sink and installed that in the kitchen. There was no place to drain the water, so he installed a fifty-five-gallon drum in a hole he had dug under the kitchen floor and then connected it to the little sink.

"If you gotta drain water, scoop it out of the sink with a pan and dump it outside. Only let the last few drops down the drain."

Then, he brought home an old Maytag washer from an auction. He was quite proud of this purchase, thinking he had me living high on the hog now. Like our sink, this washer wouldn't drain. So I had to scoop the water out and refill it every cycle. Even so, this was the first modern convenience I'd seen in years, and I was grateful. My dry, chapped hands were relieved not to have to hand wash everything. I'd always been resourceful at keeping things clean. Vinegar, baking soda, and lots of elbow grease were my secrets.

The outhouse in the backyard was an improvement over our camping toilets, but not by much. It was a long time before Walter installed a bathroom in our house. When he finally did, he made a point out of not installing a bathroom door. Walter had to know what I was doing every minute, so to offer even a little privacy would never fit into his plan of monitoring me, always reminding me I had better not run from him.

Because all of our furniture had been destroyed, burned, or left behind, all we had was a crib for Jimmy and a bunk bed Walter made.

To furnish our new house, Walter journeyed to junk yards, auctions, and garage sales. Now we had an old hide-a-bed couch, a kitchen table, and some lawn chairs.

For a high chair, we took a five-gallon plastic bucket and shaped it into a booster chair of sorts. Jimmy could sit in the bottom of the bucket with his legs sticking out of the two holes we cut near the base. About where his waist would be, we cut out an area for him to reach his hands through and feed himself. So when we strapped it to a chair, it worked well as a booster.

Walter brought home an old carpet that had been left curbside at a Wendy's restaurant. He took it to a car wash to clean it. Once dried, it found its way to the middle of our living room. The only electrical outlet in the living room now powered a discarded television set. *From tent, to bus, to house—this is as good as it gets,* I thought.

My best times were when I could find a few quiet moments to pray, and when I could spend time with the children. I'd teach them children's songs, nursery rhymes and hymns. When we were riding in the truck, I'd play guessing games with the kids. We managed to find a few books here and there and made a riddle book. The dump sometimes had some pretty good toys that I'd clean up with bleach and water, and the kids would have hours of fun.

The worst moments in our house involved my battles with dirt. The kids would play on the floor and get dirty. Our only way to wash and clean up was at the little sink in the kitchen. I scrubbed the kids every night before putting them into bed. The water was always cold; I'd try to warm the rag in my hands as best I could. How I hated washing myself in the exposed, so-called kitchen, with Walter's evil eye on me. I'd take the pan of cold water upstairs to bathe myself, away from view.

Whenever I wasn't fighting the dirt, I was busy with food preparation, a challenge in itself without a stove. I cooked and canned most anything. I even canned the deer that Walter found on the side of the road and brought home. We both knew how to check a dead animal to make sure the organs were intact, indicating the meat was safe to eat.

Eventually, I was allowed to go to the little store that stood inches away from our house. I'd buy some of its outdated, dented cans of food. The store's front window sported a huge, dusty Winnie-the-Pooh bear, some anti-government T-shirts, and a stack of cans of corn. The store had an unpleasant odor to it, like something might have died in there. Stale loaves of bread and bags of chips sat strewn haphazardly on the dusty shelves. I came to learn that it was an open secret around town that the store specialized in "hand-me-down" food.

The loud, squat woman who waited on me seemed to have a bent for gossiping. I wished that I could practice my conversational skills on her, but instead I remained as quiet as possible during my trips to there. I could tell this clerk would love to get a hold of my story. I was careful to reveal nothing to her, knowing how Walter's fury would know no bounds if he heard I was chatting it up with the neighborhood gossip. Still, I was grateful to get out of the house occasionally and visit this dismal place. After a while, Walter got to know the owner, who believed I was Walter's wife. I was told never to tell him any different.

When the weather started turning cold, we realized the propane heater for this drafty house was going to cost too much to run in the winter. Then Walter got a big idea.

"I read somewhere that people back in the old days used to insulate their houses with dirt. We got plenty of that, and it's free. I remember once seeing an old farm house burn down, and sand came pouring out of the walls. The owner told me it only took two cords of wood to heat the place, and I figured it must have been because of the sand. Let's try insulating the house the old-fashioned way."

So, while we began to dig out a basement under our house, it was my job to haul five-gallon pails of the dirt up the basement stairs, onto the main floor, then up the stairs to the upper level of the house. Next, I dumped the dirt onto the floor to dry. Once it dried, I swept the dirt back into the pails and dumped it into the spot where I had removed a damaged piece of wallboard. The dirt would fall down to the lowest level. Then it was back down the two flights of stairs to the so-called basement. I filled up more pails, one for each hand, climbed out of the hole, and went up the two flights of stairs again, where I repeated the same grueling process, over and over. Listening to the *whump* of the dirt cascading down between the inner and outer walls of the house made me wonder how many hundreds, maybe thousands, of buckets it might take to insulate the entire house, from the ground floor to the roof.

My task of hauling the dirt became Walter's main form of entertainment for more than a year. Walter would occasionally fill a pail himself, but he mostly enjoyed watching me carry them up the two flights of stairs. He continued to remind me how great it was that he had provided me with insulation and an old furnace. The fact that *I* was the only one doing most of the work never came into play. The furnace was an old one that Walter had bought from the Amish and then installed himself. The little warmth it gave us didn't really make up for the hours I had to spend listening to Walter talk. Walter loved to sell himself, to brag about all the wonderful things he had done for me. Sometimes I thought, *He may actually believe it.*

Once the winter weather began to thaw, we discovered that the insulation plan had a little glitch. Walter's idea didn't seem so good once he noticed our windows had no flashing around them. When we got our first warm spring weather, the dirt came seeping out from the cracks between the walls of the house. Brown mud oozed down the windows and walls. The same thing began to happen every time it rained. Walter was furious that he had missed this obvious problem, but he assumed I'd take on the additional scrubbing without complaint. Cleaning now became even more of a chore for me than it ever had been before. It seemed like I would just get the mess under control, and then I'd hear a crack of thunder and the process would start all over again.

It was one thing to work day and night like a slave to maintain the house, but it was another to be kept away from human companionship, totally isolated. I don't know if Walter instinctively knew it, or learned it from somewhere, but keeping a person away from other human beings is a great form of control. Here I was in this tiny little town where "everybody knows everybody" . . . except no one knew me. Any communication I had with others was rehearsed or monitored by Walter in advance. This meant that even when I was able to talk with others, I still felt completely alone. Walter told me, "If you ever hear a knock on the door, you introduce yourself as Mrs. Walter Williams and tell 'em you're too busy with the children to talk."

One day when I noticed a couple move into the house next door, I couldn't help but wonder how this might change Walter's plans for me. I stayed out of sight from these new neighbors, but

Walter strolled over like he was captain of the welcome wagon. Seeing the guy try to hoist a washing machine off the back of his truck, Walter hurried over to offer his services and then continued to help unload other items while the two introduced themselves.

As I peeked out the window I could see that this couple was young. The woman was short and chubby, and her husband was slim with brown hair, the same color as his wife's. I overheard Walter call the man Craig. Craig introduced his wife, Jane.

Minutes later, I had to go outside to dump out the water from our sink. As I crossed the patch of dirt that was our yard, I could hear Walter say, "That's Mrs. Williams." I heard Craig comment about how quiet I was. I could catch bits of conversation as I continued to drain water in the yard. Walter's response was, "She better be. Better to be seen and not heard." Walter laughed at this, but I noticed that Craig did not. It seemed to me that Craig was studying us more than one would expect.

When Craig's wife joined the men, I heard Craig say to Walter, "Why don't you get your daughter to come on out and have a Coke with us."

"Yeah," Walter responded, apparently without thinking. He let the reference to me being his daughter stand. Then, realizing his error, he added hastily, "Just remembered I gotta make a trip into town to pick up a few things, so I'll see ya later."

My sink-draining efforts were cut off by an angry Walter, who stomped inside the house and confronted me. "Don't empty anymore goddamn water until they're inside the house. This is all your fault. That goddamn Craig tripped me up about you being my daughter. You got the same witch in you your mama's got."

Walter flung my dripping pan onto the floor and slapped me. I could hear the kids stirring from their naps, but my legs were frozen in place.

Walter was pacing back and forth, mumbling about the whole incident. Then he added, "Don't talk to them. You ain't got no business being over there or outside when they're outdoors. If you havta say somethin' to 'em, make sure you don't talk about being my wife or daughter . . . well, maybe you better say you're my daughter since that's what they think."

We heard Tammy's voice calling me, which reminded Walter to add, "You tell her she better call me grandpa if those people are around. You got that? Now go get those kids to shut up."

Our life in this odd little town began with lies. I'm not sure what people might have suspected of our relationship, but what I did know was that I had another secret. I was pregnant again. I wanted to keep this hidden from Walter as long as I could, fearing he might force me to get an abortion as he'd done so many times in the past. He had forced me into so many abortions; it was hard to keep count. Just the thought upset me, so I tried to push the sordid operations out of my mind as much as possible. I had no control over my own body. Yet, I vowed to myself, *I'm keeping this baby.* So Walter could just figure out himself how he would explain his daughter's pregnancy to these neighbors.

If anyone in our little town thought Walter's story was not on the up and up, they never mentioned anything about it. It didn't take long for people to understand that it was unwise to cross Walter Williams. I had to go along with Walter's charade. Yet there was one tiny, constant thing Walter couldn't take from me. There was a voice inside of me. *This wife or daughter, whichever*

I'm supposed to be, she does have a voice. Walter had quieted that voice over the years, but he hadn't been able to silence it. *I know there will be a day that I get away from Walter.* That thought kept me going. God was still with me. But my hope was always accompanied by fear, a fear that the end to all of this might be a tragic one. Every day, I prayed I could keep the children safe.

Chapter Thirty-Four

It was in November when I felt the first labor pains hit. I did the math in my head. *It's much too early.* I think the only reason Walter decided to take me to the hospital was that he was afraid to have me die in the house. This pregnancy had been especially hard on me. For three days, I laid in the hospital bed, until one day a nurse came in and induced labor. When it became apparent the baby and I were in trouble, they performed a C-section. The baby was born on Veterans Day in 1985.

My premature baby boy weighed only three pounds. We named him Teddy. My heart leapt in my chest as I watched him being whisked away to the neonatal unit. Walter was mumbling about how much all of this might cost, but I could see that he was a bit afraid.

The doctor returned with bad news: Teddy had underdeveloped lungs, and he would need help breathing. He would have to stay in the hospital for weeks. Walter jumped in: "I'm grateful for all you can do for our son, but my wife and I have been talking. We think it's best if we return home to care for our other children. She can come visit him every day."

The doctor was hesitant but relented. "I wouldn't recommend such an early release, but if no complications from the birth arise by tomorrow, then you can come to pick her up at noon."

Once the doctor left the room Walter said, "I bet you asked if you could stay longer just so you can keep your lazy ass in bed and shirk your responsibilities at home." As Walter stepped close to me, I flinched. Then he turned and said, "They probably just want to make more money. Damn doctors. I'll be back tomorrow and you better be ready."

Teddy remained in the hospital for another month. Walter let our neighbor, Jane, take me to visit him every day. I was so relieved that he didn't stick to his threat about me having no contact with the neighbors. Jane sat in the waiting room, watching Jimmy and Tammy, while I would hold Teddy and pray for him. Jane was bossy with my children, and even with her husband and me. Not so much with Walter though. We had kind of an unspoken thing going with our relationship. I couldn't share anything about my life with Jane. I wasn't sure if this made her feel shut out or what, but that was just how it had to be.

We brought Teddy home in December. He was a five-and-a-half-pound bundle that I loved. I continued doing the chores that kept our household going while caring for our three children. My usual tasks of feeding the wood-burning stove and heating water to wash laundry and dishes took twice as long, as I had to pause and care for my baby. Teddy cried most of the time. He never slept more than an hour or two. Walter was still working as a hot oiler and came home in the evenings expecting dinner on the table, complaining about his boss, and never helping with the unrelenting work at home.

One early morning I had managed to catch a few hours of sleep and came downstairs to the living room to see Walter sitting in the old rocker. He was holding Teddy, talking to him softly, while rocking him with a fondness I didn't think he was capable of, a peaceful expression on his face. I padded softly back to my bedroom, not wanting to disturb the moment.

In January, things took a turn for the worse. Teddy grew ill. I pleaded with Walter to let me take Teddy to a doctor. Teddy's fever kept rising, and everything I tried wouldn't bring it down. Walter told me to get Jane over to watch Jimmy and Tammy, and we bundled Teddy up and rushed to the emergency room. "Pneumonia," the doctor told us. The hospital offered to set me up in a room, but Walter told them I needed to return home to care for our other children.

The next two weeks went by in a fog as Jane drove me to and from my visits with my baby. We had little conversation in the car as we went to the hospital. Jane wasn't someone I would have chosen for a friend, but it would have been comforting to have someone to talk to during all of this. That, of course, could never be.

When the pneumonia was gone, the doctor reported that Teddy wasn't showing the improvement he expected. He asked for permission to do a spinal tap. Walter was suspicious and didn't like the sound of that. We were left alone to talk. "Please, Walter," I begged. "God would never forgive me if I didn't do everything possible to help Teddy." Brushing away my tears, I signed the permission form.

Walter warned me, "You'll be sorry. I ain't got no part of this."

The tests showed nothing unusual. We were allowed to bring Teddy home. Walter told me to keep the baby quiet so he could get some sleep. "Just remember those damn tests were all your idea. Don't you forget it."

And so the long night began. Teddy wouldn't stop crying. I'd walk the floor. I'd give him a bottle. I rocked him. I sang softly to him. All the tricks that had worked with my other two children didn't seem to comfort Teddy. At seven in the morning, Teddy finally gave in to sleep. I placed him in his bassinet, collapsed into the rocker, and watched him sleep.

Suddenly I shook myself awake, noticing the clock read 8:50 a.m. *I must have dozed off!* The house was still quiet as I leaned over to touch Teddy. Terror gripped me when I realized his body was cold to the touch.

"Walter!" I screamed. He ran into the room to see me clutching Teddy to my breast, rocking him and crying, "Oh dear God, no, no, please no!" Walter stared at me, stunned.

"I'll call someone," he choked out the words. "I'll get Craig and Jane over here."

His words were lost on me. Kneeling down next to me, he said gently, "Let me put him down now . . . we havta call a coroner to confirm the death." Through my tears, I watched Walter gently place Teddy in the bassinet.

I was in a haze when Jane came in and took Tammy and Jimmy by the hand. "They shouldn't have to see this," she said softly. Craig looked uncomfortable and then mumbled something about helping Jane with the kids. I bent down to hug both of my children. "You kids go stay with Jane for a while; be good."

"I don't want to go; I want to stay here!" Tammy protested.

Hugging her, I told her, "I want you to be here, too, but Teddy had to go and live with God. We have got to talk to some people, so it's best if you stay with our neighbors for a little while."

As they turned to go, Craig looked back at Walter and said, "Call us if there is anything we can do." Turning away awkwardly, he added, "Sometimes these things are for the best. He was such a miserable little guy anyway."

I saw the fury flash in Walter's eyes, and this time I could understand his anger.

The coroner arrived a short time later, and I realized he was the same doctor who had examined Teddy in the ER, the same doctor who had recommended the spinal tap. He introduced the man with him as Detective Rainer. The next hour compounded my grief. The questions the two men asked us were brutal. The officer poked around our house, making notes on a pad, sometimes clucking his tongue. The doctor concluded the cause was Sudden Infant Death Syndrome.

Walter had stayed quiet until now, but as I was weeping, I heard him asking them to leave, saying that his wife had been through enough and couldn't take much more. I thought back to when we were at the hospital. *I think Walter told this same doctor that he was my father.* But my mind was too overwhelmed by grief to dwell on that thought for long.

The men took Teddy with them, informing us of the name of the funeral home where he'd be taken. I rocked back and forth, clutching my stomach, which was still swollen from the pregnancy. I didn't look up as the door closed behind them.

Walter's grief turned to anger as he confronted me. "If you hadn't allowed that spinal tap, that baby would be with us now."

He shoved me back into the chair and paced the floor. I felt like my grief was sucking me in, pulling me under. Now, hearing the words that my baby's death was my fault smothered me. I knew I should keep my defenses up as Walter raged on, but I couldn't focus on anything except the black hole inside me left by Teddy's loss.

"That Jane next door probably witched us. You were always borrowing things from her, and now you better damn well return them. She's witching us, just like Elaine." Walter was screaming now.

My voice rang hollow as I mechanically mumbled, "It's my fault. All my fault . . ." My voice trailed off, and I felt a longing to go and be with Teddy, to just leave all of this behind. It didn't matter to me if Walter blamed me; it just added to the suffocating grief. I went over and over in my mind each detail of how I had cared for Teddy. I kept asking myself, what did I miss?

The following days melted together into one gray fog. I had trouble eating and sleeping—just thinking exhausted me. Fragments of thoughts floated around me, leaving as quietly as they came. *SIDS diagnosis confirmed. Funeral. Tammy calling out for me. Jimmy crying. Say nothing to rattle Walter. Breathe.* I felt like I was in a trance, while Walter acted like nothing had ever happened. I could hear him talking to our neighbor Craig. I still felt the sting of Craig's remark when Teddy died. Now I heard Walter saying, "You were right, Craig, with what you said. He *was* a miserable little guy." I listened to them chuckle as they both got into the Lincoln and drove off. At times, I had had little flickers of thought that Walter had felt something for Teddy, but now I could see I had been wrong. They were off now to buy an old truck that was for sale, like that even mattered. I was left at home with a hole in my heart and Walter's sharp words ringing in my ears: "It's the way *I* say it is—and don't you forget it." *I'm so tired.*

I had to try to break free from this robotic daze I'd fallen into and make things as pleasant as possible for my other two children. I still took care of their daily needs. *If I didn't, who would? Right foot, left foot, do what needs to be done.* Tammy and Jimmy were a comfort to me, but also a constant reminder of what I'd lost.

Walter and I were the only ones who attended Teddy's visitation. I snapped out of my fog of grief for a moment when I saw Walter unsnap the little outfit I had selected for Teddy's burial. The cuts the coroner had made for Teddy's autopsy inflamed my sorrow. "I bet they did this to him just so they could sell his body parts to rich people," Walter growled.

The following day, Teddy was buried. Walter and I were the only two at his graveside. For my only comfort, I looked to God.

CHAPTER THIRTY-FIVE

Shortly after Teddy's death, Walter's unemployment ran out. Now, we returned to the familiar routine of picking up pop cans on the side of the road. With Walter driving, the kids and I would take turns jumping out to investigate anything that looked like glass or metal lying on the ground. We knew better than to protest when a shiny object Walter spotted was obviously not something that would bring us a deposit at the store. That could mean a backhand to the face. Walter would occasionally give one of the children a slap, but he never beat them. So we followed orders, and when we had U.S. 12 cleaned up and the truck bed was full of cans, we'd head to the store to cash in. Today, it was already 9 a.m., and we'd been on the job since first light. The kids were being so good. Jimmy and Tammy had played the Find the Shiny Object Game without a complaint even though they'd had no breakfast and our dinner the night before had been meager.

Walter was happy now. "We've gotta have at least thirty or forty bucks' worth here."

I filled the shopping cart with our treasure and headed into Kroger's while Walter stayed in the parking lot with the kids. With my $42 return slip, I was able to buy a few staples to keep us going for a while.

When I returned, I saw Walter leaning against the side of the truck, staring intently at something across the street. I started to apologize about the laundry soap I had bought along with our food supplies, but Walter told me to shut up.

"Look at that, over there!" He pointed to a dumpster. "We gotta get over there. I saw some guy throw out a whole cart full of food. Anyway, I'm guessin' it's food. If that's just stuff going to waste, we gotta check it out."

Walter told the kids to stay in the truck and took me with him to investigate. Lifting the lid of the dumpster, we couldn't see much of what was inside. "You gotta get in there and see what he threw away," Walter instructed me.

He interlaced his fingers to make a step for my foot. I was in a hurry to get back to the kids, so I took the boost he gave me. Grasping the edge of the bin, I lowered myself down. Inside, I found all sorts of food, most of it sealed, and some of it only a few days past its freshness date. Walter was almost giddy when I handed some of it up to him.

"If *these* guys throw out food, so do a lot of other stores. Whatta bonanza! We ain't gotta worry about eatin' ever again! You stay in there while I go fetch the truck. If anyone comes, duck down so they can't see you. And if anyone from the store comes out, tell 'em you're getting food to feed your pigs on our farm."

Hiding in the bowels of a dumpster and waiting for Walter's return gave me several minutes to think about this new endeavor. I didn't want to eat food that was spoiled, but we *needed* food. This stuff looked fine, like it was just scooped off the store shelves. I didn't hesitate long. *Survival wins.*

This became the beginning of a new adventure for me, one that would end the constant hunger in my belly and give me a chance to learn to socialize with people. For eight years, I'd spoken only to Walter and the children, for the most part. At that moment, it was hard for me to imagine how dumpster diving could lead to a little bit of socializing. Walter and I were an odd couple when it came to being business partners, but in a weird way, that is what we had become.

So the routine began: Every night, I got the kids into their pajamas and fixed Walter a Thermos of coffee. We all piled into the truck, heading out after dark. Even though I was pregnant most of the time, it was my job to climb into the dumpster and hand the food out to Walter. Having been denied any type of social life or hobbies for most of my life, not knowing what I was about to find in each dumpster became like a little treasure hunt to me. I could hardly comprehend the quantity of food that got thrown away each night. We began with bread and chips and eventually worked our way up to all kinds of food. Eventually, Walter constructed a long-handled pincher to retrieve some of the food, but most of the time, I was hoisted in, even if there was dirty rainwater in the base of the container.

Walter would observe when the various stores threw out their food, and we added more stores to our schedule as time went by. We got some of our best finds after 11 p.m. Throughout the process, I'd try to keep the kids happy when they were awake on our nightly runs, but mostly they would sleep.

When we returned home from a run, I'd carry Tammy to bed first, her tousled hair soft and sweet against my cheek. I would kiss her good night and then return to the truck to scoop Jimmy into my arms. He'd whisper the word "mama" in my ear. "I love you, sweetheart," I would whisper back as I tucked the covers under his chin.

I often wished for a quick cup of coffee before I started my nightly job, but I knew that wasn't going to happen. Our truck had a capped bed, and we would park so that neighbors couldn't see me unloading the food. I would carry the cartons I'd saved out of the house and drop them at the truck with a thud. Canned goods went into one, packaged goods into another. I carried in the gallons of milk four at a time. When the truck was empty, I'd make my final trip of the night into the house. Next, the cleaning and storing process would begin. Stifling yawns, I wiped down the groceries that needed refrigerating first and then checked the "use by" dates, making judgment calls on the items that were six months or more past their date.

It wasn't long before our cupboards were overflowing with stale bread and overripe fruit. Walter bought an old freezer at an auction to help with the storage. I wasn't sure why we kept doing nightly runs when we had more food than we needed, but I didn't dare ask. Walter had been a bit more agreeable because we no longer had to worry about putting food on the table, and I didn't want to disturb his improved demeanor.

One day near the end of May, we drove out to a Jewel store. It was about 10:30 p.m. "We'll only do one store tonight," Walter told me as I handed him a sleeping Jimmy to carry out to the truck. I nodded, taking Tammy by the hand and tucking a blanket around her as she settled herself into the back of the truck.

We arrived in about thirty minutes, parked, and followed our normal routine. We waited and watched, making sure all of the employees had left the darkened store after it had closed for the night. We'd been chased off a few times by the store manager, but he didn't call the police when Walter explained we were just taking food to feed to our pigs. When we saw that the coast was clear, Walter signaled me to get out and head to the dumpster. It was my job to lower myself in. Being only five feet tall and usually pregnant made the job rather tricky. I knew that, once inside the dumpster, my only escape out was to pile bags and boxes on top of each other so I could hoist myself over the edge. That would not be a problem this time because the dumpster was especially full. Once inside, I gasped in amazement. There was bread, blocks of various kinds of cheeses, and countless packages of other food. I was so excited that I called out, "I can't believe all the stuff in here!"

"Just shut up and start handing it out," Walter ordered. "We got to hurry and get out of here before anyone sees us."

I began counting the loaves of bread as I passed them up to Walter's waiting hands. After fifty loaves, he told me to start hauling out some other stuff. I grabbed gallons of milk, cartons of cottage cheese, packages of meat and cheese, knowing that now was not the time to check to see if they were rancid. I felt conflicted about this whole business of ours, but imagining all this food going into a landfill didn't seem right to me either.

On the way home, I fought off sleep as Walter rambled on, so pleased with himself. "Ain't it great. All that food and it's all ours. You know, all these stores have a conspiracy with the government. They just wanna keep food out of the hands of poor people. *We're* beating the government! I'm smarter than all of *them assholes.* They think they can beat us down, make us do rotten jobs, just so we can eat? Ha! They ain't got a *clue* about Walter Williams. They can't beat me, 'cause you can't beat a man at his own game. This is MY game." I tried not to let Walter's bragging dampen my wonder at all the food we had gathered.

Once we were back home, it was my job to get the kids in bed and then unload all of this food by myself. Walter sat at the kitchen table, smoking a cigarette, and watched me. Lining up the meat and cheese on the counter, I began checking the food. If there was a greenish or gray color to the edges of the meat, I cut it away. Walter usually made me eat some to see if it would make me sick. If I didn't get sick, we'd keep the meat in the freezer. Most of the time I didn't get sick. If I did, it was still my job to dig the offending food out of the freezer and discard it. I tossed out one gallon of milk that was spoiled and refrigerated the rest of the night's haul. The bread was piled on the counter. The cheeses were rewrapped and stacked in the refrigerator. Canned goods were put away in the cupboard. It was after 1:30 in the morning by the time I wiped clean and stacked the last can.

"Ain't you gonna clean up now?" Walter asked.

"I'm too tired. I'll wash up in the morning."

"You'll wash up *now*," Walter hissed as he grabbed my shirt, popping off several of the buttons. "I ain't getting near you with that smell." He pulled my shirt off and shoved me toward the sink. "Wash up, now!"

Picking up a worn wash rag, I soaked it in the cold water as I took the soap in my other hand. Walter refused to look away as I washed myself. So I turned away, trying to hide my body and my tears.

"I know what you're thinking, and you better not be thinking that way. *You* can't beat a man at his own game, either. Don't you forget it." His fingers dug into my arm as he pulled me toward the bedroom. "We're gonna go to bed and celebrate findin' all this food. You *know* you can't beat a man at his own game, don't ya?"

"You're right, Walter . . . you can't beat a man at his own game."

The next morning, I was awakened by the warmth of the sun. I was always up before sunrise, so this was startling. Every night, I kept my balance on the very edge of the bed, as far as I could get from Walter without falling out of the bed. I never allowed myself to stretch out beyond this edge. I could see that Walter was not in the room. He always expected me to have his breakfast ready, so I was confused. I examined my arms and legs, aching from the night's work, my soreness from Walter's brutality. I rubbed at the bruises on my arms. I could hear voices downstairs. This was all highly unusual.

When I entered the kitchen, I saw that Alvin was our morning visitor. He was a farmer who lived close by and I could remember meeting him. He'd invited all of us to visit his farm a while back. At the time, I had been disgusted to find Alvin's house just as dirty as he was.

"Good morning, Lorie. I was just tellin' Walter here how he might make a bundle of money from sellin' some of this here food you folks seem to be findin'."

I nodded in greeting.

"I know a bunch of Amish down the way who may want to buy some of that extra food ya got there. They ain't got a lot of money, but if you make 'em a good deal, you could be in business."

I nodded again but stayed quiet. If there were any opinions to be had in this house, they would be had by Walter. Trying to hide my curiosity, I busied myself with washing the coffee cups in the tiny sink.

"We're gonna go down to Indiana and see if he's right. I'm gonna take a bunch of this bread and see if I can sell it. Maybe we can get someone to buy this stuff. Hell, we could make a bunch of money!" Walter was almost smiling now.

Alvin picked up a loaf of bread in his filthy hands and snorted. "I know a guy down there. Name is Jake. He's got about twelve kids, maybe more. They ain't never got enough to eat."

It turned out that I was expected to join them, along with the kids. The bread was loaded into the back of the truck, and the kids were scrunched in the backseat. I was unpleasantly wedged in between Walter and a very smelly Alvin, who was rambling on about us making a pretty penny. Alvin continued talking. Now he was going on about how Jake had to do some strange stuff to support twelve kids. I started to wonder what that meant, but my thoughts were interrupted by Alvin. "That's it. That's Jake's house."

The gravel driveway led us to a gray two-story farm house. Some of the clapboard siding was rotted, and other parts were patched with tarpaper. The dirty, cracked windows were laced with duct tape or just covered up with boards. Junk, weeds, and trash were scattered about the dirt yard. Next thing I saw was Alvin introducing Walter to Jake. Jake was bearded and, from what I could see under the brim of his hat, looked a little old to be the father of so many little ones. Jake passed Walter some money. Soon Jake's arms were loaded with loaves of bread.

The memory of Walter's words from the night before rang in my ears as I watched this simple exchange. "You can't beat a man at his own game." I could see that Walter was going to win again.

Jake became a regular customer, and the word began to spread from there. Word traveled fast in the Amish community, and soon everyone knew: if you wanted food cheap, you had to do business with Walter Williams.

CHAPTER THIRTY-SIX

At first, folks would ask us where we got the food. Walter's typical answer was that it came from stores that let us take it off their hands so it wouldn't go to waste. I guess there was a little truth to that. Perhaps the Amish people found Walter convincing, or they were just too hungry to give it a passing thought. Walter was pretty savvy as he expanded his business. He listened to his customers and did his best to find the particular foods they wanted. Walter figured if the stores on our route were throwing out food, then other places might be too.

So, we added two restaurants to our route: Kentucky Fried Chicken and Dunkin' Donuts. At first, I had to scrape cigarette ashes and other debris off of the donuts. Then Walter made friends with the manager, who started saving us his stale leftovers once he understood that Walter was just a "hard-working, honest pig farmer." I couldn't help thinking with amusement that "pig" was the only part of that statement that was true.

Our night scavenging was all about the timing. We often ventured out in the middle of the night. Depending on which store employees were working, different things seemed to be thrown out each time. Occasionally we'd find fluorescent light bulbs broken over some of the food. I never knew if that was to discourage us, or just kids who worked at the store having their idea of a good time. Eventually, the Jewel store began locking its dumpsters, but by then we had lots of other places on our route.

We'd started with day-old bread and donuts, and then we graduated to cases of candy kisses and truckloads of ice cream. We discovered that the Amish loved chips, so we often stopped by the Frito Lay factory, just outside of the next large town. There was a manager there whom Walter was friendly with, and he allowed us to rob his dumpster. Walter, "pig farmer" that he was, offered the manager a pig every few months in return. Walter would find a way to buy a pig with tumors, or some other health issue, from an Amish farmer and then had it processed. Every few months, the factory manager got the pork and we got the chips. We bought a wax sealer to reseal the chip bags. Sometimes we'd make pin holes in the deflated bags and blow them back up. Often, we heated the chips to remove the moisture and then sealed the bag up.

Gordon Foods was a profitable stop for us, too. We collected giant blocks of cheese from its waste bin. We discovered that Colby didn't freeze as well as mozzarella did. We resold the cheese for a dollar a pound. If a roast puffed up in the package, stores would throw that out too. Those were good finds for us. Later on, we realized the store manager was probably on to us, as we began to find broken glass on the discarded foods there as well.

One of our best nights came when we found a dumpster the size of a railroad car that was crammed full of frozen pizzas and TV dinners. It was winter, and those packages stayed frozen in the bus parked in our yard, because by this point our chest freezer was already filled to the brim. We sold the pizzas for a dollar each, all winter long.

As we found less food in one town, we'd move on to the next. We discovered tons of crackers and cookies with no freshness dates on them. Those were easy to process and resell. Walter believed that preservatives were more dangerous than spoiled meats. I wasn't sure about that, but I kept on following orders, although even I had my limits. I was usually pregnant and thus sensitive to smells. Wet dumpsters always had maggots and flies. I refused to scrape maggots and mold; it nauseated me. So Walter took over that task. He cut the bad parts off of the cheese and cubed it. Then I would repackage it onto paper plates. I tried to make it look good. Presentation was everything. Sometimes Walter would insist that we put bad parts on the bottom and good parts on the top. I didn't like doing business like that. It seemed like a metaphor for our life: Walter schmoozed the customers and made it seem like we were a happy couple, and then he'd make me miserable when we were hidden from view, just like the rotting cheese.

Walter would give freebies to his customers too, to guarantee their loyalty. They seemed to like him. They called him "Wally, the Bread Man." The Amish women were easy for him to win over. They were so innocent, and they always seemed to be pregnant too. Some of them befriended me, especially those who could speak English. I found myself speaking to them a little more each time they shopped out of the back of our truck. Eye contact was impossible for me at this point, as I couldn't shake Walter's threats about not talking to people. But because it was good for business and probably harmless, Walter made an exception for the Amish women. The chances of one of them reporting Walter to the authorities were pretty remote. I did appreciate their small kindnesses to me and looked forward to peddling our food from farm to farm. One of the women even made a little pillow for Tammy. It was a small gesture for her, but for me to receive a gift was such a memorable thing. It made me want to try to recover my ability to communicate with others.

Carrying on a conversation felt so foreign to me each time I tried. For eight years, I'd said few words to anyone in the outside world. The words I said to Walter were either forced agreement or attempts to say what I thought he wanted to hear. I'm not sure if conversation was a skill I had never learned, or if I was just relearning what had used to come naturally. I started with simple comments about the weather or ways the women could prepare the food we were selling. Eventually, I found that we were having short conversations about our children. It may not have seemed like much, but coming from my long years of silence, it felt wonderful.

It was refreshing to be outside the confines of our little house, but my newfound freedom was always overshadowed by the exhaustion brought on by all of the additional hours of labor our new business brought my way. My last ounce of daily energy was spent falling into bed each night.

It also became my responsibility to record the sales and the amount of money collected. Once the bookkeeping was completed, I had a little time to do the household chores, cook, and see to the children. Then it was time to start our nightly routine all over again. We were making two hundred dollars a week, but my life during this time was a constant struggle just to keep going. The loss of Teddy still left a dark shadow inside of me, and I had no outlet for those feelings. As much as I tried to keep those feelings to myself, Walter noticed.

"What in hell is wrong with you? Why won't you talk to me? Don't you know that's all you're good for? You better snap out of it. You're starting to get *me* depressed. You better get out of this truck and smile at those Amish women."

The irony was not lost on me. For all those years, Walter had kept me in the woods or in the house, forbidding me to talk to anyone, and now he wanted me to talk, for the good of our "business." The little flicker of hope that had always lived inside of me felt like it was almost extinguished. Yet the tiniest little glow refused to leave. Maybe it was because I was able to talk to people now, little snippets of conversations with these Amish women. I guess it was a good thing Walter forced me to do so. These women certainly were not liberated by any stretch of the imagination, but they were women, and I found myself looking forward to our talks.

Days later, Walter yelled at me about something else: Apparently, our neighbor Craig and our farmer friend, Alvin, had compared notes, and they had realized something wasn't right with Walter and me. They had begun to suspect that maybe I wasn't actually Walter's wife. Walter told me the Amish people might have gotten ahold of the story too. Walter had to do his best to convince them that we were just a normal couple. In my fog of exhaustion and grief, there were moments when I thought Walter might be right. *Maybe I'm really not his daughter.*

But in the end, despite these thoughts, I always knew it was true. I couldn't forget my own memories of my childhood and the few moments in which I had thought of Walter as a dad. Then I'd feel guilty and pray to God for help. I still believed God would find a way to deliver me from Walter.

Yet I found that I couldn't just snap out of it. Feelings of depression were pulling me under. Walter noticed and asked me, "What's your problem? You got nothin' to complain about. You got plenty of food now and a nice home to boot. Read your Bible, girl. You ain't living any different than those people. You don't hear them complainin', do ya? Lot treated his daughter the same way."

I knew I couldn't beat Walter at his game, but maybe because I felt I had nothing to lose, I found myself wanting to fight back in little ways. Now, when Walter insisted that I talk to him, I didn't always parrot back what he wanted to hear. Sometimes I'd just say, "What is there to say?" Or "I don't know." Even when it made him angry or violent, it felt good to fight back, even if it was in such a small way. But then there were other times when Walter's training wasn't wasted on me. I'd cry and beg for forgiveness. Walter always liked to say that there was a war between angels and demons going on inside of him. If that really was the case, it was obvious which side was winning that war. I was pretty sure the angels never even had a chance.

Chapter Thirty-Seven

I couldn't hide my surprise when, one day, Walter confessed to me that he felt something pushing him to go to church. So we set off to an actual church service. Walter had taken a lot of things from me, but he could never take my belief in God. Getting to attend church was one of the best things that ever happened to me. Even though I couldn't say much, I was able to meet some new people who were kind to me. I loved listening to them talk about God and faith. Hearing the Bible read out loud lifted me up, and the hymns were comforting to me. I had always carried around my own faith in my heart, but now it was able to flower a little, and I got to experience the joy of sharing it with others.

Since Teddy's death, I'd been forced to have two more abortions, and I also had another miscarriage. I was twenty-two years old now and I knew I was pregnant again. Again I decided to hide it from Walter for as long as possible in hopes of keeping this child. I could feel that I was coming to a new turning point in my life. Over the past few years, I had been living in fear of losing another child, but I felt stronger now since I had attended church and found some quiet time to meditate on my faith. I felt at peace, as much as a person could in my situation. I could feel God watching over me and my children. I was not alone. The fog that had enveloped me for the last few months started to lift.

So it was with a sense of calm that I gave birth to my daughter Robin. I felt blessed that she was a healthy baby. The children and the processing and sales of the dumpster food made the days sail by. I would carry Robin in a sling so I that I could do more chores while also keeping her happy. Even when she grew too big for the sling, she was content to play on a blanket, as long as she was close to me.

Before I knew it, Robin was almost one, and she was such a joy. Tammy was now almost seven, and she was progressing well in school even though she could be a handful at times when she was home. Having no way of knowing what experts would say about child behaviors at certain ages, I just had to use common sense. Six-year-old Jimmy was still happy to attend school, even though sometimes he grew frustrated with the lessons and he'd just up and leave the room. A teacher would have to go find him outside the classroom, sitting by himself. Brother and sister both loved hopping off the school bus at the end of the day and running into the house to see their baby sister, Robin. My joy in watching my children grow was soon interrupted by nausea and exhaustion as another pregnancy began to wear on my body.

One Saturday evening after Walter, the three children, and I returned from a church service, Walter announced that we would be leaving in a few days to go to Florida for a church celebration called the "Feast of the Tabernacles." I'd heard others at church mentioning what a wonderful experience this was, but I never dreamed we would ever be able to attend. To escape my daily grind and embark upon a spiritual adventure seemed too good to be true. The children were grinning ear to ear as we loaded them into the truck for our journey. I'd almost forgotten what joy felt like, but I thought it might have been what I was feeling as we began our trip south.

As we made the drive in our crowded little truck, I showed genuine interest when Walter told me a story about how he had been baptized in Alaska, but then he went on to grumble that it had caused problems for him. When I read in the flyer from church that people would be baptized in the Gulf of Mexico, I knew that this was something I wanted to do; in fact, I longed for it. I made sure to keep my voice low and even when I asked, "I've never been baptized, Walter, and I would really like to be. If I have the opportunity, will it be okay if I go ahead with it?"

Walter shrugged. "I ain't gonna mess with that. Ain't no way I'm telling you no on that. It ain't my place to say. I leave that between you and God."

Walter was good on his word. When I stepped into the Gulf waters on that sunny Saturday, our faith's Sabbath, I could see him and the children watching from the beach.

"As Jesus went to John in the Jordan River, so you come now. . . . You are baptized in the name of the Father, the Son, and the Holy Spirit." The minister dunked me in the warm, salty water.

With tears and ocean water on my face, I prayed, "I am a sinner and in need of God's help and forgiveness. Please help me and lead me, Lord."

Suddenly, I felt Walter splashing through the surf to stand next to me, Robin in his arms. Looking at the minister, he asked, "Sir, I was baptized in 1973, but I didn't receive the laying on of hands. I was wondering if you'd do that for me now?"

The minister put his hand on Walter's head and said, "May He make His face shine upon you and be gracious unto you. May He lift up His countenance upon you and give you peace."

Then Walter turned to me and said, "Let's get the hell out of here."

Even after the trip was over, I felt an inner calm as we resumed our hectic life. We signed on as official members of The Church of God International and Walter made regular donations. I felt more at peace now that I had made a new commitment to God. My faith was the only thing I knew would be the same for me yesterday, today, and tomorrow. My faith kept me from falling in my slippery life. Yet, at the same time, I began to fear that Walter might use religion as just another way to control me.

We began receiving tapes from our church in the mail. We'd listen to them in the evening. Walter felt driven to do so. It turned out that many of the tapes were about incest and its sinful nature. In time, I realized that this was not a coincidence; someone at the church must have figured us out. When I'd first heard the word *incest* on the Oprah Winfrey show, I didn't even know what it meant. I had to go look it up. I'm sure Walter knew what it meant, but he didn't want to face that fact. He'd turn off Oprah whenever her show dealt with incest or abuse, and he turned off the tapes after that too.

"This is a bunch of crap. This guy doesn't know what he's talking about. I don't know why the hell we listen to this shit."

I knew that the words he was hearing must have made him think at least a little bit about how he was living his life. Walter had tried to convince me for years that we were husband and wife, but his reaction now was very telling. We both knew I was his biological daughter. I knew how we were living was not right. I prayed every day that this madness would stop.

My faith continued to make me feel stronger about standing up to Walter. I wondered if I would cower when I was put to the test. I knew it wouldn't be long before that test would come. One night, after four hours of repackaging food to sell to the Amish, I heard Walter call me to come outside: "Come help me pull this cap off the truck. I gotta put in this extra seat for the kids."

I did go outside, but I told him, "I need another hour to get the rest of this food processed so it won't spoil. Could you wait just a bit?"

"Don't you ever question me!" Walter backhanded me across the face. "I oughta knock the shit right out of you, teach you a lesson about arguing with me." His hands wrapped around my throat.

"Go right ahead. Go ahead and hit me again. What difference does it make? I'm used to it anyway."

Walter's head snapped up in surprise at my backtalk.

"Don't you hurt my mommy!" My heart sank when I realized that Tammy was witnessing this violence.

"Go to bed, honey; it's all right," I reassured my daughter. "I'll be in later to tuck you in. Go ahead; everything's going to be all right, I promise."

Walter sneered, "Aren't you such a good person, la-de-dah, a sanctified pillar of the church, *and* one who is saved? You're so full of shit! Maybe you ought to read the part in the Bible about wives honoring their husbands."

He was right in my face now. I could feel his hot breath while flecks of his saliva hit my cheek. I didn't turn away. I looked straight into his eyes, which were flashing with anger.

"You think you're honoring and obeying me right now? God ain't gonna be any too pleased with the amount of backtalk you've been giving me lately, little Miss High-and-Mighty. You better do a little more listening to those sermons. I think you missed the part about honor and obey. I think you're the biggest sinner around when it comes to the terrible way you treat me. But you're probably too stupid to understand what the words on those tapes the church sent us even mean."

I pulled away, turned my back to him, and went to my daughter. Mercifully, she had fallen back asleep. I brushed the hair from her forehead and kissed her good night. I sat down on her bed, taking a few minutes to calm myself and pray.

Sometimes, when I had a moment to myself, I'd just scream as loudly as I could, full of frustration with how Walter treated me and overwhelmed by the hopelessness of ever escaping this man. I knew no one could hear my screams—except Walter, who probably enjoyed them—but just letting it out helped sometimes. This quiet time, the few minutes to meditate, felt even more soothing to my soul. God was listening and would not forget me. I found the strength to go on.

The next day after the food sales were complete I got Robin down for a nap. I picked up my Bible, hoping to read a bit before Tammy and Jimmy got home from school. After a while, I realized I'd lost track of time. I jumped up to get the Kirby and vacuum up the chip crumbs that were left on the rug from our latest batch of re-packaged Frito-Lays. Then I got started packaging the foods I hadn't completed earlier. I saw a shadow darken the doorway and heard Walter's voice: "What in hell is wrong with you? You ain't got this stuff packaged up yet, and you been sitting here with nothin' else to do?"

He backhanded me, and I could feel blood trickle from my lip.

"I was reading the Bible. I'll get your work done now. I always do, don't I? So don't worry about it."

I picked up the old Kirby and walked past Walter, amazed when he actually let me pass. He followed me into the living room and started ranting.

"You're such an ungrateful, worthless little bitch. Don't be tellin' me not to worry about it! The kitchen is a mess, and you haven't even got the food finished. How many times do I gotta remind you that I own you? Don't you forget that!"

The calm I had felt while reading the Bible was such a contrast to my pounding heart as I took in Walter's brutal words. *I am God's child. I will not be owned by Walter or anyone.* A flood of emotions that I'd kept buried for years erupted to the surface with a frightening speed. *I just have to do something, but what?*

I felt my hands tighten around the handle of the Kirby as all of my muscles tensed. I lifted it up and thrust the vacuum cleaner at Walter with all my might. He reached up to block it, and his eyes looked wild as I began to scream at him: "You just don't get it, do you? If you want it done, do it *yourself*!"

All of the pent-up emotions came rushing out of me, all at once. I could feel my body being flung to the floor, but Walter hadn't touched me. Through my twitching and writhing, I heard myself scream: "Dear God, in the name of Jesus, help me. I can't do this anymore. It's too much for one person! I'm living with Satan! If you want to kill me, God, then just *do* it, because I can't go on like this any longer. Just let me *die* and be done with it!"

Some seconds, maybe minutes, passed. For once, Walter Williams was at a loss for words. I could see Robin out of the corner of my eye, confused by what she had just seen. Walter scooped her up, and I heard him say, "Your mom isn't feelin' so good." He tucked Robin back in bed and returned to tell me, "God ain't gonna listen to a sinner like you anyway. Your prayers are just a waste of time." I didn't think Walter sounded quite as convincing this time. I thought he'd storm out of the house, but instead he sunk into a chair and seemed to gaze at nothing.

A moment later, I picked myself up off of the floor, realizing how sore my whole body felt. *I don't know what just happened to me.* Had that been a seizure? Was I having some type of breakdown? *That just can't happen. My kids need me, and there is no one else to care for them if I fall apart.* I felt heartbroken that Robin saw my outburst. I had tried my best to keep the children from witnessing Walter's acts of violence, along with my desperation. But this time Robin had been exposed to something a child should never have to see. This filled me with a greater determination to break free. I knew I had to find a way out for my children's sake. I had no idea how to begin.

CHAPTER THIRTY-EIGHT

I think Walter was a little bit afraid of me after that day. He kept prompting me to tell him that what we had been doing was right, but I wouldn't tell him that. Walter had spent a lot of years molding me into the obedient wife. Fear and intimidation were his teachers, but I had now reached a point beyond fear. Now when he'd tell me he should knock the shit right out of me, I responded, "You go right ahead!" I could no longer be silenced. I could feel my faith in God fanning that little flicker of hope I still held inside of me.

Walter's next tactic was to play on my guilt, blaming me for Teddy's death, but that still didn't stop me. I'd lived most of my life with a ticking bomb only inches from me. For years, I had done everything I could not to disturb it. Soon after the Kirby vacuum incident, Walter again berated me for not completing my chores on time.

"You've been so lazy, moping around ever since Teddy died. It's your own goddamn fault he's gone. You just *had* to let that doctor give him a spinal tap. Now you expect *me* to pick up the slack around here after all I've done for you. Well I'm sick of it. I wish I had a gun. I would just end it. I'd end it for all of us!"

Walter had spewed millions of words at me over the years, and I had tried my best to dismiss them as the rantings of a madman. But suddenly, this time, Walter had gotten my attention. He had never made a threat like that before. I tried to think of things to say to distract him from that thought.

"It's going to be all right, Walter. I'll snap out of it, just like you asked. You know you don't want to hurt yourself, or your children."

Saying soothing words to Walter required some of my best acting skills. I had to do whatever I could to appease him—for my children's sake and for my own survival.

After that day, there was another change in Walter. Now he began to use his "nice guy" act on me, that ploy I'd seen work on so many people, countless times. That certainly was a surprise, and a transparent one at that. Apparently he'd taken notice when I had gone off on him. These latest theatrics were his way of keeping another scene like that at bay. I decided to play along. Walter began to do small, helpful things such as cleaning up the kitchen all by himself. He still expected my undying gratitude for such a small act, but I just told him, "When I clean up the kitchen, I do it for myself and the kids, but not for you." I looked Walter right in the eye, and he said nothing in response. Making eye contact after years of intimidation was huge for me. I felt myself getting stronger each day. I gave God the credit for that.

Not long after those encounters, my current pregnancy reached its term, and one afternoon I felt my water break as I was doing chores. My labor pains came on quickly, the intensity increasing by the minute. I hurried Robin over to Jane next door and asked Jane to call Becky, my midwife. Jane jerked her head around quickly, swinging her long brown hair across her face as she grabbed the receiver from her telephone. In the bossiest of voices, she instructed the midwife to get over here, and then she wrapped a chubby arm around Robin and hugged her close. We exchanged "the look," the one that meant *I can't tell you anything but the briefest of words, and you know better than to ask.* Tammy and Jimmy wouldn't be home from school for hours. Walter was out which was fine with me.

Four hours later, I'd delivered a baby boy. "Does he look all right?" I asked Becky, concerned. I tried to push the thought of Teddy out of my mind and stay in the present, but I suspected my midwife could hear the fear behind my words.

"He doesn't look like the other three, and he's very small, but the heart sounds good. His lungs don't sound as clear as I'd like them to be, so you should call the pediatrician today. It may just be because of his size—but you want to be sure."

The kitchen door slammed, and Walter boomed, "Lorie, where in hell are you?"

"She was busy giving birth," Becky answered, with more than a little disdain in her voice.

"I didn't know you was here. *My*, look what we have here."

I thought to myself, *How fast the chameleon can change colors,* as Walter examined the baby closely and then nestled him in his arms.

"I'm sorry I wasn't here. I shoulda been. I got tied up doing that job I told you about."

His eyes sent a silent message: *Don't let on that I never told you a thing about a job.* Walter must have thought Becky needed a second performance, so he continued on: "You must not think much of me, not being here for Lorie and all. I try to be a good husband to her, but I didn't do right this time. You just rest, Lorie; I'll take care of everything else."

"Becky says we need to get him to a doctor soon and get his lungs checked out," I protested.

After that, it wasn't long before Walter rushed Becky out the door and then turned on me. "What was you thinkin' just now? We ain't takin' this baby to no doctor! Remember what happened last time I let you talk me into that?"

Tuning out Walter's reprimand, I kept my eyes focused on my baby boy's face. Walter's voice softened a bit. "We'll call him Michael. That's a good name. You rest for a while. The kids will be home soon, and you'll need to start fixin' supper."

Walter turned and walked away.

CHAPTER THIRTY-NINE

By January of 1991, our business of selling to the Amish community had grown by leaps and bounds. On the best weeks, we could take in as much as seven hundred dollars. Walter was well known in the Amish community now. The customers thought he was a conscientious salesperson. He would go out of his way to bring any family the treats they might have a particular craving for, and he presented the food he sold to them well. He stayed friendly about refunding money to anyone who was dissatisfied with a purchase, and he was generous about giving away free food to new customers. For the most part, his Amish customers liked him. Perhaps they thought I was a lucky woman to have such a husband.

The school's winter break had ended, and Tammy and Jimmy were happy to be back in the classroom. After school each day, I would ask them to tell me what they had learned. I hadn't been able to attend school regularly, but I was bound and determined my children would all graduate from high school someday.

At home, I balanced my time between Robin and Michael. The bookkeeping for our business helped my mind stay sharp when the babies were napping. I enjoyed the challenge of math. It always made me think about school. Sometimes I thought about the fact that many of the students I had met during my limited school experience must have been graduating from college by now. For me, though, the bookkeeping and my Bible study were the only academics that I squeezed in between the endless sea of pioneer chores, parenting my four beloved children, and, of course, catering to the demands of a maniac.

One evening, when Michael was being especially fussy, Walter took Tammy and Jimmy with him to snag some snacks from the dumpster at Frito Lay. I tried all my remedies to comfort Michael that evening, but he wouldn't stop crying. I borrowed Jane's phone and called my midwife, Becky.

"I need advice; Michael won't stop fussing, no matter what I try. It's not going to work out for me to take him to a doctor. What can I do?"

I knew Walter would never allow a visit to the hospital after what had happened with Teddy. "I know a chiropractor you could visit, if that would work," Becky replied, and she gave me his phone number. I knew I had to find a way to get the baby to him; something definitely wasn't right with Michael.

Walter returned home with a truckload of food for me to prepare, but I refused. "Michael needs me. Something is wrong with him; he really should see a doctor tonight."

Just as I suspected, Walter still blamed the doctor for Teddy's death. Finally, he agreed that if Michael wasn't better by morning, we could make a trip to the doctor the midwife had recommended.

After a sleepless night, we fit the whole family into the truck and drove to a nearby town to see the chiropractor. We were soon met by a pleasant doctor who said, "This seems like one unhappy fellow." The doctor determined that Michael had a disc out of place and passed me a form for us to sign. I took the form outside to the truck, and Walter agreed to sign. The doctor performed a simple procedure, and Michael's crying ceased.

"He should eat and sleep well after this," the doctor told me. "Sometimes, a disc can get pushed out of place when the infant travels through the birth canal." I returned home with a relieved heart, baby in arms.

That evening, I got the other three children settled in bed. Then, I attempted to nurse Michael, but he wasn't interested. Soon, he fell asleep peacefully, and I stayed by his side, listening to his breathing. Hours later, a strange gurgling sound startled me. Reaching for Michael, I saw that he was a strange color. I screamed for Walter. Within minutes, the three children were loaded into the back of the truck. Walter fired up the ignition, but as he began to back out, he let out a string of obscenities. "We've got a goddamn flat tire! You have to get out while I change it." I begged Walter to hurry as I ran to the back steps and began performing CPR on Michael. A few minutes later, Walter yelled, "It's done, let's go!" Walter drove as fast as the truck would go, and we got to the doctor's office in record time.

The next few moments passed by in confused turmoil. I found myself yelling at the receptionist as she tried to talk to me about insurance forms and registration papers. "My son has stopped breathing. Doctor, please, help him now!" The doctor appeared, and we rushed to the examining room. I could hardly bear waiting the agonizing number of minutes it seemed to take for the doctor to carefully scrub his hands. Walter mumbled something about this being the very same room they had put Teddy in when he died. My grief pushed all other thoughts aside. After a brief exam, the doctor called for an ambulance. Michael was still alive, but only barely.

Minutes later, two paramedics had Michael in the back of the ambulance, but they refused to let me ride with him. We followed as closely as we could but were soon caught in traffic, lagging behind the ambulance. We arrived at the hospital only to be told we had to provide some information before we could see our baby. Walter stepped up to fill out the forms while I paced the floor, asking every few minutes if I could see Michael yet. My head was spinning, and I felt faint. *You have to stay strong for Michael*, I told myself. My prayers became deeper, more desperate with every moment as I began to fear that I might not be bringing Michael home.

Finally, a somber-looking doctor appeared to tell us that Michael was on life support. "It doesn't look good. There could be a possible injury to the brain. We need to rush him to a larger hospital nearby." I tried to focus on the words he was saying.

"Please, doctor, may I please ride with him. I have to be with him!"

"No, you will have to drive over and meet us there. We will take good care of him."

I couldn't tell if his promise was sincere or not, but Walter's voice snapped me back into reality. "We gotta let them do what they need to do. We'll pack a few things and head to the intensive care unit. Thank you, doctor, I'm sure you did your best."

We rushed home and explained to Craig and Jane what was happening. They assured us our kids would be fine with them. Minutes later we were on our way. We arrived at the hospital around 8 p.m. We rushed in, hoping to see Michael, but we were taken to a conference room instead. There was a table and office chairs set up in the colorless room. We were both too anxious to sit. My silent prayers were interrupted when two men in business suits entered the room.

"I'm Detective Rowse from the State Police, and this is Mr. Wells from the Department of Social Services. We need to ask you some questions," one of the men said, gesturing for us to sit down. The detective got right to the point. "Your baby shows signs of some type of abuse. Michael has a blood clot on the brain, which could indicate some type of trauma to the head. What can you tell us about that?"

I couldn't wrap my brain around what he was saying. Michael had been in my care only, and I'd never been anything but gentle with him. My throat was tight with anxiety, but I managed to find my voice. "We'll answer any questions you might have, but can't we please see Michael, or at least talk with his doctor?"

"I'm sorry, but you'll need to provide us with some information first."

For over an hour, the two men grilled us with questions. I answered them all honestly. They wanted to know why we had taken Michael to a chiropractor instead of a regular doctor. I explained that our midwife had recommended this doctor. I knew I had nothing to hide, so I answered each question as best I could.

The social worker had been silent up to this point, but when he finally decided to speak, he dropped a bombshell. "We are aware that you are Walter's daughter. We do have your records available to us."

Maybe these people will help me get away from Walter, I wondered, but the social worker didn't question me further about that. I hoped they would ask me if I wanted to be in this situation, but they didn't. I prayed that they would ask to speak to me alone, but they didn't do that, either. All that happened was that the social worker gave me a disgusted look and informed me that our case would be turned over to the county. Then the two men turned and left.

Minutes later, a doctor entered the conference room. He gave us a venomous look as he spoke. "Your son has a massive hematoma on the brain. It is apparently the result of some trauma. We have him on life support. He may be brain dead. We'll monitor him for the next twenty-four to forty-eight hours to see if there is any brain activity. If not, we'll pull him off life support and allow him to die." He turned and left.

His words chilled me to the bone. I couldn't take it all in. The words *ALLOW HIM TO DIE* were screaming in my head as I rocked back and forth, sinking deeper into the black hole that was swallowing me alive.

I'd forgotten Walter was even in the room until I heard his angry voice. " You and the goddamn doctors. Just like with Teddy. You just *had* to take him to a son-of-a-bitch doctor, and *this* is what happens. Now they think we murdered him, and it's all your fault."

"It's always my fault, Walter, always my fault." I parroted his words, hoping to make the noises coming from his mouth stop, as I felt myself free-falling into a black fog.

On January 16, 1991, a day and a half later, Michael was pronounced dead. I was informed in the most matter-of-fact way possible, and I buried my face in my hands after I heard. *Another son – dead.* Teddy had died two years ago, almost to the day. *I don't know how I'm going to go on.*

The only words of comfort I heard in the dark days that followed came from our midwife. "You have been a good mother to all your children, Lorie. There are other things that could have caused Michael's medical problems." Becky's words sounded soothing, but nothing could comfort me.

An hour after we returned home, a social worker and two police officers came to our house. They told us they would be taking the children to foster care until Michael's case was resolved. Tammy, at nine years old, understood what this meant and began to scream. I wasn't allowed to go to her and comfort her. Jimmy, eight, and Robin, three, looked scared and clung to me. I packed the children's things, and the three men took them away. I stood at the window and watched the car until it was just a speck on the horizon. My world was gone. My heart was breaking. I turned to see Walter in the kitchen, fixing himself something to eat.

"We *have* to find some way to get them back. Please tell me you'll help," I begged.

"If you just would have had them aborted, we wouldn't be in this mess. Next time you get pregnant, we just won't tell anyone. Besides, it ain't so bad being alone at last."

The visits and questions from police and social services continued over the next two weeks. Through my grief, I was chilled by the irony in my situation. From when I was seven years old, I'd begged representatives of these two agencies to spare me from Walter's abuse. My pleas were ignored. Now that I was twenty-four years old, a grown adult, we had daily visits from both. Finally I had their full attention, but there was still no escape for me. If these public servants had freed me from Walter's grasp one of the ten times my case had been reported to them, I would be as far from Walter as I could get right now.

Walter made it through the next few weeks eating and sleeping just fine. I could barely believe it when he'd be in the kitchen, grilling himself steaks and humming happily. I had no appetite at all. Walter busied himself sorting through our food bags and containers and making multiple trips to the dump.

Soon after Michael's death, Walter took our dog and cat and dropped them off at a rest stop. I prayed that kind people would rescue them. *Does he see this as some kind of a new start in life? Out with the old and in with the new?* For me, it felt like the end. He still expected me to help him with the dumpster business, and I robotically went through the motions. If a word of desperation happened to slip from my lips, he reminded me that losing the children was my fault.

I knew this wasn't true. I had only cared for Michael tenderly. I also knew there had not been any times he had been out of my sight, so I knew no one else had hurt him. I told Walter that I would go to the police voluntarily to try to settle this and get the other children back. He agreed to go with me. After two hours of questioning, Walter requested lie detector tests.

The police set up a date for us to come in and take our tests. We were happy to comply. At the station, we were sent to separate sterile-looking rooms. The officer secured something around my waist and attached another device to my fingers. All of the cumbersome equipment rattled my nerves, but I stayed calm. *I don't lie, so all I have to do is answer honestly.* Soon the detective told me we were ready to begin.

"What is your name? How old are you? What are your sisters' names?"

My answers were short. More mundane questions followed, but then, just as I expected, the questions took a turn. "Have you lied before?"

I gave this some thought, and there was only one time I could remember lying. "I broke a paper towel holder once, and when my father asked me if I did it, I didn't admit that I did. I just said that I was out in the woods picking berries."

"When you hit your child, do you hit him more than once?"

"I don't hit my children."

"Did you shake your child to wake him up?"

"I don't shake my children."

The questions felt more like an interrogation, and it continued on and on. I could tell that the officer was trying to trip me up by repeating some questions in different ways, but I took my time and told the truth. Finally, I was led back to a waiting room where Walter had been taken after his test. We waited in silence.

When the detective and lieutenant reappeared, I was amazed to see that they were both softly crying. They made no effort to wipe the tears from their faces. In a broken voice, one of them delivered the results. "You both passed."

We turned to leave, and Walter couldn't resist glancing back with a sneer, satisfied to have the last word: "You oughta give the test to the chiropractor who adjusted Michael. I bet he wouldn't pass!"

Our lie detector tests supplied enough evidence for the prosecuting attorney to drop the charges. I never knew whether Walter lied or told the truth during his test. I knew Walter could be capable of hurting anyone, but I didn't believe he ever hurt our baby.

I'd kept Michael close to me during his short life, and I vowed that I would always keep him close in my heart.

The days crawled by, dark and lonely. I could think of nothing else but getting the kids back. Their absence was worse than anything Walter had ever done to me.

A few weeks later, a car we'd never seen before pulled up to the house. I saw three smiling faces appear as Tammy, Jimmy, and Robin scrambled out of the backseat. I scooped my children into my arms, feeling the gloom that had enveloped me shattering to let in the sun. The day they returned home was a day of gratitude and such happiness. God answered my prayer. I felt as if I couldn't get enough of the kids, and they couldn't get enough of me. Even the most basic things we did—brushing teeth, buttoning pajamas—sparkled with smiles and laughter. The only shadow that hung over my joy was that recurring feeling that something else terrible was going to happen. Now I understood: that was what it would take to attract notice from the authorities and get me out of this situation. This fear slipped into my heart like a secret I begged not to be told, and there it stayed.

CHAPTER FORTY

By March of 1991, the kids had adjusted back to school, and spring was beginning to show its face. As the snow melted, our normal routine of dumpster runs and early morning food sales to the Amish returned with the same rhythm as before. In the months following Michael's death, Walter became mellower. My days were easier with his anger at bay. In the wee hours of the morning, once the work was finished, Walter would demand that I clean myself up. It was then I knew that the most difficult part of my day was about to begin.

Walter's rapes were silent, angry, savage. When he was through, he pushed me out of bed and demanded that I follow a certain procedure. I was to douche with vinegar following each of his rapes. I didn't know if this was actually a birth control method. Then I willed myself to go to sleep. Survival came first; there was little time for pouting. The demands of my day would begin all over again at first light, and there was no such thing as a day off—ever.

It wasn't long before Walter's mellow mood changed into something different: suddenly he was full of ideas, and he had a new topic of conversation. He became obsessed with the "energy" he claimed he could feel emanating from everyone he met. He'd return from the tiny store next door and start in on his new pet theory. He'd say that one guy had good energy, but someone else gave off bad energy. The prickly, static energy he felt from others took on an ever-greater importance to him.

Walter also felt more driven to attend church after this discovery. So off we went. We'd sit in the back of the church. Walter would ignore the minister's words as his eyes darted wildly from one member of the congregation to the next, muttering about the good or bad energy he could feel from each person.

On the ride home, he continued his tirade. "Couldn't you feel that energy today? Everyone in there had energy just bouncing off of them! It was either good or bad. No in-between! Could you feel it too?"

"No, Walter, I couldn't."

"That's because you ain't as good as me. You just ain't got the gift that God gave me."

Walter became consumed by this whole energy thing. I couldn't figure out what had triggered his obsession. I only hoped it was short lived. Once the kids were out on spring break he wanted us to go other places to see if he could feel the energy just as strongly in different locations.

When he told me he wanted us to go on a trip his eyes shone with manic energy as he paced around the house, grabbing objects we might need. "We're gonna head over to the big grocery store and get some stuff for you and the kids. Then we'll go mushrooming. Tomorrow we'll head up north. We can stay in motels along the way. We'll throw in a tent just in case. It'll be good for all of us." Walter's offer to shop at a store and buy for us was highly unusual.

After packing the food and clothing in the truck, I secured Tammy and Jimmy in the jump seat Walter had rigged for them in back while Robin sat between us in the front seat. I tried to think positively and hide my concern over the glee Walter felt about this trip.

We weren't more than a few miles out of town when Walter stopped the truck on a hill, pulling the window between the two seats down so the kids in back could hear him. "Watch this, Tammy and Jimmy."

He jumped out of the truck without shutting his door and raised his arms, pointing to our tiny town below. "Look at *all* that evil down the hill there! See all that bad energy? It's about to be destroyed by *me*! Look, kids, just like Sodom and Gomorrah. Look at that big fireball down there! God is destroying all that bad energy—through *me*! I am God's go-to guy!"

Walter shook his arms toward town and laughed a strange, guttural laugh. Then he cackled and hopped back into the truck. Minutes later we drove through the next town and he did the same thing. His laugh grew more evil. "You're destroyed, too, you good-for-nothin' crazy-ass sons of bitches!" he howled as we screeched off to his next target.

As Walter's antics continued, Tammy and Jimmy started to laugh and imitate their father's bizarre behavior. The kids were mesmerized by the repetition and flair of his words and gestures as he "cursed" each little town on our drive. They couldn't resist joining in what they must have thought was a theatrical game. Seeing the children imitate *anything* Walter did was horrific for me. I couldn't wait to get them home and take them upstairs with me, away from his demented influence.

I was mute with fear as this ride of insanity continued, with Walter's behavior growing stranger along the way. As we drove, he reached his hand down to his crotch and then pretended to hand me something. "Here's what you want, bitch, go on, take it, goddamn it. You *know* you want it."

He continued pointing out the window at the houses we passed. "I'm gonna blow up *all* the towns from here to the lake. All those godforsaken sons of bitches . . . social workers, doctors, lawyers, cops, everyone . . . they're *all* gonna find themselves dead! *Dead*, I tell ya."

As I closed my eyes, recoiling against the window on my side of the truck, Walter grabbed my arm and screamed, "You better damn well open yer eyes, 'cause you're gonna see this, bitch! I got the power. You gotta see all these evil people get blown away by me."

I felt like I was losing all sense of time. How long had we been at this horror show? I turned to the children and gave them a gentle nod, hoping to reassure them without Walter noticing.

Hours later Walter pulled into a gas station. While he was pumping gas, I was astonished to see him wave and smile at a police officer who pulled up in front of us. When the officer returned to his squad car, a smiling Walter rushed up to him, arm outstretched for a friendly handshake. Seconds later, they were having a brief conversation. I was pretty sure Walter wasn't telling him about all the towns he had just "blown up."

Walter returned with chips and drinks for the kids, and we continued up U.S. 12. "Look at all the serenity. We've destroyed all that evil, and things are better now."

Soon, Walter pulled into a motel and returned to the truck with a key to our cottage. To the other guests at our motel, Walter may have looked like any other dad traveling with his family on a road trip.

The truth was that Walter could never just drive us from one point to another. Any time we were out on a car trip, he had a comment about everyone he saw passing by. "If she would walk more, she wouldn't be so fat." Or a remark Walter believed was positive was really shaded with the negative. When passing by an African-American man, he might say, "Not all black people are bad. I had a buddy in the army who was black and he was a good guy." It was even worse when Walter decided to act on his contempt for others. He was mad at a neighbor once and poured a quart of motor oil all over his steps and porch. When he was mad at a doctor for how she'd treated us, Walter pooped into a brown paper bag and threw it on her porch. If I had had the power, I would have stopped his random acts of meanness.

When we returned home the next day, Walter's disturbing behavior on the trip had me thinking even more about a possible escape plan. What if I couldn't figure out how to leave before Walter went completely ballistic the next time? I knew I would need money, a vehicle, and ample time for Walter to be away from home. For years, I'd been aware that Walter was always staying one step ahead of me. I knew he kept his money and the keys to the truck hidden in various places. The chance of me finding both of them was impossible. He kept those items on him when he was gone, and he hid them immediately when he returned home. An escape at night would be equally impossible. Even if I got up to use the bathroom, he would always ask me where I was going. So I'd return to bed and crawl back in, hanging on to the edge where I always slept. If I heard Walter stir and waken, I would pretend to be asleep, hoping he would leave me alone. It was obvious that his antiquated form of birth control didn't work, because I was pregnant again. It felt like I was always pregnant, even though there were a few months here and there when I wasn't.

Pregnant or not, our nightly work had to continue. In and out of dumpsters I went, with aching legs and back, sick from the maggots and the rotting meat.

CHAPTER FORTY-ONE

Despite the relentless exhaustion, I found joy in caring for the children. I was especially proud of the healthy meals I could prepare for them. Laundry and dishes were the most time-consuming chores.

Washing clothes for five people involved carrying pails of water to our half-functioning washing machine, then siphoning the water out into five-gallon pails for the rinse cycle. Now it was winter again, so our clothes would freeze solid when I hung them outside. My hands stayed chapped and cracked for months. Meanwhile, scooping water out of the tiny sink in the kitchen and pouring it out onto our frozen backyard added hours each week to cooking and dishwashing… and so it went. Winter also made all these chores more time consuming because I had to continually run outside to gather firewood.

Once the chores were done, I could devote my time to the children. I'd give them little jobs to do and teach them their colors and numbers. We worked on the alphabet, and I read to them daily. One afternoon before we began a little reading time, I asked Tammy to put her art supplies away and encouraged Jimmy to carry a few toys to the toy box.

"I don't want to. Jimmy can do it," Tammy insisted.

"Tammy, Jimmy is helping with the toys. You need to gather up your books and crayons and put them on the shelf."

"No!" Tammy persisted.

As I took Tammy into the other room to sit by herself for a few minutes, I heard Walter come in and begin speaking to her. "Mommy is mean, isn't she, Tammy? *I'll* let you have your way. Mommy is a big, fat monster. You don't have to put your things away if you don't want to, honey. Don't listen to that monster. She doesn't know what she's talking about."

I cringed at Walter's words. He frequently undermined me when we were alone together, telling me I was ugly and fat and stupid. Lately, he had added a new twist. I knew children needed boundaries, and I always had a few rules I expected them to fol-low. This past year, Walter had been trying his best to turn the children against me. Robin was too bonded to me to let that hap-pen and Jimmy always gravitated toward me. Even at his young age, I was afraid Jimmy sensed that Walter favored the girls over him. Tammy, being the oldest, liked to try her hand at defiance. When she was alone with me, she was usually well behaved. Now, when Walter tried to turn her against me, I saw that she found this situation interesting. She was giving it some thought.

I knew that Walter was a sick person and I shouldn't give any validity to what he said about me. I remembered my sisters telling me I had a good complexion and my green eyes were pretty. My shape was not what it had been before all the pregnancies, but it was still passable. I'd been told I had a nice smile, though that had been years ago. Yet, after years of hearing almost daily that I was a horrible, ugly person, I found that I avoided looking in mirrors. I was afraid I might see the person he described. If he could do that to me, it wouldn't be long before he was able to convince Tammy she didn't have to listen to me. *I need to get her away from him before that happens.* I knew my plan of escape had to include a high level of safety for the children, and their basic needs would have to be met throughout the process. *A penniless pregnant woman running away with three young children in tow is not going to work.* I even wondered if Tammy would willingly leave her dad now that he was playing his game of overriding my authority. Maybe that was why he had started this diabolical trick, to use her as insurance so that we couldn't flee from him, even if we got the opportunity.

My next labor began on a cold February day in 1992. Like Michael, this baby would be born at home. This time, there would be no midwife. Becky wouldn't return after the tragedy of my last birth, and Walter wasn't allowing any alternatives for help with the birth.

So, I prepared the sofa bed in our living room. I covered it with plastic and topped it off with a clean sheet. I tried to keep the children entertained during the early contractions, and I was able to do some light housework. As I began to transition, I stretched out on the bed I had prepared. Walter was busy with one of his many projects. Today, he was outside extending the cab of our truck. He'd taught himself how to bend scrap metal. He soon became the least of my concerns as I breathed into each contraction, while doing my best to keep the children calm and secure during the process.

Walter breezed into the house just in time to wash his hands and catch the baby when it came out. It was a beautiful little boy. Walter was careful to push the precious liquid in the cord back into the baby before cutting and tying it. I was left on my own for the post-labor, pushing the placenta out. *Last night, I was in and out of dumpsters. Today, I have my new son in my arms*, I marveled.

Daniel was a healthy baby, and oh so handsome. This blue-eyed, blond little boy with even features captured my heart as soon as I first touched his smooth skin. He was a chubby little guy with especially big hands and feet. I couldn't help but smile about that. He was still considered a newborn when we started our dumpster runs again, nestled in a car seat with all the other children in the back of the truck.

During all our years of nightly runs, we had only one accident. Danny was still a baby in a car seat when we flipped the truck over. Some Amish people came to our aid, and they were able to flip it back right side up again. The children seemed all right. Daniel had a small cut on his head. Walter wouldn't let him go to the hospital. I cleaned and bandaged his wound as my smiling boy watched my every move.

Sometimes, as I dreamed of escape, I wished I could get more channels on our old TV with bunny ears so I could expand my knowledge of the outside world. Walter was the only one with spare time to catch some shows now and then. His opinions were always strong and over the top. He hated Barbara Walters. I think this came from one show he watched where she interviewed some serial killers and her questioning got pretty deep. I suspected that Walter's interest in these criminals was more involved than that of the average TV viewer. He was always drawn to shows about serial killers. He rooted for the wrong guy. He acted like he knew what was going on behind the scenes of these shows, and as if he knew the motives of the interviewers. When I tried to imagine Barbara or Oprah interviewing Walter, I didn't know if I should laugh or cry.

Never wanting to be like Walter was an ever-present desire for me. Doing the opposite of what he did always seemed like the right thing to do. I didn't know what I would do if I ever found myself thinking like Walter. How could anyone be so diabolical? Sometimes he'd slip and give me a glimpse of some of the things that could have made him that way.

He remembered being bullied by other kids, and that had taken a toll. His father pretty much hated him. In addition, Walter had ADHD, and his dad thought he could beat that out of him. Walter had made it through only tenth grade, but he'd managed to teach himself to read and find his own odd strategies to figure out math problems.

I also knew that Walter had a brother, six years older than him. One time, he did admit that his brother had sodomized him when they were young. Knowing how horrible that abuse was, how could Walter ever want to repeat it? When I thought about this tragic and sad behavior passing down through generations, I once again promised myself that this madness would stop with me. Nothing would keep me from preventing a third generation from repeating these atrocities, not even Walter. Knowing I was firm in my resolve gave me the courage to go on.

Daniel's recent birth had brought back the flood of memories of Michael's and Teddy's deaths. I still tried to find ways to remember them both. Our church friends had planned a funeral for Michael, and that eased the pain a little. Not a day went by that I didn't pray about the loss of my two boys. Too often, I'd be reminded of how old they would be now. I'd lose myself in thoughts of what they might have been doing at that moment if they had still been with me. It made me hold baby Danny even tighter.

CHAPTER FORTY-TWO

One afternoon, our usual routine was broken by an unusual sound: someone was rapping on our door. When I stepped outside, I was surprised to see my oldest sister's daughter, Terri. It had been years since I'd seen a family member. Walter had a post office box, and he was very careful that no one who might know our family learned our address. Terri looked like she must have been about nineteen. Her voice quivering with nervousness, she told me that Emily and Cheryl were both working now. *Is that code to let me know they'd be able to care for us if we could get away?* I felt so conflicted. I couldn't endanger my sister and her children, and I didn't want Walter to find out Terri had been there.

Soon after Terri's visit, Walter did indeed find out. I couldn't figure out how this had happened, but Walter was always on high alert, and his sixth sense was always sniffing around, looking for any sign of cracks in my prison walls. Now he kept accusing me of wanting to run away, and he began watching me more closely than ever.

When my sister Cheryl turned up at my door next, I was overjoyed to see her, but I was concerned for her safety as well. My niece was able to get word back to my family of where I was living. Days later Cheryl showed up and told me, "Mom is over at that store next door. Can you sneak out and talk to her?"

I knew that my mother couldn't be the person to help me. It would be too risky to try to get away with Elaine being my Moses, trying to lead me to freedom. One glance from Walter and she would buckle and side with him.

I hesitated, but after a moment I decided to go over to the store and talk to my mother. Now that I had been a parent for a while, I did want to express my appreciation for what she had done for me. The last time I had seen her, Tammy had been a baby. I had had five births since then. *I should at least acknowledge that being a mother is not an easy job and that I'm thankful for the few positive things she managed to do for me before Walter took over my life.*

Walter was away, so I looked both ways before leaving the house and then dashed to the store, which was only a few steps from my front door. Upon entering, I immediately noticed Elaine looked worn but did manage a faint smile when she saw me. Elaine told me she wanted to help me get away. I asked her, "How can you possibly help me?" We both knew the answer to that.

I thanked her for the good things she had done for me—the garage sale clothes she managed to buy, the cake she baked me for my eleventh birthday when we lived in the woods, the cooking lessons I learned vicariously through her. We exchanged a few more words, and then I rushed back home before I could be missed. My head swirled with a hurricane of emotions after seeing my mother for the first time in so many years. I knew that she was a victim too, of her own father and Walter, but regret tarnished the sympathy I felt for her. I tried to let it go and open my heart to the peace I felt when I shared my gratitude with her. I hoped that no harm would come to her as a result of her feeble attempt to rescue me.

Of course, Walter somehow found out about my brief encounter with Elaine. It was like he had a detective agency all his own, or at least eyes in the back of his head. He tightened his hold a bit, even though he knew there was no way Elaine could get me and my four children out of his grasp. Soon it would be five children; there was a new baby waiting to make his or her way into the world.

On a hot summer night, one year and a few months after Daniel's birth, I went into labor again. After a long night of contractions, the new day dawned, and there was still no baby. I was getting weaker. I asked Walter to break my water, and fifteen minutes later a beautiful baby girl presented herself. We named her Rachel. It was July 18, 1993.

In the days following her birth, Rachel needed to nurse every hour. She couldn't seem to get enough to satisfy her, and she'd fall asleep quickly, only to awaken soon after and need to nurse again.

When the baby was thirteen days old, her nursing problems still hadn't improved. Then, while holding her, I was alarmed to see her have a small seizure. We took her to the hospital. I stayed there with her while they ran all kinds of tests. Walter took the other children to the park to play while I stayed with Rachel, nursing her on demand. The tests showed nothing unusual, so two weeks later she returned home. Rachel continued her hourly nursing. I kept her in bed next to me so she could conserve her strength while breastfeeding. At the time, I didn't know that she was tongue tied, and that may have affected her ability to nurse.

I introduced formula and cereal earlier than usual to help Rachel flourish. She was not gaining weight as fast as she should have. When she grew a little older and I introduced solid food, the challenge continued. One day she liked peaches, and the next day she wouldn't have anything to do with them, and so it went with a variety of fruits and vegetables. We were able to get some help from a homeopathic doctor. She did some tests on Rachel that were helpful, and I followed her advice and discussed my concerns with some of the Amish mothers.

Next, we took Rachel to a doctor the Amish women suggested I use. She didn't seem to believe that I was trying everything I could think of to get Rachel to eat better. The doctor was also unhappy when Walter told her he would not allow Rachel to be immunized. He believed it was harmful and was suspicious of the whole process. "I wouldn't bring a dog to you for medical help," Walter said as we left the doctor's office.

The pediatrician sent a county nurse to our house to check on Rachel's progress. I welcomed her visits, but as soon as Walter arrived at home he cut her visits short. After three times of being rushed out the door by Walter, the county nurse sent a Children's Protective Services worker to see us. At first, Walter got along well with this man who said that it looked like I was trying hard to help Rachel. I was thankful that this caseworker could see the lengths I went to with my baby.

It wasn't long before Walter got tired of the CPS worker coming around so much. Walter's true colors emerged, and he told the man to leave. All I wanted was help getting my baby to eat well, but it had turned into a game of tag. First the homeopathic doctor, then the pediatrician, followed by the county nurse and now the CPS worker. I figured it would be just like all the other times when Walter had thrown social workers out when I was a girl. This worker would just leave and never come back. For two decades,

Walter had ordered social workers off his porch and we never saw them again, so why should this time be any different?

I was completely shocked when this CPS worker came back with the sheriff. I'd given up on this scenario long ago, but there they were. When Walter saw the two cars pull up to our house, he rushed inside and grabbed Rachel.

I realized that the doctor, or the county nurse, or the CPS worker had reported that Rachel still wasn't gaining weight fast enough. Failure to thrive is what they called it. I was sure that Walter's behavior to all of those professionals must have stirred up suspicion.

The sheriff looked down at Walter, who was cradling Rachel. "You have to give me the baby. She's going to go with us. We have a car seat in the CPS worker's car, and a foster mom lined up to care for Rachel."

"She's not going anywhere with you. You have no right to take my child," Walter insisted.

The sheriff reached down and took the baby from Walter's arms. Walter jumped up, fists clenched, and lunged toward the sheriff.

"You son of a bitch! You come into my house and take my kid? There is *nothing* wrong with this baby! My wife feeds her all the time."

The sheriff didn't arrest Walter for doing this. I wished that he would have, but I couldn't even think about that as I watched my baby being taken away. *I wish I could go with them and continue caring for Rachel. I feel like a piece of me has been torn away.* It reminded me unpleasantly of the time the older kids were taken to foster parents after Teddy's death, and how grief had swallowed me up.

I turned to see the frightened faces of my other four children as they embraced me all at once, and I felt the hollow words fall from my lips once again: "It's going to be all right." We watched until the car carrying Rachel was no more than a speck in the road.

"We gotta get the hell outta here before they come back for the rest of the kids." Walter's frantic words caused the children to clutch me even tighter. I didn't know what we should do next, but I knew I had no say in the matter. In my grief, I was struggling just to think straight. I tried to appear calm in front of the children as I packed our things. *I wonder who is taking care of Rachel. Will she transition well to all formula while my milk is drying up?* My breasts ached as I felt a surge of milk filling them from the mere thought of my baby. I knew this would be just the first of many physical and emotional aches that I'd feel with the sudden loss of my child. I turned back to the task at hand as I followed Walter's orders.

"Help me get this tent into the truck and then pack up the rest of our camping gear. I'll get our important documents while you finish packing what the kids might need."

I helped Walter load the truck and urged the children inside. "Kids, we're going away for a little while; it will be like a little vacation."

I buckled Danny into his car seat and was grateful to see him smiling up at me. I gave him a big smile back and then turned away from the older children so they wouldn't see me tearing up.

Walter had always trusted the Amish, so I wasn't surprised when we stopped at a home that belonged to an Amish family. They let us set up our tent in the woods behind their open field. We were no strangers to camping, and the kids were excited about the prospect.

We continued our nightly runs to the dumpsters; only now, we turned over much of the food we gathered to this family, our new landlords, so to speak. Where this food came from remained unspoken in this exchange.

As we grew accustomed to our surroundings, I began to notice some things about this family that I hadn't realized before. The children were afraid of their father. He'd reach out and smack them at mealtime for doing the tiniest little thing. I was thankful that our children didn't show that kind of fear toward Walter. The irony of that thought was not lost on me.

Word travels fast in the Amish community. I could see why they didn't need telephones to know what was going on with their neighbors. In spite of Walter's friendly manner and the occasional free food he gave out, there were some Amish families who didn't have a good feeling about "Old Wally, the Bread Man." One family in particular did not want to pay their bills on time. They demanded cheaper prices for the food we sold to them. Maybe this family had reported us to someone, or maybe the sheriff and CP worker could tell by the items left behind at our house that we had been selling illegally to the Amish. Either way, Walter felt that the law was hot on our trail. After a month of hiding out in the woods, we packed up and left. We were on the run.

Walter was nervous that CPS would find us. I wanted them to find us, but I didn't want to be separated from my children. Walter had ranted for years about how the state would love to get its hands on our children and do experiments on them. Knowing he believed that confirmed for me that he knew full well he was their grandpa and their father, even though he denied it. My concern was that the children would be taken from my care. In spite of Walter, I knew I was a good mother.

My thoughts kept returning to my premonition: *something terrible has to happen before I can get away from Walter.* I had never thought I would live to be twenty years old, yet here I was, twenty-six, and I'd survived Walter so far. My will to care for my children was stronger than my fear of Walter. *I must stay alive to be here for my kids. I must proceed with caution.*

We went to a town farther away and asked a couple from our church if we could stay with them. They let us set up camp. Walter was careful to make sure our tent was not visible from the road. I couldn't remember a time in my life when my adrenaline had not been pumping. Now it was going full force. I could feel a new twist to this churning inside of me. "Fight or flight" screamed through my veins more powerfully than ever, but I didn't know which to choose—fight or flight. My path wasn't clear, at least not yet.

We just tried to make it through one day at a time at our new hideout. Rita treated us kindly, as did her husband, Josh. That man was a big eater, all 450 pounds of him. Walter felt he should contribute something to our upkeep. We had run out of money, and the food we'd packed was running low. Walter took the risk of going back to our house and retrieving all the meat from our freezer to give to our latest landlord. Josh was pleased with this gift, and it didn't take long for the numerous roasts, the dozen steaks, and the ample pounds of hamburger to disappear.

Each day was filled with more tension than the last. I kept a close eye on the children and was thankful they seemed to be faring well. Walter always had one eye on the road. *The clock is ticking. How much longer can we hide from the authorities?* I felt so conflicted. I wished for someone strong to step in between Walter and me. I had spent all of my life hoping for that. But more than anything else in the world, I wanted to keep my children. Losing Rachel was wearing on me, and I found myself holding my other four children tighter than ever. Not knowing from minute to minute how this would all play out was excruciating.

About a month later, Walter suddenly decided to move our tent so that it was visible from the road. I was confused by this move, but I didn't ask him why he did it. Maybe on some level Walter was hoping to get caught, but that certainly seemed out of character for him. All I could do was hug my children close and just wait.

One morning, a few days later, I woke up and went inside Rita's house to join her for a cup of coffee. The children were still asleep in the tent, and I knew they would be spilling into the house soon, four little bundles of energy, wide eyed and innocent of what might soon be at hand.

It was comforting to have a female friend to sit and chat with, such a rarity for me. Rita was older than I was and had taken me under her wing ever since we had begun attending church. Josh was a scary guy, huge and bearded. He carved Bible verses on the gate to his house and painted biblical texts on the side of his Suburban. He certainly wasn't your run-of-the-mill kind of guy, yet he had always treated me decently. Someone looking in the window at that moment might have thought this scene was typical of one you might see all across the country: two women having a cup of coffee together. I suppose to most people this would feel normal, but I had never known normal. I was grateful for this little bit of quiet time with Rita, even though nervousness and fear permeated my every waking moment. I tried to center myself for what was yet to come, and my prayers were continual. No matter where we hid, I knew God was there.

The word was out on the television and in the newspapers: we were fugitives of the law. *It's only a matter of time now.* I clutched the warmth of the coffee cup and took a few deep breaths. I heard the door bang. "I just saw a state police car pass the house," Walter snapped. He couldn't hide how jumpy he felt. My prayer was that the police would take Walter away, not the children.

The state police car Walter saw must have been going to get more officers to join them. It wasn't long before we saw several police cars pull up in front of Rita's house. The minute I saw them, I knew. It was over. This was not just one social worker or a single school official. This was half a dozen armed officers. *If they incarcerate Walter, that will mean freedom for me.*

Chapter Forty-Three

This was what had to happen to change my life. I could hardly comprehend the thought that it was finally over. It was my birthday: I was twenty-seven years old. Walter was fifty-four. My other birthdays had been pretty much like any other day, but this would be one for the books. All of the years I had waited for this moment, my fears that something terrible would have to happen to free me from Walter's prison: that time had finally arrived.

I would have been so relieved if I knew the authorities would just let me keep the kids. But I knew that wasn't going to happen. That was the terrible something that cast a dark shadow on my day of freedom.

Walter was arrested and put in the back of one of the police cars. I was handcuffed from behind, but I was grateful that the children were allowed to ride in the squad car with me. Through my tears, I saw the face of the lone female cop. She told me her name was Jill. She would be driving the children and me while the other cops hauled Walter away. Jill turned to me and said, "I know your mother and I know who you are. I want you to be able to stay with your kids. I'll do my best to keep them in foster care together until that time comes. I don't know why no one has helped you before. I know that you have lost two children. I read reports about your case and connected the dots. I spoke with Walter years ago. He said you were his wife. I noticed that he did all the talking and you never spoke. Remembering that incident helped me figure out who you are. I know you have been through a lot, and I'm glad for you it is finally over. Now I'm going to read you your rights. You have the right to remain silent. Anything you say . . ."

As she read me my rights, I tried to let the words wash over me. I had never felt like I had any rights to begin with anyway. Yet I was also strangely comforted to discover Jill knew me. She seemed kind, but maybe she was playing a game of "good cop, bad cop." I tried to hold it together for the sake of the children. Robin was frightened by my handcuffs. She yelled at the officer, "You better take those off my mommy!" Danny was crying. Jimmy and Tammy were scared and silent. I wished I could touch them, hug them, but all I could do was try to comfort them with my words.

"It's going to be all right. Mommy is here. I love you. Tammy, please hold Jimmy's hand. Robin and Danny, lean in close to me. I can't put my arms around you, but I'm hugging you all with my heart." *How can I make my words count? Will they remember what I am saying to them today?*

"Mommy wants to always be with you. No matter what happens, I want you all to remember that I will never rest until we are all together, I promise. Remember that I love you. I will always love you. Tammy and Jimmy, you're the oldest. I know you can't understand all of this, but remember to be strong. Never stop believing that I will be with you as soon as I can. I hope you will feel me holding you in my heart and God holding you in His hand until we can be together again. Remember to say your prayers every day, just like I taught you."

While she drove us, Jill told me what would happen next. "Your children will go to foster homes nearby. Robin and Rachel will stay together and go to the same home."

We reached the police station. I could see that there were cars there, waiting to take my kids. The hurt of being separated from all of my children was so deep that I couldn't feel relief that I had escaped Walter. For sixteen years we had lived together as man and captive wife. For twenty-seven years Walter had controlled my every move. The abuse, the isolation, fifteen pregnancies. Yet I survived. I know that God didn't bring me through all those years for me to give up now. I saw the children's faces turn toward me as they were being driven away. The squad car I was in turned in a different direction. I was alone.

When we reached the police station, another officer led me inside and handcuffed me to a metal heat register. My handcuffs were so loose that I could slip them off if I wanted to. *Maybe this is some kind of test. Do they think I would slip them off and run?* I had a long history to teach me that running wouldn't work. I knew I had to cooperate with the police. After all, it had taken twenty-seven years to get their attention. I understood that my journey to get my children back started this minute. *My first step is to make sure these darn cuffs don't fall off me!* As it turned out, the problem was only temporary. After a few hours, I asked permission to use the bathroom. When I returned from relieving myself, the officer tightened the handcuffs on my wrists. Then he fingerprinted and booked me. From there, the sheriff took me to a jail for women.

As the door to my cell closed, I wondered if my freedom was beginning or ending. My ordeal with Walter was over. Now that he was finally in jail, he would be monitored from this point on. At least, I hoped that was the case. This was the first time that the state had gone far enough to actually put Walter behind bars. The bars that protected me from this madman I once called my father meant freedom for me. I prayed I would never see him again. I knew I would get a restraining order against Walter the second I was allowed to do so. I had to keep telling myself, *It's over*, trying to convince myself that it was really true. My mind was also racing with thoughts of my children. *I will fight with everything I have in me to get them back. And what about the new child I'm carrying in my belly right now? I won't let them take him, either.*

Though I had no idea how it would end, as I took the first step on this journey, a new chapter was beginning for me.

Part 2

Chapter Forty-Four

I look up from the book I'm reading when I hear footsteps coming down the corridor of my wing of the jail. "What are you lookin' at?" one of the inmates sneers at me.

I turn my eyes away from her, only to look up again when I notice a guard standing at my cell door. "On your feet, Williams. It seems your bail has been paid."

The moments that follow go by in a blur of papers to sign and forms to fill out. Through my confusion, I learn that my church has put up the bail money for me, and Rita has come to take me to her home. That was where the police had found me two weeks ago, and that is where I shall return. I verify Rita's address so my parole officer will know where to find me. I am allowed a minute of privacy to slip into the dress I was wearing the day I entered this place. It's a well-worn, cornflower prairie-style dress, one of the only two dresses that I own. It has seen me through my last few pregnancies, and now it will see me through this new day of freedom.

I blink at the bright sky as Rita and I walk across the parking lot together. The sight of the old Suburban she is driving never fails to shock me a little. Even more remarkable are the words that her husband, Josh, has painted on every inch of the truck's body. His cryptic writing can be read from a block away: *In the beginning was the Word and the Word was with God . . . The Word*

became flesh is the verse painted across the driver's side of his old Chevy. ***You shall not bear false witness against your neighbor*** adorns the back of the vehicle. As I approach the passenger side, I see a jumble of words. The ones that catch my eye are painted in a bright red across the door: ***Honor your father and your mother***. I swing the door open, making a gap between the words of this commandment.

After sharing a few pleasantries with Rita and assuring her I am all right, we ride along in silence. I know she is concerned about driving Josh's car, and she seems a bit nervous. She keeps her speed below forty miles per hour, making the trip longer than expected. As the trees and houses slowly travel past my view, my thoughts turn to the children. Are they safe and well cared for? I try to imagine them happy for the time being. I have been thinking about what I need to do to get them back. It's the same thing I'd planned on doing if I was ever free. I will secure a job and make a good home for them. I try to imagine what it will be like to have the children back in my care, and me free from Walter's grasp. It's all too much right now, so I close my eyes and lean back in the seat, thanking God for my church and my friend Rita.

CHAPTER FORTY-FIVE

I spend the next month helping Rita with household chores, as I have no way to pay her rent or buy any food. The rest of my time is spent working for my pastor and my church. It's the only way I can pay back the bail money they put up for me. I am delighted when my brother Bruce comes to visit me one day.

"I have some money saved up, Lorie. I'd like to give you a loan, if you'll accept it."

"Thank you, Bruce. You're such a good brother. I'll pay you back every penny, I promise."

"If you do, it will be the first time anyone has ever paid me back for a loan." Bruce smiles. "I'm just glad you made it, Lorie. There were times I feared I would never see you again."

Bruce pushes his glasses up on his nose, combing back a shock of brown hair with his fingers. When he smiles, I am reminded of how handsome my brother is. I can't help but marvel how he, too, managed to take good care of his teeth all these years. His offer of help reminds me that Bruce is a good man. He's living proof that it is possible to have good character, even when no role model is available during childhood.

Because I am now house hunting in a larger city that is several hours from Rita's home, Cheryl lets me move in with her. I think back to that night in the snow when we said goodbye, both of us knowing she could never go home again. *I'm so happy she turned out to be a kind, responsible person!* The next day, Belinda stops by with some clothes and a few essentials for me, and I am pleased to see how pretty she looks now that the strain of surviving Walter is gone from her life. I haven't seen her in years, and I thank God she survived. We haven't been together since we were kids, and we find joy in getting reacquainted.

My oldest sister, Emily, offers to drive me around town to look for a job. I'm so grateful for all of the help my siblings are offering me; I learn that all of them knew I was a captive. They also knew they were powerless to help me and each of them carries the burden of that knowledge. Unfortunately, they knew all too well from their childhoods that reporting Walter to any type of authority only brought more trouble for Walter's victims. We all feel such relief that Walter is behind bars, but the threat of his release lurks in the shadows, waiting for all of us. If any of them fear that my presence will lure Walter near them again, they never say so.

"Pull in over here, Emily. See that sign at the dollar store? Looks like they might be hiring."

I smooth my clothes and tuck my hair behind my ears as my sister watches me head into the store. When I return to her car, Emily can tell by the smile on my face that I was hired. "They need help restocking, with the Christmas season coming up and all. I told them I'll be glad to work any hours they can give me. You know, Emily, it seems so weird, making a decision on my very own."

My sister's sad smile reminds me she was the first to flee our home as a young teenager.

My housing search leads me to a mobile home that is in pretty good shape, and the price is right. Bruce's loan gives me enough to purchase it, along with the rent of my new little yard at the trailer park. There is even enough money left over to get the utilities hooked up. *Thank God Bruce has a bent for saving money and a kind heart to lend it.*

I shop at Goodwill and local garage sales to buy beds for the children. A bunk bed goes into the boys' room for Jimmy and Danny. I pick up some cute sheets at a garage sale along with a few more odds and ends to make the room inviting for my sons. Next, I purchase a full-size bed for Tammy and Robin to share and a crib for baby Rachel. The three girls will have the larger bedroom at the end of the hall. When Elaine finds me a sofa bed at a garage sale, I am grateful to have something in the living room for me to sleep on. I'm conflicted about seeing my mother again. I am very careful to set boundaries with her, and I don't let her get too close. She gives me an old Chevy, too, and I am able to find a rebuilt transmission and soon have it running. I know I will return this to Elaine as soon as I am able to purchase a vehicle on my own, but for the time being, I can't turn it down. I need transportation to get to work.

A working refrigerator came with my trailer, and I get a good deal on a metal table and chairs for the kitchen. I can't wait to cook the kids their first breakfast in my new kitchen. Until then, I am on the road to self-improvement. The DSS is in the process of changing its name to FIA, Family Independence Agency. Whatever its name might be, the big surprise is that Child Protective Services finally sees me. *The invisible woman is back in town!* I try not to look back on all the times that my siblings and I reported Walter's abuse. Now that Social Services is involved with my case, I am no longer the abused child. This time, I must fight to prove that I am a fit parent, and I intend to do exactly that. I know that Rachel's failure to thrive was not because I didn't feed her. God knows I tried every way under the sun to get her to eat a balanced diet. Yet that is the charge I was brought up on and it led the way to Walter's arrest as well as mine.

I'm required to take various parenting classes, and I try to see this as an opportunity to better myself. So I grab a bottle of water, jump into my now-workable car, and head out to class.

Today's lesson is on breastfeeding. I breastfed all of my children, but that doesn't mean I can't learn something new. I am so grateful that, during this pregnancy, I can actually see a doctor regularly and take prenatal vitamins for the first time. This is my fifteenth pregnancy. When I finish class today, I sit in my car and eat the sandwich I've packed, and then I log my hours into the journal I am keeping. I show the records of my class time to my social worker each time we meet. Of course, I get the instructor's signature as proof I actually attended class. I haven't missed a class yet, nor have I been tardy.

On my own, I set up appointments with a psychologist. My story is a bit much for both of us, but somehow we muddle through our sessions. I know it is God who has seen me through these nearly three decades under Walter's control, but I want to do all I can to keep my mind healthy now that I have my freedom. I know I can't make up for the years lost, but I want to get myself to a good place as I try to manage the swirl of new events I find myself facing each day. One day at a time, I keep reminding myself.

Once my lunch is gone, it's time to work my shift at the dollar store. Then I drive into town for night class. I am working on earning a high school diploma. I may be a decade late on graduation, but I believe I'm embracing these classes in a way that I never could have as a teenager. We're studying the Civil War right now, and I am fascinated by the topic. I feel such a connection to the people who were forced into slavery. I know that slavery was so much worse than being under Walter's control. My heart goes out to anyone who knows the pain of being in bondage. It goes against human nature and must be stopped at all costs.

Finally, the day comes when I'll have my first visit with my children. I feel a prickle of excitement during the entire hour-and-a-half drive to the FIA building where we'll meet. I've packed some art projects and some healthy snacks for our time together. On the way, I pray that the foster moms are feeding the kids healthy foods, saying prayers with them each night, and treating them kindly each day.

The room where I wait is small and nondescript. The only thing worth noticing is the big mirror that covers most of one of the walls. I am sure my caseworker will be on the other side taking notes of everything I say and do. I arrange the art supplies on the table and set bowls of blueberries and cut-up apples in the center. Then I wait.

When the door opens and the kids spill into the room, I try to hold back the tears, but it's impossible. We hug, and kiss, and hug some more. The kids are all talking at once, except for baby Rachel. Tammy is anxious to hold her; this is the first time she's seen Rachel and Robin since the day of my arrest. The boys haven't seen the girls, either, since the day we were all sandwiched in the back of the police car. I wonder if they notice the same little changes in each one that I see. Rachel has a new tooth. Danny is a tiny bit taller, and Robin's speech has become a little more mature. Tammy is even prettier than before, and Jimmy is as agreeable as ever. The time for goodbyes comes all too soon, and I stare longingly at the backs of their heads as they are ushered out of our visiting room.

The next time I meet with my caseworker, Paula, I ask if I can see the report from my first visit with the children. Some of it is just basic stuff, but I see that she noted that I allowed Danny to make marks on the table in the visiting room. "I thought it was more important to praise Danny for the picture he made," I explain. "You know I cleaned the washable marker smudges off the table after the children left. I didn't want to waste a minute of being with them, and I didn't want Danny to feel like he did something wrong." I can tell by Paula's lack of reaction that she is not going to make any changes to this report.

Next, I see that the report says I let Tammy babysit Rachel during the visit. My eyes sting as I try to explain that Tammy hadn't seen her baby sister in a while, and she just wanted to hold her. Paula brushes my comment aside, changing the subject: "Can I see the records for the classes you've been attending?" I show her my accounts from both of the parenting classes and from my high school classes. She doesn't remark on all of the positive statements the instructors wrote about me or the A grades I've earned in both of my classes. It almost seems like she is a little irked by the positive information. Trying to ignore this thought, I decide to stay positive. "I want to thank you for getting Danny into that special school that can help him with his learning. Robin seems to love her preschool, and I'd like to hear more about it. Is Rachel eating better? Jimmy and Tammy both said they like their new schools, but Jimmy seemed to hesitate a little bit. Have you talked to his teacher?" I try to be grateful for the little bits of information I am given. At least it makes me feel a little closer to the children when I can't be with them.

Chapter Forty-Six

Still thinking about yesterday's encounter with Paula, I park my car and head into work the following morning. It's a quiet day at the dollar store as I take an inventory of the new holiday supplies. When I see a customer enter the store, I feel myself do a double take; I recognize her! She walks straight to me, and we embrace.

"So, you *do* remember me! I've been searching for you. Your night school teacher told me I would find you here."

Looking into Mrs. Macon's face, I can see the concern, just as I did decades ago when I told her at school about Carl abusing me. *So here she is, my second-grade teacher, and she not only remembers me, but she was actually looking for me!* "The second I heard of the arrest on the news, my heart stopped," Mrs. Macon explains. "They withheld your name, but I just *knew* it was you. I never forgot you, Lorie. Not so much because we share the same name and you were in my class, but because of what you told me that day. I have thought about you often these last two decades. It has been unsettling not knowing what happened to you. Can we get together soon and talk?"

A few days later, I welcome my former teacher into my home. I keep calling her Mrs. Macon, but she tells me to call her by her first name. When she was my age, she still went by her nickname, Laurie, but now she uses her given name, Laurel. The last name we used to share is now her middle name, and her married name is Macon. We sit together on my sofa and sip coffee in my living room, which is also my bedroom. "So why were you arrested? I have no doubt that you were feeding your baby as best as you could. What happened to bring you to this point?" Laurel asks.

So a new chapter in my life begins as I start meeting with my teacher. I finally have someone to talk to, someone who wants to hear my entire story. It takes countless visits before I get her fully up to speed on the twists and turns my life has taken. We take new versions of teacher/student field trips, as I show her some of the places from my past.

"That little white house on the corner is where my mom left me with those men that time," I tell Laurel as she drives her car through my old neighborhood. "I kept fighting them off, and eventually they left me alone. When Elaine came to get me, with absolutely no explanation of why she left me with a bunch of strange men, I could feel some of my love for her dissolve."

I see Laurel shiver when she notices that the school where she teaches is only a stone's throw away from that house. "I pass by that house when I go to teach each day. I'll never be able to look at it again without thinking of you."

I can see that I'm only adding to Laurel's concern for me, just as I had done when I told her my story at age seven, but it certainly feels good to tell someone all the things that have happened to me, especially someone who cares.

We drive on for more than an hour to our next stop, chatting along the way. I can see that my teacher—now my friend—is trying to put the pieces of the puzzle together. When we pull into the yard of the house where Walter and I had lived most recently, I feel a prickle of fear move up my spine. I know Walter is incarcerated; otherwise, I never would have come here. But I still feel his menacing energy lingering in this place.

"Is this old rusty scale the one you used to weigh your newborn babies? And is this the tool that resealed the cellophane on the chips you sold to the Amish?"

My teacher is incredulous now that we're actually inside the house I'd tried to describe to her in words.

"Some Show and Tell, huh?"

When I lead her up the steep stairway and we find ourselves staring at the double bed I had to share with Walter, I see Laurel has become quiet. She is staring at the heavy black oxfords parked at the foot of the bed.

"Archie Bunker shoes," she finally says, trying to make light of things, but I can see the tears welling in her green eyes.

When we turn toward the bathroom with no door on it, I see her stop and grip the wall a moment before she can go on.

She also takes note of the streaks around the windows from the hundreds of buckets of dirt I poured between the walls, following Walter's command to insulate. "This all brings such a new reality to your story, Lorie. I see an Avon sign in the yard across the street and wonder why the Avon lady didn't call someone to investigate. The ball was dropped so many times... I wish I had never lost contact with you after you left my class." As we head to Laurel's car we stop a moment and silently stare at the rusty old school bus that was my home for so many years.

Days later, we venture into the county park, and sure enough, there are still souvenirs left over from our stay here when we returned from Canada. The rusty Lasso insecticide cans we found in the weeds could very well be the same ones we used when cooking here.

Weeks later, we journey up north to a wooded area where Walter and I lived for a while, and in this place, we find even more evidence of our camping trip. "See those old boards over there? They must be part of the frame Walter built and covered with heavy-duty plastic. It was a homemade tent. That was our home for quite a while."

A few yards away, I spot a can that Walter had rigged for us to use like a stove burner, and I'm reminded of a few more stories to share with Laurel.

On the way back home, we stop for a bite to eat. As we sit across from each other in the cozy booth, I check my wallet, in case Laurel will let me pay this time. "What are those yellowed slips of papers you have in your wallet?" she asks. "They look like you've had them for decades."

I take them out and show them to her. "I always thought if I ever had a little extra money, I would like to buy Adelle Davis's books about healthy cooking and eating," I reply.

The following afternoon, Laurel is brighter than usual when she shows up on my stoop after a day of teaching. "I got into Adelle Davis's books when I was pregnant with my first child. This nutritionist is so ahead of her time. I want you to have these."

I open the sack to find new copies of the book titles I have carried with me for so many years. I'm so excited. "I've wanted these for *so long*. I know the basics of healthy cooking and eating, but having this information at hand will help me to expand. I can't wait to try out some of these recipes on the kids. Paula, my caseworker, is bringing them for a visit here tomorrow. I hope they like their future home. Would you mind looking around and telling me if you think everything here will pass inspection? There are always negative things in my reports, so if you see anything out of place, please tell me."

Laurel takes a careful stroll through each room and then concludes, "It's warm and homey. Everything is neat and clean, so organized. I love the little stuffed animals you've arranged on all the beds. I can't imagine anyone finding something that is not kid friendly here."

"Well, we'll see. Come check out my plans for food and activities for the kids, too."

Laurel seems caught up in the excitement of the very first visit, too. This is my home, the very first time I can have the freedom to be with my children without the fear of Walter walking in the door. After a few hours, we say goodbye, and I assure Laurel that I'll tell her how the big day goes.

A few days later, Laurel and I settle our coffee cups on my kitchen table, and she insists I tell her everything. "The visit was wonderful. The kids were so excited about their new bedrooms and being reunited with each other. I thought it couldn't have gone better, but then the next day I asked to see the report. Paula stated that there was a lamp in Jimmy's room with a burned-out bulb, which the report said created a fire hazard. It was like she *had* to find something to make me look like a bad mother. I just don't get it. She's got to know I have done everything I'm required to do, and so much more. And not because I have to—but because I *want* to."

Laurel's brow furrows as she stirs her coffee. "Something is wrong here. It's like you're being sabotaged. I would like to come along on your next visit."

CHAPTER FORTY-SEVEN

The following week, Laurel joins me in the crowded observation room at the FIA. It's the first time she has met the kids, but they seem like old friends before the hour is up. Laurel asks if she can join me for the following visit, also. That one I'm especially excited about, because I get to meet the kids in a park on a Saturday. That day can't come soon enough for me.

The anticipated day finally arrives. The kids pile out of the social worker's van and run to embrace me. I see that Paula is not the one who brought them this time; instead, it is a male social worker. Laurel is good on her promise. She arrives on time, and I notice that she has someone else in the car. It has been several decades, but I'm amazed to recognize the kind face of my elementary school principal, the other person I told my story to at age seven. Mr. Sass was loved and respected by all of the kids in my school, and I feel honored that he would take the time to join us today. He is now the director of a children's agency in the town where I live. He is wearing a flannel shirt rather than a suit, and his manner is casual as he shakes hands with the caseworker. Relief floods over me as I realize I have two professionals observing this visit with my children.

We're in a park with picnic tables surrounded by beautiful trees. The day feels glorious to me as I hug my kids. My baby is due soon, but I manage to keep up with the children as they run from the swings to the slide and then back again. "I'm hungry," Robin calls to me, smiling. She's noticed the picnic basket full of snacks I brought with me. I unpack the food, and we have a picnic together.

I can't help but notice that this new caseworker gives off a strange energy. "Bad energy" is something I would rarely think about on my own, but for some reason I can't help but feel wary of this man. But under the watchful eyes of my former teacher and principal I feel safe, and I just try to savor every moment with my kids. I know I will ache for them tonight when I'm home alone.

The next week, Laurel stops by my house and is barely in the door before she's anxiously asking about the report of our park visit. Frustration makes my voice sharp as I explain several negative remarks the report contains. "The caseworker said that I let Danny eat a whole *box* of graham crackers. There's no way that could have happened; I have the rest of the box of crackers right here. The only thing is I was doing that little plant study with Robin and Tammy when Danny was at the picnic table with you. Did you notice how many he ate?"

"I don't remember, but there was nothing remarkable about it. I certainly would have noticed if he ate the whole box. I'll call my principal right now. He's in his office at the children's agency. I'll let you know what he says."

He answers on the second ring. Minutes later, Laurel hangs up and then turns to me.

"Wow, what a guy. He remembers the cracker count *exactly*. He says that Danny ate two and a half crackers, and he's willing to write a letter stating that. You can show it to the judge at your next evaluation. There's no doubt in my mind now; it seems like your caseworker is willing to lie to make you look bad in these reports."

I spend the next few days thinking over everything that happened during my visits with the kids. The petty things that aren't even true must be more than careless errors. *My caseworker is setting me up so that I don't get my kids back.* That grim reality almost sucks me back into the darkness I felt under Walter's control. *I have got to pray about this and keep on showing these people who I really am.* My thoughts are interrupted by the ringing of my phone. It's Paula, my caseworker. My heart races when I hear what she has to say. "The social worker who observed you on your visit to the park is no longer with our agency. It seems he molested some of the boys he transported to various places. I know he drove Jimmy several times, and we are hoping he was not touched in any way by him. He has been fired and won't be in contact with children again."

My last shred of confidence in these people is slipping away. *They're supposed to be protecting my children!* I demand to see Jimmy, to talk to him and make sure he is all right.

"You'll have to wait until your next assigned visit for that," Paula says bluntly, and then she hangs up.

I feel the strain in the relationship with my caseworker, but I don't let up. I document every class I attend, and I also continue collecting letters of recommendation from work and places where I volunteer. The stack of complimentary statements from professionals that I interact with has become so large that I have to buy a bigger three-ring binder to hold them. I bring the binder with me every time I go to see the judge who is in charge of my case. My lawyer flipped through this book once and complemented me but the judge never looked at it.

With all the changes in my life, I'm thankful I called a psychologist a few months ago and have started meeting with her. I'm not so sure about how any of that is supposed to go, but I always show up on time with a smile on my face. The doctor tells me we are making good progress. However, things turn a bit awkward at my next appointment. The counselor asks me repeatedly about the anger I might feel toward Walter. "You must hate him. The anger must be overwhelming. Perhaps you even wish him harm."

I ponder this for a while before I answer. Of course I feel anger toward Walter. I've even hated him. But all I've ever wanted was freedom from him, and I have that now. So I measure my words.

"I am a Christian. I know my heavenly Father has forgiven me. All He asks of me is that I love Him, and love my fellow humankind. Of course I don't *love* Walter. I don't ever want him near my children or me again. If he gets out of jail, I'll get a restraining order on him. But if I just wallow in anger and hatred over this man, that's not going to do me any good. It would be just one more way he could keep me captive, and it would hinder my relationship with God. The Bible asks that we forgive others just as God has forgiven us. So that is what I've done. I'm in control of my life now. It has been a journey working on forgiving both of my parents, but it is something I must do, and it is helping me to move on. I have enough to focus on as I begin a new life for myself. All my strength is going toward getting my children back and providing a good life for them and myself. If I spend time hating Walter, then he'd win again. Walter loved to say that 'you can't beat a man at his own game.' If I have a peaceful home with my children and show them the love my parents never showed me, then I have won."

"But surely you must be very angry. We should talk about that." My psychologist seems troubled with my response.

"This isn't working for me. I appreciate your time and know you want to help me, but I have no place in my life for anger."

As I walk out the door, I call back a quick "Thank you." The sun is high in the sky as I approach my car. I look up, and it fills me up. I say a little prayer and then steer my old car toward home.

Eventually, another caseworker from a different agency is asked to step in occasionally and monitor how my situation is going. I hope she'll speak up when false claims are filed against me. My hope doesn't last long; I can see that this woman is Paula's ally. In her reports, she zeroes in on Laurel and how she has been helping me out. She looks under my porch and sees a box from a new television Laurel bought me, and she also spots the new picnic table Laurel's husband delivered to my yard. Both of these gifts take on a suspicious nature in my reports. It isn't stated directly, but the caseworker is hinting that my relationship with my former teacher is a bad thing. Now I see that Chris is on the same page as Paula. I'm faced with two people who are here not to help me establish my new life, but rather to prevent me from succeeding. Whatever I do, no matter how perfect, will somehow be twisted to make me look bad. Laurel's husband speaks with a social worker who is in an administrative level with the state. This friend asks, "I've been reading some of the reports on the Lorie Williams case. Why does the name Laurel Macon pop up in some of the reports?"

Harold answers, "Let's just say they stacked the cards against her but they didn't know there was a joker in the deck!"

The reports are frustrating, but the rest of the time I'm too busy to let negative thoughts fill my head. When I'm not working, in class, visiting with the children, or attending services at my church, my time is filled with getting ready for the new baby. Sitting in this waiting room at my doctor's office may feel routine to the other moms sitting across from me, but for me it's a glorious experience. Each day when I take my prenatal vitamin, I thank God that my eighth child is my first to have this advantage.

Chapter Forty-Eight

The first day of March comes in cold and blustery in 1995. I'm at home washing baby clothes and blankets I've bought at numerous garage sales when the first labor pain hits. Bearing into the pain, I say a prayer. I thank God that this baby will be born in a hospital and then brought to a home where there is no Walter. If I want to forget housework and sit and hold this tiny one for hours, I'll be able to do just that. My baby will never have to hear Walter's voice ordering me to scrub a floor or clean up food scavenged from dumpsters. My head is filled with these happy thoughts as I check myself into the hospital.

When my new baby boy is placed in my arms, I feel the full force of my emotions pour out in a flood of tears. He is healthy and beautiful, and my heart is full. On my next visit to see my children, I will introduce them to the newest member of our family, Christopher.

My three sisters all come to see us in the hospital. Elaine comes too, and of course, Laurel. She has worked hard helping me, and now we can just sit back and count little fingers and toes, smiling each time Christopher makes the tiniest squeak. The baby catches on to nursing right away, and I breathe a sigh of relief, remembering how difficult this process was for Rachel. I feel so peaceful as I close my eyes to get a little sleep, knowing I'll wake up many times in the night to check on my new son.

The following day, I am again struck with the thought that it feels so luxurious to just sit and hold my precious little bundle.

In the afternoon, Paula comes to visit. I expect her to tell me about some of the available services to help me with my new baby, but I can tell by her face this is not a routine call. "We have to take your baby. He will be put into a good foster home, and you will be allowed to visit. You can have a little more time to hold him, but then you will need to give him to me."

A dark flood washes over me. I should be telling this woman how I made every doctor's appointment, how I ate only healthy foods. I should remind her that I have a nursery all ready for Christopher's homecoming. I should scream, *HOW CAN YOU TAKE A CHILD FROM A MOTHER WHO HAS DONE NOTHING BUT LOVE THE CHILD?* I should remind her that Walter is gone forever to me, and this baby will know only good things from me. But I don't say any of these things to her. I don't fight her when she takes Christopher from my arms. I just feel broken. I have survived so much, but I don't think I can survive this.

When Laurel arrives a little while later, I can't find the words to tell her what has happened. She is wet from the rain outside, and for some reason, she's still clutching the case that contains her big car phone. "My husband called the school and told me they were taking the baby. You or someone in your family must have called him while I was at school. I don't know how I even managed to drive here. As I ran across the hospital parking lot, I had the husband of the lawyer from a famous baby case that got national attention on the phone. I don't know *how* I even got his number, but I thought his wife could help you. It was a last-ditch effort, I guess. He was kind to me on the phone, but he said they couldn't help us. Her area of law is to protect children, not mothers. We need to figure out another route to get your baby back. You did everything right. *How* can they do this?"

Laurel sits and holds my hand, and we say nothing for a long time. My mother has been sitting quietly in a far corner all this time. Laurel gets up and pats my mom's hand and says, "I'm sorry for you too. I know this is very hard for you also."

Elaine answers, "I've been through lots worse than this."

Laurel comes back to my bedside, and after a long silence I can feel her energy revive a little. That's good, because I feel numb. *I have nothing.*

"We *will* fight this," Laurel encourages me. "I know your lawyer has told you time and time again not to go public. Not to go to the newspapers. Not to accept invitations to appear on the talk shows. Now, I think it's time. I think you should write a letter to your lawyer and tell him the people of this state won't stand for it when they hear about how you've been treated. Do you want to do that? Are you ready to put your story out there publicly if it will help you get your children back?"

I only nod. I *do* want to do that. I've played by every rule my caseworker suggested, and it has gotten me nowhere. I agree with my friend, but I don't have the strength to put it into words.

The following day, I return to my home empty handed. I call Paula and tell her I want to visit my baby right away. Then I go to Christopher's crib and pick up the blanket I have sewn for him. I sink to the floor and bury my face in his quilt. It still smells like the baby detergent I washed it in, and that makes me cry even harder. My breast milk is flowing along with my tears, and the thoughts in my head swirl but never seem to land. I'm not sure what to do next.

Does the Department of Social Services think I spent sixteen years with Walter Williams out of choice? Do they think that during the one day they allowed me to have Christopher, I was an unfit mother? Are they punishing me because my parents were investigated by them seventeen times, and now I'm guilty by association? These are the thoughts running through my head when I get word that I am being summoned to court. Christopher's name has been added to the list of my other children, and the charge is neglect. I am told that Walter will have an attorney there, and his custody rights of the baby may be discussed.

Laurel and I meet with my court-appointed attorney for the first time. I spend less than ten minutes with this woman. We try to cram all of the injustices about the baby being taken away into those few minutes. I'm relieved Walter won't be in court himself, only his court-appointed attorney. I'm surprised to hear that Walter's lawyer claims Walter will give up rights to the baby if that will help me to keep custody of him. For this I am grateful.

Stepping into this courtroom again brings back dark memories for me. I was seven when I sat in this room, describing the things Carl had done to me. I felt so small then, but I still feel small today, like I have no power over my own life or the lives of my children.

Within the first few minutes of the hearing, Paula takes the stand, and she says anything she can to make me sound like I am not capable of caring for a baby. She even says I would be incapable of operating a nebulizer when I know she has seen me use it on the baby. Then there is my lawyer, the one who has known me for ten minutes. My lawyer just sits there. She doesn't object or question anything Paula is saying. It's actually Walter's lawyer who comes to my defense. "How complicated can a nebulizer be?" he asks.

Then he inquires about my recent grades from my high school classes. Paula says I have a 4.0 GPA, but then she adds more comments to discredit me. I am not allowed on the stand. I feel like I'm drowning. The summary of Paula's final statement: I cannot care for this baby. At this point, I notice Laurel standing up in the back of the court. She is holding up a big, yellow legal pad with *4.0* written in large, dark letters. My attorney doesn't pick up on her not-so-subtle hint. The only good thing that comes from my day in court is that Walter willingly gives up rights over Christopher.

I return home feeling just as defeated as I did the day I was released from the hospital. I was so happy when "the system," as Walter liked to call it, finally intervened. I thought this time professionals would actually help me. I wanted to put all my energy into learning things Walter wouldn't let me learn, bettering myself as a person, making a home for my kids and me, and going back to school. But instead, I fill my days countering these little lies that are told about me in reports—how many graham crackers Danny ate, a burned-out light bulb—and then the really big falsehood: *I am not capable of caring for a child.* I just don't know where to turn. God help me! I am in the middle of a pity party when I hear my door open.

"Lorie, are you there? It's me."

Laurel finds me, and we sit down together on my sofa. "Let's get started on that letter to your lawyer."

It's a hot day, and we go to Laurel's house so we can use her computer. The purpose of the letter is to inform my lawyer of all of the things I have done to regain custody of my children and also to reveal the unfair treatment I have received by the FIA of the small town where Walter and I once lived. Laurel sits down at her computer. "Do you think this agency has treated you fairly? Have you met all of the demands you were told you must complete to get your children back?"

It feels good to finish the letter and see all of the injustices in writing, but I'm not confident this will do any good. It seems like the cards are stacked against me. We drive the letter to the post office, and I whisper a little prayer as we drop it in the box.

The next day, I get to visit my baby. I try not to hold him too tight as I breathe in his smell. I touch his soft skin and try to hold on to the memory of how it feels. It was painful for me to stop nursing suddenly, just as I had to do when Rachel was taken from me. I ask about the kind of formula he is on. I know Christopher is showing some mild respiratory issues, so I set up the nebulizer for his treatment and hold him as he breathes in the moist air. I'm grateful for this. If I were still under Walter's control right now, I would be desperately begging him for permission to take the baby to a doctor. It still stings that Paula claimed in court that I wasn't smart enough to set up this simple machine.

Chapter Forty-Nine

A few days later, I have a break between my school and work. I'm busy planting some herbs just outside of my mobile home when I hear my phone ring. I almost trip as I dash into the kitchen to answer it. A familiar voice is on the line—my lawyer. "I received your letter. I immediately took it to the judge who has been presiding over your case these last six months. He read it. He asked me to give him a reason to give your baby back to you. He asked about that big notebook you bring to every hearing, the one we never look at. Now he wants to see it. If that contains the positive records you've told me it has, then I think there is a good chance you may get Christopher back. Bring those records with you, and be here tomorrow at ten."

I hang up the phone and drop to my knees in prayer. As soon as the clock reaches 3:45, I call the school and ask to speak to Laurel. "You won't believe this . . ."

As Laurel's van pulls up in front of my trailer, I can't help but wonder if she broke the speed limit getting here. I repeat the words from the phone conversation to her again.

Laurel is pacing back and forth in my living room. Her hands gesture everywhere as her words come pouring out with passion.

"So all this time you jumped through every hoop your caseworker threw at you. You went way beyond the requirements, and it didn't help your case. But we do the *one* thing your attorney asks you not to do, threaten to take your story to the press, and suddenly, everything changes! Don't get me wrong; I am so happy about this, but I just can't ignore the fact that you are still the same person you were before this phone call. You've always been a good mother. I don't blame them for not wanting the way they treated you sensationalized in a newspaper article, but if they knew what they were doing wasn't right, why did they do it in the first place?"

Laurel looks at me, and we both break out in smiles.

"All right already, let's just celebrate this moment. We should look at your notebook and see if there are a few things you want to highlight, because there are *dozens* of things in there that show how remarkable everyone but your caseworker thinks you are. Hey, have I mentioned lately I think you are pretty remarkable, too?"

We hug and exchange smiles and then turn to our task at hand. Together, we review the papers. Marilyn, the nurse who is in charge of Christopher, wrote wonderful things about me. So did Delia from a different agency that I have been working with recently. She hopes to get my case switched over to the town where I now live. There are dozens of letters to choose from, as well as only positive reports from my high school classes and the classes required by the FIA. I wish the judge would read them all.

I smile at the thought that our threat to go public was such a big success. When I first met with my attorney, he told me talk shows such as *Sally Jessy Raphael* had called him and wanted me to appear. National and even some international talk shows were interested in my story. Each time, he advised me not to contact any of these people because he didn't want my story to be aired in such a public way. Likewise, I refused offers to interview with various newspapers. Who knows? Perhaps I'll take my story to my grave. Or maybe a day will come when I feel ready to tell my story to anyone who will listen.

After I park next to my attorney's car in the lot beside the courthouse, it's all I can do to keep from running down the hall to meet the judge. I take a seat next to my lawyer. He asks to see my notebook and I gladly hand it over. While he flips through the pages, I take a moment to consider this man.

He was assigned to my case, and I'm guessing he never thought it would be this complicated. When, at one point, Laurel called him and asked if we should hire a second lawyer to assist in my case, he didn't become defensive. He said, "I don't think the judge will act any differently if you have a high-priced attorney from out of town take on the case, but if that is what you want to do, it's all right with me." I'm glad now that we followed his advice. He steps up and hands the binder to the judge, who examines it and asks me a few questions. It takes only a few minutes. Then he confers with my lawyer while I sit in prayer. We are dismissed, and my lawyer and I walk out together. Just outside the door, my attorney turns to me and says, "You are getting your baby back. We will arrange with your caseworker and the foster mom, but it should be very soon."

I can't just accept what he says. Not after all the years where things went wrong in my life. I can't just say thank you. "Are you sure that is what he said, that he really means it? Can my caseworker stop it from happening? Is it really true?"

"It's a done deal."

He smiles, and I manage to choke out a "thank you." It feels like my old car is driving on clouds as I head back to my home. I can't wait to get things freshened up for Christopher. And I can't wait to call a few people. My first phone call is to Laurel. "You won't believe this . . ."

My case has been turned over to Children's Family Services in my new town, so it's goodbye to Paula and Chris and the FIA in the community where I once lived with Walter. It seems my case has sent Paula to job stress counseling. When I tell Laurel, I catch the hint of a smile on her face. "It's a good thing if she feels stressed about not doing the right thing. I just wished she would have acted upon those feelings." Laurel had gone out of her way to have a few words with Paula and Chris, both of whom lied on my reports. "You had to know Lorie is a good person who loves her children. Why did you make everything so hard for her? Why did you put things in your reports to discredit her? What was really behind all of this? Why did you do it!?"

Sadly, they both had the same answer: "I had to; my boss made me do it."

CHAPTER FIFTY

Today is a game-changer. It's April of 1995. I have the car seat secured in my car. I'm leaving soon to go get Christopher, to bring him home. I thought my day couldn't get any happier, but Laurel arrives with more good news: "You're going to have a posse riding with you to get that baby. A whole caravan of cars, and every driver is some kind of professional who has worked with you here in your new community. Here they come now: Christopher's nurse, Marilyn, who has always believed in you; your principal, Mr. Sass, who believed in you when you were in second grade and still does today. Then there is Delia from CFS, who is now taking your case and has been totally impressed with you so far. We're all going to be there, not only to make sure there is no monkey business this time, but also to see your face when that beautiful little boy is placed in your arms."

We all gather in the hall of the FIA to wait. I hear my principal whisper to his former teacher, Laurel, "Which one is she?" Laurel nods toward Paula, who looks pretty uncomfortable. She certainly is outnumbered. I look around at the faces of the wonderful people who are here with me today. A united front, I guess you would call it. It's a short list of people who brought me out from under Walter's dark control to a new life for my children and me. But it's the quality that counts. All the disappointments from those who could have helped but never did fade away as I see this coalition of friends. My thoughts are interrupted as my lawyer steps over to me. "It's ludicrous how this case has been handled, just ludicrous, but I am very happy for you today."

I thank him and turn to Laurel. "What does *ludicrous* mean?"

"You make your teacher proud. Always learning."

Christopher is brought to me and gently placed in my arms. My posse walks with me to my car where I secure him into his car seat. There are more than a few tears. I don't believe it's for real until I drive away from the office.

I talk softly to Christopher as I drive. I tell him how much he is loved. I tell him that he opened the door. Now that he is back in my care, it won't be long before his brothers and sisters will be joining him. Until then, I will treasure the time just the two of us have to get acquainted again.

EPILOGUE

Twenty Years Later

As I turn the key to the door of my new massage salon, I can't help but smile at the creative job Rachel and Robin did decorating this place. I smooth a clean sheet out on my massage table and give a little prayer of thanks that Cheryl liked my massages enough to suggest that I make a career of it. Minutes later, my first client of the day arrives, and soon she is toasty warm under a sheet as I begin to work on her. "How are all your kids doing, Lorie?" she asks.

"You know Tammy and Jimmy each got married years ago and left the fold, so to speak. Chris graduated recently and is working. My youngest four children live with me. Danny manages to keep busy at home knitting and doing puzzles. Robin is a joy who never met a stranger and works part time dog sitting. Rachel makes jewelry, and her photography is lovely. She has had two small strokes but she has completely recovered. Right now, they are all having fun working on the huge family garden. I'm thankful they all get along so well."

"I know you got your Habitat home paid off years ago, but it seems like you and the kids are always doing new projects at your house."

My mind wanders back to all of the years since the day Christopher was returned to me. Soon after that, Tammy and Jimmy came home, and a week later Robin and Rachel came spilling into the house, full of hugs and giggles. Our family was complete the day Danny joined us. If I had a dime every time the children told me that they loved me, I would be a rich woman. But I am already rich, blessed with a loving family and a peaceful home. Seeing the kids grow up in our home—the meals we've cooked together in that kitchen, all the pets we've had over the years, all of us piling into the van and heading off to church—it all makes me feel so blessed to have given my children a loving and safe home. God has been good to me.

As I help my client turn over and begin working on her back, I say a little prayer of thanks that, even though it took me twenty-seven years, I finally did escape.

"I am starting to feel so much better already, Lorie. You have such healing hands. I've had massages by others before, but there is something special about you. You must have lived a charmed life to be able to give so much love and healing with just the touch of your hands. You know, Lorie, everybody has a story, and sometimes I wonder about yours."

Lorie

Lorie has a successful business and resides in her Habitat home with four of her grown children. She has not seen Walter since the day the police took him away. She remains close with her siblings and Laurel. Her faith in God and humankind remains strong.

Walter

Walter was sentenced to serve twelve months on the charge of the baby's failure to thrive. He was released a month early for good behavior. The statute of limitations had expired on his alleged abuse of his daughter when she was a child. Because incest was not reported until after Lorie's sixteenth birthday, Walter could not be charged. Incest between adults was not illegal in the state where they lived at the time. He has had no contact with Lorie or her six children. He resides in the same house where he last lived with Lorie.

Elaine

Lorie did find out from her siblings that Elaine sometimes drove around aimlessly looking for her. Her children understand that her fear of Walter prevented her from being the mother she might have become. Elaine died in 2005.

Carl

Carl did manage to shake off some of the anger he felt from the years of Walter's abuse. He works two jobs but still manages to help his siblings with various projects. He is kind to his family and like his sisters and brother, he has no contact with Walter.

Bruce

Bruce proved that a son can grow up to be the opposite of his father. Bruce is a good man and a wonderful uncle to Lorie's children. He lives a quiet life and is still helpful to his sisters.

Belinda

Belinda married and had children. She was close to her husband's family, was successfully employed, and was a good mother to her children. She died unexpectedly in her sleep at the age of forty-five in 2011.

Emily and Cheryl

Emily and Cheryl are both married and employed. They are lovely women and the best of friends. They enjoyed raising their children and are involved in the lives of their grandchildren. They both remain supportive of their little sister Lorie.

Laurel

Laurel and Lorie remain close friends. Laurel sees this book as a second chance to keep a promise. She believes that when a seven-year-old girl asks for help, we as a society should do all we can to make things right.

Laurel Williams Macon is a retired school teacher. This is a heart-felt book about a beloved student whose fortitude and courage inspired her to share this ultimately triumphant story. She and her husband are Michigan natives and the parents of three grown children.

CPSIA information can be obtained
at www.ICGtesting.com
Printed in the USA
BVOW06s2136211216

471577BV00008B/183/P